The Life of
WILLIAM APESS,
PEQUOT

ALSO BY PHILIP F. GURA

Truth's Ragged Edge:
The Rise of the American Novel

Jonathan Edwards:
Writings from the Great Awakening

The American Antiquarian Society, 1812–2012:
A Bicentennial History

American Transcendentalism: A History

Jonathan Edwards: America's Evangelical

C. F. Martin and His Guitars, 1796–1873

Buried from the World:
Inside the Massachusetts State Prison, 1829–1831

America's Instrument:
The Banjo in the Nineteenth Century
(with James F. Bollman)

The Crossroads of American History and Literature

A Glimpse of Sion's Glory:
Puritan Radicalism in New England, 1620–1660

Critical Essays on American Transcendentalism
(with Joel Myerson)

The Wisdom of Words: Language,
Theology, and Literature in the New England Renaissance

Apes

The Life of

WILLIAM APESS,

PEQUOT

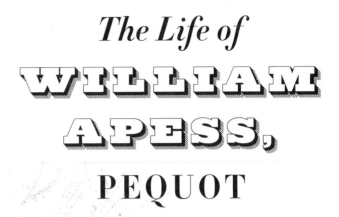

PHILIP F. GURA

The University of

North Carolina Press

Chapel Hill

Illustration on the jacket and the title page:
frontispiece to William Apess, *A Son of the Forest* (1831);
collection of the author. The signature appears in
the author's copy of the book.

© 2015 The University of North Carolina Press
All rights reserved
Designed by Richard Hendel
Set in Miller, Didot, and Sutro types
by Tseng Information Systems, Inc.
Manufactured in the United States of America

The paper in this book meets the guidelines
for permanence and durability of the Committee on
Production Guidelines for Book Longevity
of the Council on Library Resources.

The University of North Carolina Press
has been a member of the Green Press Initiative
since 2003.

Library of Congress Cataloging-in-Publication Data
Gura, Philip F., 1950–
The life of William Apess, Pequot / Philip F. Gura.
pages cm
Includes bibliographical references and index.
ISBN 978-1-4696-1998-9 (cloth : alk. paper) — ISBN 978-1-4696-1999-6 (ebook)
1. Apess, William, 1798–1839. 2. Pequot Indians—Biography. 3. Methodist Church—New England—Clergy—Biography. 4. Indians, Treatment of—New England—History. I. Title.
E99.P53G87 2014
974.004′97344092—dc23
[B]
2014026609

For DDH

There once, lost,

now found again,

a miracle

CONTENTS

PROLOGUE

New York City, 1839

On April 10, 1839, Dr. J. S. Hurd, a New York City medical examiner, performed an autopsy on a man at William Garlick's boardinghouse in lower Manhattan.[1] Garlick's boardinghouse stood at 31 Washington Street, two streets east of the Hudson River and bordered by Battery Place and Moore Street. Washington Street was one of several thoroughfares in a neighborhood that was home to crowds of low-paid workers, a population mirrored across the island along the East River, where eighteenth-century Dutch and English inhabitants had built sturdy homes adjacent to flourishing slips, piers, and warehouses. As commerce increased, though, the "East Ward" had become overcrowded. Wealthier families moved uptown, as far north as Fourteenth Street along Broadway, into neighborhoods delineated by the "grid" plan that the city's Streets Commission had instituted for more orderly development. Their previous homes then became boardinghouses for an ever-shifting population of clerks, craft apprentices, cart men, dockworkers, sailors, and various day laborers.

Just above the Battery—the tip of Manhattan—on the west side of the island, enterprising businessmen eager for more commercial space filled the low land along the Hudson River to create Greenwich, Washington, and West Streets, where they constructed wharves and two- and three-story brick warehouses and boardinghouses that eventually catered to the dense nexus of workingmen and women. Not as notorious as the city's "Five Points" district in the East Ward, where an impoverished population lived and worked amid all manner of vice and crime, by the 1830s the area around Washington Street, part of the new "River Ward," was synonymous with a transient working class.[2]

The deceased had lived at this address since January with his second wife, Elizabeth, to whom he had been married for at least two years. Within days of the inquest into his death, scores of newspapers in New York, New England, and down the East Coast were reporting his demise. But bespeaking the man's obscurity, what publicity there was surrounding his death initially lay more in its circumstances, signaled by a notice in the *Philadelphia North American*, than in his identity. "LOBELIA AGAIN," the column read, for the inquest had uncovered that a "botanic physician," Dr. Asher Atkinson, had administered lobelia, a homeopathic drug, to his patient shortly before his death.[3] Many people, particularly members of the established medical profession, regarded botanic medicine as quackery, and the headline implied that Atkinson's ministrations had evidently contributed to another patient's demise.[4] In such cities as New York and Philadelphia, where tensions between botanic and allopathic physicians were especially great, many readers viewed this individual's death as but another example of the failure of unregulated medical practice.[5]

But the coroner's report fills in more of the story.[6] Catherine Garlick, the daughter of the boardinghouse owner, and an unnamed neighbor testified that the couple who rented from her father seemed "affectionate and kind to each other," but Garlick also claimed that prior to the deceased's illness he "had been some days on a frolic," that is, a drunken binge. Another boarder, John Wight, seconded this report. This behavior was not uncommon, Wight testified, for his neighbor would "sometimes get on a Frolic and continue a few days and then would abstain from liquor all together."

The deceased's wife added to the mystery. She recalled that on the Friday before her husband's death, he had visited Dr. James Veer nearby at 117 Varick Street and was prescribed some sort of medicine. The next day her husband seemed better. He took tea at his usual hour, but the prescribed medicine, whatever it was, operated so "very powerfully" that in the morning he could not get out of bed to dress.

Only then did the family turn to Dr. Atkinson, who administered lobelia to "turn his sickness downwards." An annual plant with pale blue flowers, lobelia was a staple among the botanic physician's curatives, prepared as either an ointment made from the plant's root or a tincture from its dried seeds. Also called "Indian tobacco," recalling the plant's traditional medicinal use among Native American tribes, lobelia was a powerful emetic and particularly useful in treating patients with asthma—hence, another of its common names, "asthma weed." In addition, lobelia is a psychoactive drug, and some cultures believed that its ingestion, often by smoking, induced spiritual transcendence. Thus, though botanic physicians commonly prescribed lobelia, they also warned that it could be "very prostrating to the system" and, "when given alone, sometimes cause[d] alarming appearances."[7]

Atkinson gave his patient two doses of fifteen grains each—one grain is about sixty-five milligrams—which "operated copiously as an emetic."

The doctor returned the next day, but finding his patient little improved, administered some "black powder," a mixture of mandrake root, charcoal, and ground-up whitewood and dogwood bark. Mandrake, or "may apple," was a strong purgative; the mixture of bark was a powerful tonic.[8] At first this concoction made the man feel worse, but a short time later he seemed improved. He got up, brushed his teeth, and ate some toast. Then, two hours later, he was dead. The inquest concluded that he had died of "apoplexy," a diagnosis commonly used to describe something akin to a stroke and whose symptoms were congruent with what Dr. Hurd had found in his examination.[9]

The inquest absolved Dr. Atkinson of any blame and dampened further attempts to place the lack of effectiveness of botanic medicine at the center of the story of this individual's death. Instead, reports shifted to who he was. The notice in the *Philadelphia North American* described him as "a Narragansett Indian . . . otherwise known about the country as Apes the Missionary Preacher." "The deceased in his lifetime was an author," the *Albany Evening Journal* noted, who "wrote the Life of '"King Philip,'" several sermons, &c, which he sold for his own interest." The same paper mentioned, albeit erroneously, that the man's wife was a "good looking white woman," a fact that, though titillating to some genteel readers, would not have made the couple unusual in lower Manhattan neighborhoods. Five Points, for example, was notoriously multiracial. No newspaper, however, mentioned that six years earlier the deceased had begun a meteoric rise as a spokesperson for Native American rights and liberties.

The deceased was forty-one-year-old William Apess. Two years earlier, he had been one of the country's most important Native American intellectuals, having published more than any other indigenous writer before the twentieth century and attained fame and notoriety for championing his people's tribal rights. In 1829, he had issued his autobiography, the first Native American to do so. He had led the successful challenge of the Mashpee Indians against the state of Massachusetts, through which the Mashpees sought to restore some measure of self-governance. Apess subsequently had embarked on a lecture career in New York, speaking on the history and culture of Native Americans.

Despite Apess's extraordinary significance, today he is known primarily among scholars of Native American studies, with excerpts from his writings taught in some surveys of American literature. But for both his historical importance and his foundational role as a Native American intellectual, Apess deserves the same widespread recognition as others in the antebellum period who questioned the sincerity of the nation's ongoing commitment to democracy, a cohort of reformers that includes Margaret Fuller and Elizabeth Cady Stanton, champions of women's rights; Frances Wright and Orestes Brownson, of the dignity of labor; and William Lloyd Garrison, Wendell Phillips, David Walker, and Frederick Douglass, of African American freedom and equality. These were reformers who were unafraid to speak the truth about the emperor's new clothes.

By challenging the treatment of those people impoverished and disenfranchised because of their race, gender, or class, these reformers risked vituperation, condemnation, and even imprisonment, not because they despised their country but because they loved it so much. In the 1820s and 1830s, Apess stood both with this cohort and yet apart and above, his voice raised in protest particularly against the plight of the Native Americans, who all too many white people wanted to believe were, by God's fiat, doomed to extinction and, for the moment, increasingly forced out of sight. But how and why did Apess end up as he did, perishing not only from the face of the earth but also almost completely from historical memory?

No one could have predicted Apess's success during his life. He was born into abject poverty in 1798 in rural Colrain, Massachusetts, of what the census reported as "colored"—probably mixed-race—parents who had moved there from southern Connecticut, near lands given in the eighteenth century to remnants of the Pequot Indians. His parents returned to Connecticut a few years later only to separate, but not before physically and psychologically abusing their young son, William. Subsequently, when his parents wandered away from the area, he lived with his grandmother but found little more stability there. She beat Apess so severely that the town's overseers of the poor placed him with various white families before formally binding him out to a series of masters as an indentured servant. Given the general predilection for strong drink in that period and Apess's own trying circumstances, in his teens he compounded his difficulties by becoming (as he later admitted) an alcoholic.

His life changed, however, when he experienced a powerful conversion as a result of Methodist preaching. Beginning to assume control of his life for the first time, at the beginning of the War of 1812 he fled his indenture and enlisted among New York troops. Still only a teenager, he became a drummer and marched forthwith to the Canadian front, the most important theater of the war.

Before long, he was needed as a soldier. He traded his drum for a rifle and saw action in several battles around Lake Champlain and in expeditions against Quebec, the staccato of gunshots replacing the percussion of his drum. After the Treaty of Ghent ended the war, Apess remained in the north woods, spending time among the Haudenosaunees in upstate New York and eastern Ontario. When he returned to Connecticut months later, he formalized his commitment to Methodism through baptism and began to work as an exhorter. He also visited his mother, whom he had not seen in twenty years, and married Mary Wood, another Indian, with whom he had at least two daughters.

In 1825, the Methodist leadership assigned Apess to a circuit that took him to Long Island, the Hudson River Valley, New Bedford, Providence, Boston, and the islands of Nantucket and Martha's Vineyard, where he ministered primarily to Native American and mixed-race congregations. He became more and more confident in his self-expression, and four years later he self-published *A Son of the Forest* (revised two years later), a spiritual autobiography that related the story of his life up to that time. He also preached and lectured in Boston and soon came to the attention of prominent reformers like William Lloyd Garrison, who in his influential journal, the *Liberator*, noted Apess's speaking engagements along with those of the city's abolitionists. In 1833, he published a well-received sermon and the *Experiences of the Five Christian Indians; or, A Looking-Glass for the White Man*, in which he recounted the biographies of recent Indian converts and condemned the prejudice to which they and other Native Americans remained subject.

Apess's commitment next brought him face-to-face with the Massachusetts government. As part of his ministerial duties, in 1833—when the nation was increasingly exercised over the seizure of Cherokee lands and the tribe's forced removal to west of the Mississippi River—he visited a Native American congregation on Cape Cod that was fighting on a smaller scale the same battles that the Cherokee tribe had fought against usurpation of its tribal rights and privileges. Apess thereupon assumed a leadership role in the Mashpee fight to regain control of tribal lands that white overseers were pilfering. He vociferously argued the tribe's case for more self-government to the state legislature and subsequently was arrested and jailed for several months for his part in what became known as the "Mashpee Revolt." He subsequently published an account of this struggle in his *Indian Nullification of the Unconstitutional Laws of Massachusetts* (Boston, 1835), whose title signaled his awareness of recent public debates in national politics over the right of state nullification and in which he continued his autobiographical narrative, his life increasingly defined more by politics than by religion.

After the Mashpees won the right to self-government, Apess returned to Boston, where his influence and notoriety grew. In 1836, he delivered a remarkable "Eulogy on King Philip," in which, overturning the filiopietism through which his contemporaries celebrated the achievements of the Pilgrim Fathers, he touted the seventeenth-century New England Indian leader during King Philip's War (1675–76) as one who was as great a patriot as George Washington. By request, he repeated the speech in that city and again in Hartford. In its call for white Christians to acknowledge that God embraces people of all colors and its refiguring of how one should rewrite New England history, the published *Eulogy* stands with Frederick Douglass's "What to the Slave Is the Fourth of July?" as one of the most searching indictments of the nation's institutional racism. First delivered in the Odeon, Boston's largest and most elegant hall, this address marked Apess's full emergence as a public intellectual.

But as happened for so many others caught in the growing financial depression, the Panic of 1837, Apess's luck then turned. By 1836, he had left the Methodist ministry. Without regular income, he also became embroiled in lawsuits on Cape Cod and had his goods attached for debt. Eventually, he mortgaged all his property in an attempt to remain solvent. To escape this new turmoil—and perhaps his creditors—he moved to New York with his new wife, Elizabeth, where he appeared in the city's lecture halls as a speaker on Native American history and culture. In that city, in a crowded boardinghouse on Washington Street, a lifetime of hardship caught up with this brilliant casuist for Native American rights.

William Apess was an extraordinary man, and his story deserves a larger audience. To be sure, beginning in the 1970s and particularly after 1992, with Barry O'Connell's republication of Apess's complete writings, scholars of Native American history and literature have exhaustively studied Apess's writings, but they have too often aimed such works at scholarly communities rather than at the larger public, which needs a straightforward account of Apess's life and times.[10]

Apess was not some sport or relic—another example of the nation's vanishing "Indians"—but someone who strove to understand himself as a member of an indigenous nation within the United States of America, and so to claim for himself, his tribe, and Native peoples in general a place in the new nation. Thus, unlike, say, Frederick Douglass, who dreamed that African Americans might participate fully as American citizens and so urged his people to grasp the still-unfulfilled promise of democracy, Apess's loyalties were to tribe and people, not to the United States per se.

He left a legacy whose recovery has only recently begun to have its full effect. Native American activist and intellectual Robert Warrior puts it best. Apess, he writes, is "the Native writer before the twentieth century who most demands the attention of contemporary Native intellectuals," and, I add, of contemporary Americans.[11] Dr. Hurd's examination at 31 Washington Street, dispiriting as it appears, thankfully marked the end of only the first phase of Apess's influence.

The Life of

WILLIAM
APESS,

PEQUOT

ONE

Cruel Beginnings
{1798-1812}

PEQUOT HISTORY AND CULTURE

On the first page of *A Son of the Forest*, written when he was thirty-one, William Apess proudly claimed that he was a "descendant of one of the principal chiefs of the Pequod tribe, so well known in that part of American history called King Philip's Wars."[1] By 1800, the Pequots were a remnant—numbering no more than a few hundred—of a population originally centered in southeastern Connecticut and Rhode Island. Almost from the beginning of European settlement in these regions, the Pequots' relations with the newcomers had been antagonistic, with altercations breaking out particularly frequently over access to or appropriation of traditional hunting and fishing grounds. In 1637, the Massachusetts Bay Puritans finally waged outright war against them and, in a surprise nighttime attack on their fortified encampment near present-day Mystic, Connecticut, massacred several hundred, including many women and children.[2]

This was a decisive blow; most survivors of the Pequot War drifted west or north to seek survival among other Native peoples. Moreover, the Puritans' subsequent actions even amounted to an attempt at cultural genocide, for by the terms of a treaty at Hartford, Connecticut, in 1638, they remanded the remaining approximately 200 Pequots to the Mohegan and Narragansett tribes, forbade them ever from identifying themselves with the name "Pequot," and forcibly incorporated their lands into the colony of Connecticut.[3]

But by the late eighteenth century, the remaining Pequots persisted in two locations in what had become the state of Connecticut: on colony-granted lands in Groton (a group later known as the Mashnantucket Pequots) and across the Mystic River in adjacent Stonington (later, the Eastern Pequots). On tribal reserves established by Connecticut as early as 1666 (the acts themselves giving the lie to the Natives' putative "extinction"), only footpaths connected domiciles, and no colony roads passed through, lending the area an aura of isolation.[4] Seasonally, following tribal patterns set for hundreds of years, the surviving Pequots moved among these two locations and other little-settled areas, following river bottoms to fish and hunt and harvest wild foodstuffs. As resources on the reserves grew scarce, some Natives traveled seasonally to lands further to the north and west, where white settlement pressed in less. Still others moved near or into white communities and worked at low-paying tasks, eventually becoming part of the region's emerging multiracial working class even as they maintained their tribal identity.

In their habits and general appearance, surviving Pequots were increasingly inconspicuous. Many dressed in English-style clothing and by the early nineteenth century lived in small huts or houses, as well as in traditional wigwams. Their diet combined English and Native foodstuffs. Most commonly they stewed food rather than roasted it, and they threw into their pots a variety of stock: deer, sheep, pigs, raccoons, dogs, clams and mussels, and both freshwater and saltwater fish. Maize, oats, peas, potatoes, and squash were their common vegetables.[5]

What most distinguished these people from Europeans and their American descendants, however, were their attitudes toward work and the land. Given the Pequots' wish to continue to hunt and forage seasonally, to Euro-Americans they appeared transient and unreliable, which the former attributed to an inherent laziness. Moreover, on their reserves, the Natives practiced tenancy in common. Even though "proprietors"—those born into the tribe—could cultivate and build on sections of the lands and pass on any improvements to their children, the tribe itself retained overall stewardship of the parcels. Any member, though, could use unclaimed lands for pasturage, wood gathering, hunting and fishing, or harvesting shellfish, but it was understood that the natural world was a common inheritance not to be permanently parceled among individuals.[6]

Pequot women frequently remained on the allotted lands while their husbands periodically moved to hunt, fish, or find work for wages. Labor for others (this meant for whites) became increasingly common as the Pequots, like Native people throughout New England, depended more and more on manufactured clothing and other store goods for which they could pay cash as well as barter.[7] Thus, after the turn of the nineteenth century, the Pequots were inexorably pulled into the market economy that now defined nineteenth-century New England, even as they struggled to retain elements of traditional lifeways.[8] Attempts to maintain cultural and political independence, however, were made more difficult, because,

Cruel Beginnings

unlike the Cherokees or Seminoles, who argued their sovereignty on the grounds of the federal government's treaty relations with them, the Pequots (and other New England tribes) used their common culture to support claims to sovereignty.[9]

COLRAIN

William Apess was not born on one of the Pequot reserves established in the colonial period but in the northwestern Massachusetts town of Coleraine (now Colrain), in Franklin County (which until 1813 made up the northern tier of Hampshire County). For good reason, Franklin County is described as part of the state's hill country, for almost every town within it, with the exception of a few along the Connecticut River, which bisects it, has considerable heights of land surrounded by boulder-strewn fields, geological markers that the retreat of glaciers left 10,000 years ago. The oldest towns in the county are Deerfield and Sunderland, in Franklin County's south-central region, along the Connecticut River, where rich alluvial soil lent itself to agriculture and pasturage for cattle. By the eighteenth century, residents had grown wealthy by shipping surplus grain and livestock downriver through Northampton, Springfield, and Hartford, to Long Island Sound, and then to New York City. With more difficulty, they also drove goods and cattle eastward, along the Bay Path through Worcester to Boston and its surrounding towns. Subsequent economic development in the region followed the Connecticut River northward to Northfield, or it followed one of its tributaries—the more turbulent Deerfield River, west, from Greenfield, or another, the Millers River, east. The last part of the county to be settled was the mountainous northern region bordering Vermont and making up the present-day towns of Leyden, Heath, Rowe, Monroe, and Colrain.[10]

By the mid-eighteenth century, as economic opportunities became scarcer in Hampshire County's older towns, ambitious and impatient residents, facing either very high prices for available land or a long wait to inherit it, began to settle this remote region near the Vermont border, in a section watered by the Green River on the east and two branches of the North River, a tributary of the powerful Deerfield River, in which salmon still ran. Clearing the land for farming and pasturing, the first settlers also marketed lumber and cordwood, maple sugar, and (eventually) livestock and sheep to generate extra income.

This area was first known as Boston Township No. 2, because it was made up of lands granted to some of Boston's residents after they had successfully petitioned the Massachusetts General Court for compensation for the town's regularly paying a fifth of the entire colony's taxes and providing more than its share of support for the entire state's poor. The settlement eventually became the town of Colrain. Adventurous speculators and new emigrants from the Irish province of Ulster (known as "Scots-Irish"—hence the town's name, after the Irish Lord Coleraine) found the region more suitable to agriculture than some of the other uplands. They brought in a Presbyterian clergyman as early as 1750, and by 1786 there were enough new residents to support two Baptist congregations as well. In 1800, the Troy (New York) Conference of Methodists sent missionaries to neighboring Rowe and two years later established a class of a dozen or so believers on Catamount Hill, one of the more remote and less settled regions of Colrain where the North River cuts through a steep, narrow gorge. This spot became a regular stop on the Methodist circuit.[11]

In this hardscrabble environment, economic success did not come quickly or easily. In the eighteenth century, raids by Native Americans remained common, with several townspeople killed or taken into captivity in the decades immediately after settlement. During the American phase of the Seven Years' War (1754–63) against the French and the Indians, some inhabitants joined the fabled Roger's Rangers and saw action at the Battle of Quebec. Shortly after the end of those hostilities, emigrants from the east and down along the Connecticut River flooded into the area, so that by the end of the 1760s Colrain had about ninety farms. In the inflationary years in the immediate aftermath of the American Revolution, though, many of these pioneers (like others in western Massachusetts) fell into debt and lent support to Shays' Rebellion (1786–87), centered in Hampshire and Berkshire Counties, thirty miles away. Economic recovery was slow, and the ranks of the town's poor increased when African Americans, whom some of the settlers had brought to the area as slaves before the Revolution but whom state law had freed in 1783, remained in the area, forming the nucleus of an interracial community that eventually included Apess's parents.[12]

EARLY YEARS

Tracing William Apess's genealogy is difficult, for records of Native Americans—and of people of color generally—from this period often are fragmentary or lost. Apess heard his grandmother describe his grandfather William Apes as a white man who married "a female attached to the royal family" (that is, King Philip's), but to what "degree of affinity" Apess did not know (8).[13] Extant records suggest that this William Apes was born around 1730 in Stonington, Connecticut, married a woman named Jerusha Maria, and served on the British side in the French and Indian War; he died sometime after 1814 in Colchester, Connecticut.[14]

Apess's father, William Apes (b. 1770), from Colchester, Connecticut, was thus of mixed descent, but by his son's account, he always strongly identified with the Pequots. "As soon as he attained sufficient age to act for himself," Apess remembered, his father (as was typical in the Natives' matrilineal kinship system) joined the tribe to which he was connected through his mother, in whose veins "not a single drop of the white man's blood had ever flowed" (9). Apes worked as a servant to Captain Joseph Taylor in Colchester and married Candace Taylor (b. ca. 1777), one of Joseph Taylor's freed slaves, of mixed African and Native blood. Candace, however, probably was not Apess's mother because Joseph Taylor did not free her (as he did with two others, all referred to as "Negro slaves" or "blacks") until 1805, when she was twenty-eight. It is unlikely that she was in another state with William Apes for the birth of Apes and at least one other sibling, an infant brother who died in Colrain of dysentery in an epidemic in 1803.[15]

With Candace, and living in the Colchester area, William Apes had three sons, Elias, Griswold, and Gilbert, whose descendants were termed "coloured," "mulatto," or "black."[16] At some point before May 1815, Candace had moved to Hartford, where she died in 1838. With a probable third wife, Mary, William Apes had Elisha, born in May 1815 in Groton, Connecticut; Solomon, born in 1818 in Preston, Connecticut; Leonard, born in 1820 but dying within a year; Abby Ann, born in Colrain, Massachusetts, in 1822; Sally George, born in Colrain in 1823; and a second Leonard, born in Leyden, Massachusetts, in 1824. These children are recorded as either Indian or white, but never as mulatto or black. In 1820, when the family was living in Colrain, the U.S. census counted *all* of them as white. As this fragmentary genealogy suggests, in this period, racial categories in New England were very imprecise and fluid, probably dependent to some degree on the predispositions and preconceptions of individual census takers.[17]

By the late 1820s, Apes and his family had returned to southeastern Connecticut, where three of William and Mary's sons became whalemen.[18] The family's frequent movements suggest that Apess's parents, particularly his father, maintained a peripatetic lifestyle, typical of Native Americans in that period. "My parents were of the same disposition of the Indians," Apess later wrote (with an odd locution), "that is, to wander to and fro." William Apes had so much Native blood, Apess continued, that when he moved, he even "fashioned after them [the Indians] in traveling from river to river, and from mountain to mountain and plain to plain," rather than following the white man's roads.[19] Apess himself never totally embraced this lifestyle but did follow it somewhat in his future labors as an itinerant preacher.

One of William Apes's moves took him to "Colereign," in the "back settlements," where he remained for some time and where Apess was born, on January 31, 1798. The little we know of his few years in Colrain comes from his autobiography. The family lived on the steep slopes of Catamount Hill, on the outskirts of town, where most newcomers had settled after the Revolutionary War. Like other mixed-race inhabitants of New England, his father may have hired out to work on a local farm; he also made shoes, a craft he later taught his son. William Apes also very likely hunted, fished, and grew subsistence crops on the outskirts of town, where, Apess said, they lived in a "tent" (9).

We know little else of the physical conditions in which the family or their neighbors dwelled; but Yale president Timothy Dwight, who traveled extensively throughout New England and New York in the first decade of the nineteenth century, offered insight into contemporary housing for the region's indigenous people. He visited an area called Lanthern Hill in a remote part of Stonington, Connecticut, on the Pequot lands where Apess's grandfather had lived. "Some of them lived in wigwams," Dwight observed, and others "in houses resembling poor cottages, at the best small, ragged, and unhealthy." Still others "lived on the farms of the white inhabitants in houses purposely built for them, and pa[id] their rent by daily labor."[20] Recent archaeology in this Lanthern Hill area has uncovered the foundations of sweathouses and animal pens, and also indications of cornfields and gardens, wells, storage facilities, stone walls, middens, and cemeteries.[21]

Dwight unfortunately has nothing to say of the language and customs the Pequots might have preserved, though, and his overall portrait is decidedly negative, informed as it is by white Americans' increasing sense that Natives in New England were a degenerate race whose time was passing.[22] All the "energy" of the original Pequot warriors had "vanished," he continued, leaving in its place what he regarded as laziness and prodigality. The people, for example, quickly squandered their wages on "ardent spirits or cider," for which they would part "with everything they possess." The tribes' seeming lack of familial responsibility similarly chagrined Dwight. Presumably unaware that Pequot men periodically left

　　　　　　　　Cruel Beginnings

their spouses in charge of the homes and farms while they traveled to traditional hunting and fishing grounds, he deplored that they seemed to have "no such thing among them as marriage, but cohabit[ed] without ceremony or covenant, and desert[ed] each other at pleasure."[23]

———

COLCHESTER

The Apes family remained in Colrain for only a few years. When Apess was just a few years old, his father moved the family to Colchester, Connecticut, twenty-three miles southeast of Hartford and the same distance north of New London at the mouth of the Thames River on Long Island Sound.[24] Colchester was an uneven, hilly township with fairly rich soil and a large and lucrative deposit of iron ore. Wigwam Hill, one of its neighborhoods, was home to a small Native population. The town also boasted well-regarded Bacon Academy, established in 1805 through the generosity of town resident Pierpont Brown. Children of members of the local Congregational Church attended the school free of charge, and it also welcomed students from throughout the region, who boarded with local families. At the time the Apes family moved to Colchester, it was best known for its iron ore and this academy.[25]

Colchester also had a significant number of slave children, who, according to the Gradual Abolition Act of 1784, were to be freed when they were twenty-one; town officials wanted to ensure their literacy and funded an institution, which they founded a few years prior to Bacon Academy, where they could be educated. Thus, on the town common adjacent to the academy was a more modest building that was home to the only school in the state specifically earmarked for "colored" children. When the Apes family moved to town, the school already had about thirty students, who were taught by Prince Saunders, a "colored" man who was beginning what became an extraordinary career as an educator.

Saunders was born in 1775 in nearby Lebanon, Connecticut; he taught at the "colored" school and at the same time received instruction in Latin and Greek at the academy. He, too, may have been of mixed African and Native blood, for in 1807 he left Colchester to attend Moor's Charity School in Hanover, New Hampshire, affiliated with Dartmouth College and founded expressly for Native American students who wished to become missionaries.[26]

Saunders stayed at Moor's Charity School for two years, long enough to impress Dartmouth's president, John Wheelock, who put him in touch with prominent Unitarian clergyman William Ellery Channing, a strong supporter of a Boston school established for "the elevation of the colored people."[27] In 1809, Channing hired Saunders to teach students primarily from the "tumbled down tenements" on "Nigger Hill" behind the Massachusetts State House. He taught there for four years in rooms in the African Meetinghouse made available by the Reverend Thomas Paul, founder of Boston's black Baptist Church.[28]

In Boston, Saunders entered fully into the social and intellectual life of a sizable community of free "blacks." He joined the city's African Masonic lodge, served as its secretary, and in 1815 traveled to London as a representative of the Negro Masons of America. There Saunders met British abolitionists William Wilberforce and Thomas Clarkson and with the former's recommendation in hand, traveled to the recently established country of Haiti—the first independent nation in Latin America, the first postcolonial independent black-led one in the world, and the only one whose independence was gained as part of a successful slave rebellion—to offer his services to its then-emperor, Henri Christophe.[29] Impressed by Saunders's intelligence and regarding him a fit representative of Haiti's political experiment, Christophe named Saunders his personal courier to London. The emperor also charged him with the reorganization of Haiti's school system, a task Saunders undertook with his usual enthusiasm for education.[30]

As it happened, Apess received his first formal schooling from this soon-to-be prominent figure in New World African American history.[31] But despite such unusual opportunity for people of color as Colchester offered, Apess's life in Colchester was difficult. For example, although his family remained together "in comparative comfort" for a few years, it then began to splinter (9). His parents separated, his father returning to Colrain. In 1811 (probably after he had started a new family), William Apes sold thirteen acres of land in Colchester to Daniel Taylor, the neighbor of Candace's former owner.[32] Through these family changes, Apess was left behind; he did not see his mother's face for the next twenty years.[33] He and his siblings lived with his mother's parents in one-half of a house; an uncle, likely Lemuel Ashbo, lived on the other side of the building.[34]

The children had little to eat and were clothed literally in rags, "so far as rags would suffice to cover our nakedness." They often went to bed hungry or having eaten at most a cold potato, and they slept "on a bundle of straw without covering against the weather." Occasionally, Apess recalled, charitable white neighbors brought frozen milk, thawed to make porridge that the children "would lap down . . . like so many hungry dogs." On one occasion, during a heavy rain, his grandmother told the children to go into

Cruel Beginnings

the cellar and, when they complained of cold and hunger, told them "to dance to keep warm." Psychologically and materially bereft, Apess and his siblings lived this way "for some time" (10–11).

Following a pattern common among New England tribes, Apess's parents wove baskets to support their family, a craft his maternal grandparents also practiced so that they could exchange them for those things "absolutely necessary to keep soul and body in a state of unity," even as they withheld such comfort from their charges (10). By the early nineteenth century, as settlers progressively took control of lands that the region's tribes had used seasonally for agriculture, hunting, and fishing, basket making and other weaving from local reeds and rushes constituted a common way for Native people to supplement their incomes. In a new, increasingly interconnected marketplace, a traditional craft like basket making assumed new significance, particularly because of easy access to the necessary raw materials—willow, wood splint, rushes, cornhusks, cattails, and sweet flag—none of whose harvest required land ownership.[35]

Many nineteenth-century town historians testified to the ubiquity of such activities as Native American families supplied local and regional needs for food containers and other such commodities as straw brooms and cane bottoms for chairs. One local historian described Anne Wampy, a Pequot from Ledyard, Connecticut, as carrying "upon her shoulders a bundle of baskets so large as almost to hide her from view." Because her craft was so highly regarded, she found "customers at almost every home."[36] Native artisans made circuits—Wampy traveled a circuit of "a dozen or twenty miles"—through various communities, staying with other Native people on state reserves or at the edges of settlements, becoming part of what the authorities called the region's "wandering poor."[37]

ABUSE AND RESCUE

Parental abandonment was not the worst of Apess's worries. Apess and his siblings endured heart-breaking abuse. One incident from Apess's autobiography is especially haunting and marked him for life. On what proved to be the final occasion before his rescue from his grandmother's home, in her stupor and self-loathing she asked the young boy if he "hated" her. The young Apess did not know what the word meant and, wishing to please her, responded affirmatively. Thereupon she began to beat him with a club, asked the same question again and again, and when he innocently answered the same way, continued to strike him, the scores of years of pent-up rage from hearing others direct the word at her exploding against the young boy's body. When his Uncle Ashbo tried to intervene, Apess's grandfather attacked him with a firebrand, but he finally succeeded in securing and hiding the child.

This horrific episode likely happened in 1802, for that year the town reimbursed Ashbo for caring for Apess for ten days.[38] On February 18, 1802, a charitable white neighbor, David Furman, a cooper (barrelmaker), encountered the boy, his arm broken in three places and his body covered in bruises from the beating, and took him to Laban Gates, a local doctor, whom the town later paid for "reducing the fractured arm of William, an Indian boy" (12–13).[39] Shocked at what the child had experienced and having no children of his own, Furman subsequently applied to Colchester's selectmen to have Apess and his siblings removed from their grandparents' home and put under his family's protection. The town fathers granted the request, and, as was the custom in New England communities in dealing with the indigent or incapacitated, Colchester periodically reimbursed the Furmans for their expenses.[40]

Apess's foster family was devoutly Christian. Mrs. Furman was a "close order" Baptist—that is, one who strictly adhered to church doctrine and discipline—neighbors considered her "very pious"(17–18). She and her husband treated Apess as "tenderly" as though he had been "one of the elect," not only just "one of their sons." After a year that brought him much-needed stability, they had become so fond of the boy that they requested to have him formally bound out to them, to work on their farm until he was twenty-one, in exchange for room and board, clothing, and schooling (13). Settled in his new home, from the age of six Apess began to attend the nearby "colored" school and stayed for "six successive winters," that is, during the season when boys had the most free time from farmwork. During this time, he acquired all the formal instruction he was ever to have. For three of these years Prince Saunders was his teacher (15–16).

Living with the Furmans, Apess entered an extensive and varied "pauper apprentice system" through which post-Revolutionary New Englanders assisted children with special and long-term needs.[41] Before the proliferation of public institutions like orphanages, asylums, special schools for the deaf and blind, and almshouses, communities cobbled together necessary assistance for needy individuals within their borders. Specific funds for such relief were appropriated at town meetings.

But Apess's placement differed from the more formal indenture parents made for a child with a skilled craftsman such as a printer or cabinetmaker, in which the chief purpose was the child's eventual mastery of a trade. Rather, after negotiations between town magistrates and the host family (ones in which neither Apess nor his birth family had any say), he was required to live in his master's home and work at whatever tasks he was set, a temporary servitude that greatly benefited the host family and lasted until the ward reached maturity.

The system benefited the town as well, for in this way its magistrates could monitor and control potentially unruly or disruptive members of their community. Not surprisingly, they tried to place children in well-ordered, fairly prosperous two-parent households. The town fathers also believed that an attentive woman like Mrs. Furman was central to a child's moral development. If the mother in a foster arrangement happened to die, the magistrates usually moved the ward to another two-parent home to ensure a caregiver whose concern was the child's spiritual well-being.[42]

Despite the good this system did by removing children from untoward or dangerous situations, it was not intended for their social amelioration. At the end of such foster care, for example, someone like Apess had labored at menial tasks but not necessarily acquired special skills to raise him above the position of any other day laborer in the regional economy. If a boy, he probably learned the rudiments of reading and writing but usually would not attend an academy or read with a clergyman to prepare for college—his physical labor, usually agricultural, was too valuable. If a girl, housekeeping, basic sewing, and farmyard husbandry were the rule, not music, embroidery, or painting on velvet—and she was not raised to think that she could marry a college graduate or professional man. Moreover, in addition to reinforcing existing class and gender boundaries, the magistrates respected traditional racial lines. The Furmans, for example, considered Apess "a person of color," not a Native worthy of any special consideration, and thus would never have considered sending him to an institution like Moor's Charity School, even if they had known of it.[43]

Indenture among white families like the Furmans would likely have worked to distance Native wards from their heritage, even though in Apess's case any efforts to make him relinquish his Indian ways ultimately proved unsuccessful. On the first page of his autobiography, he relates that his maternal grandmother taught him about his Pequot forebears, something she clearly thought of great significance and worthy of passing on to him (7). Of the crucial matter of language, however, we know little.[44] Whether Apess knew and used Pequot, a dialect of the Mohegan tongue (the speaking of which the Puritans had made a capital offense after the Pequot War), remains moot. It is significant, however, that he later wrote from firsthand conversation the biography of an elderly Pequot woman who had retained parts of the tribe's language; and at one of his lectures on New England's history with the Indians, he recited the Lord's Prayer in King Philip's—that is, the Massachusetts—language, something so unusual to whites that newspapers saw fit to mention it.[45]

Once indentured, Apess confronted new rules and customs. He was immersed in domestic farm labor, living on and cultivating a plot of land considered to be, according to European custom and law, Mr. Furman's sovereign possession. The boy dressed in English clothes and shoes. Even his diet changed, for Natives still consumed such traditional foods as corn stews and roasted fish, with a few vegetables such as peas and potatoes. With the Furmans, Apess ate mutton, beef, cheese, more potatoes and other vegetables grown in the farmer's kitchen garden, and apples; and the family would season food with salt and occasionally sweeten it with molasses or sugar. The beer, cider, and rum that had destroyed his grandparents' lives were ubiquitous, for before the 1830s there was little concern with temperance.[46] Even the discipline the Furmans administered was different, for, despite Apess's severe beatings at the hands of his relatives, in general the region's Native people frowned on corporal punishment or even scolding their children, fearing that such actions destroyed a young person's self-confidence and sapped the life force. In a white household, Apess did not escape lashing, verbal or literal, nor the resentment, depression, and self-loathing they engendered.[47]

In one way, however, Apess was more fortunate than many of the poor children and adults whom towns supported through this voluntary system, for by his own testimony the Furmans lived comfortably. It was not so in every foster home. One scathing critic of New Englanders' treatment of their indigent complained that too often those who stepped forward to help the less fortunate themselves occupied a social station barely above those whom they assisted. Some foster parents were "desperate, hardened, and intemperate" common laborers whose family members were "scolds, rough and overbearing," and thus from whom "kind words and gentle demeanor" were rare. Worst of all, because the local poor system rewarded families who bid the lowest to maintain a needy individual, those who offered assistance were often "a class of mere and much-loving money-getters" and frequently not scrupulous in fulfilling their obligations. To them, supporting the poor was not charity but a way to supplement their meager incomes.[48]

Cruel Beginnings

Before moving in with the Furmans, Apess had never been inside a meetinghouse and was ignorant of the Christian religion. When he was about six years old, Mrs. Furman raised the issue of death and a "state of future existence," subjects that frightened him because he could not yet comprehend what they meant. This conversation and Mrs. Furman's subsequent repeated "pious admonitions" to good behavior made a lasting impression on him and marked the beginning of a lifelong concern with his soul (23–25).

Part of Apess's initial exposure to Christianity included his guardians' and other whites' constant injunctions not to persist in "Indian" ways. So assiduously did the Furmans attempt to wean Apess "from the interests and affections of [his] brethren," he recalled, that a mere threat of being sent away "among the Indians into the dreary woods" became a stronger incentive to obedience than any threats of corporal punishment. Because Apess remembered how his own relatives had mistreated him, he believed that he could expect no better (and probably worse) from other members of his race who knew him "in no other relation than that of a cast off member of the tribe" (20–21). Such thoughts tragically led to deep-seated fear of any of his own people whom he might encounter.

To emphasize this visceral example of what amounted to self-hatred, Apess related an anecdote as harrowing as that of his beating at his grandmother's hands when he said that he did "hate" her. One day while gathering berries with some of his adoptive family, Apess encountered a group of women at the same task whose complexion was "as dark as that of the natives." We do not learn if they were indeed Natives or African Americans, for all Apess relates was his reaction: he was so terrified that he left his party and ran all the way home, a behavior prompted by the many stories he had heard of the Natives' cruelty to whites, of "how they were in the habit of killing and scalping men, women and children" (22–23).[49]

At this time, Apess also thought it disgraceful to be called an "Indian" because whites so often hurled it "as an opprobrious epithet at the sons of the forest" (20–21). Even Mr. Furman used it. Hearing from "one of the girls belonging to the house [presumably another needy child the Furmans had taken in]" that Apess had threatened her with a knife (a lie), he called his ward to him and said, "I will learn you, you Indian dog, how to chase people with a knife." Despite Apess's vehement denials, Furman severely whipped him. The other children subsequently assured their master that Apess had not done the thing of which he had been accused, but the stigma of the word "Indian" had done its psychological damage.

Christianity taught Apess to resist the self-loathing such treatment engendered. But it was not Mrs. Furman's Baptist brethren who first pointed the way. Rather, when he was eight years old, some people whom he described as "the Christians" visited his neighborhood. "Their hearts were warm with the cause of God," he recalled, and they would sing hymns to Zion and "pray earnestly for each other." He was very much taken with the emotional appeal of their worship, and having "very strange feelings for a child of [his] age," he resolved to become better. It worked. He had been known as a "rude" boy, but now his neighbors recognized a change (24–25). After a short while, these traveling evangelists left the area but not before having whetted Apess's interest in a religion of the heart of the sort they preached.

The way Apess names this group, "the Christians," suggests that he did not mean the term generically. Rather, these were likely followers of Elias Smith, a Vermont native and strong Jeffersonian who in the 1790s had left his Calvinist Baptist faith to espouse a doctrinally simplified Christianity based in radically democratic principles. Smith claimed, for example, that every individual should read the New Testament for himself or herself and not blindly follow inherited dogma as interpreted by the priesthood. Further, along with others of this persuasion, such as Barton Stone in Kentucky and Alexander Campbell in Pennsylvania, Smith rejected all notions of civil hierarchy, linking his religious beliefs to the nascent political culture whose champions sought to extend the boundaries of American democracy.[50]

A master of publicity and communication, in 1808 Smith took advantage of the explosive expansion of print culture to start the nation's first religious newspaper, the *Herald of Gospel Liberty*, to proselytize his cause. Through it, he urged Christians to follow religious liberty wherever it took them despite any objections from established clergy. Indeed, Smith permanently earned their wrath by calling their seminaries nothing but "Religious Manufactories" established for "explaining that which is plain, and for the purpose of making easy things hard."[51] The Christian Connexion, as his denomination came to be known—later, the Disciples of Christ—proved an appropriate faith for budding democracy; the very term "connexion" implies the sense of an extended, loving family relationship among all believers. Not surprisingly, when Apess was able to read the Gospels for himself, he focused on those passages in which Christ preached the equality of all men and women under God, regardless of skin color.

Cruel Beginnings

The visit of "the Christians" made Apess ponder further the mysteries of death and the afterlife. His fear and confusion was increased when Mrs. Furman's mother, who lived with the family, died. This was the first corpse that he had seen, Apess remembered, and he was "much affected." He and the woman had been very close, compounding his sorrow; and she even had allowed Apess to call her "mother." Shortly after this, his "distress of body" and "anxiety of mind wore [him] down," and he became quite ill. Neither the local physician nor anyone else in town could diagnose his symptoms and were helpless to assist him. Whenever Apess lay down, for example, it seemed as if something were choking him; when he sat up, "the wind would rise in [his] throat and nearly strangle [him]." Apess felt continually as if he were being suffocated, and someone from the family had to attend him constantly (27–28).

What followed was even more unusual, if also indicative of the superstition that still reigned among lower-class New Englanders. With the persistence of the boy's sickness, Mr. Furman decided to try to "frighten" the disease out of him. He explained that the Devil had possessed the boy and had to be flogged out. Furman truly believed that this would "cure" the boy, and when it did not, he gave him a dreadful whipping.

Things only got worse. One morning, as Apess was helping to milk the cows, he felt "very singular" and began to make a strange noise, prompting him to run back to the house because he thought he was dying. Mrs. Furman followed, fearing that he was indeed near his end. The strange noise, so loud that it could be heard "fifteen or twenty rods off," accompanied every breath. It was perhaps that of whooping cough or croup, but because of his newfound fear of death, it caused him irrational fright (28–29).

METHODISM

Shortly after this episode, Apess slowly began to mend, but rather than rejoicing in his deliverance and thanking God that he had found Christianity, he began to resist all discipline, secular or religious. For one thing, Apess again sought out some "old school fellows" and with them began to profane the Sabbath. When he was eleven, things took a more serious turn. It was "fashionable" for boys to run away at about that age, and the oldest ward on the Furman's farm encouraged him in this. Apess "thought it was a very pretty notion to be a man," that is, to leave his situation, work for himself, and make money. He made plans to run off with this friend to New London, where he believed he would be "metamorphosed into a person of consequence." But, instead, the older boy betrayed him to Mr. Furman, who decided to rid himself of the growing trouble Apess had begun to cause him by selling his remaining term of service. Judge William Hillhouse (1728–1816), of Montville, near New London, a prominent citizen who had served in the Continental Congress, purchased it for twenty dollars (29–30).[52]

The Hillhouses—strict Presbyterians—treated Apess well, even surprising him with a jackknife, but only to "promote their interests," that is, to ingratiate themselves with their new worker. After two weeks, it was clear that Apess was no longer the family's favorite; for example, now they dressed him in tatters. As Apess's circumstances became more trying, some of his early religious impressions returned, and for consolation he frequently hid behind the barn to pray. He also began to attend evening meetings of an unnamed religious group, but Hillhouse very quickly prohibited it.

In response, Apess ran off briefly and was flogged severely on his return, which only prompted him to consider a more decisive break. He headed for New London and then, a few days later, went on to Waterford. When he learned that his father was living only about twenty miles farther, he made his way to him, intending to stay but a week. At the end of that time, Apess's father told him to return to Hillhouse, which he did, only to run off again after a few days. When the judge realized that he could no longer control the boy, he resold his indenture, to General William Williams (1781–1853), a prominent New London resident.[53]

At first, Williams treated Apess well, and his assigned labor was not difficult. But it soon was apparent that his new guardians considered him nothing but their servant, "from the cook to the clerk" (30–34). His reaction to such menial service reveals much about his own sense of difference from the African Americans with whom whites often lumped Natives like him. Apess would not submit, he later wrote, to being treated like "the poor African," answering yes, "'Massa, Massa—Mister, Mister,'" at their every command. He pointedly called the Williamses "by their regular names."[54]

Hillhouse had warned Williams that Apess was likely to run off, and thus from the outset his new master brooked no infraction of the rules. A devout Presbyterian, Hillhouse insisted that his charge go to meeting, but Apess soon realized that the services of "the Christians" had been much more rewarding. In particular, he disliked the Presbyterian minister's habit of reading prepared sermons. "The Christians," he recalled, "depended [only] on the holy Spirit" for their inspiration (36–37).

Apess endured Williams's regimen and, presumably, Presbyterian ser-

Cruel Beginnings

vices for a few years. Then an itinerant Methodist began to hold meetings in the neighborhood, even as members of other denominations ridiculed him and his followers for their erroneous doctrine and overly emotional services. People of "character" did not attend such meetings, Apess was told. But he found the services moving and believed he had "no character to lose," and he attended whenever he could, for the Methodists' sincerity deeply impressed him. They seemed to be kind and gentle people, their manner was plain, and their hymns were beautiful. The power of God attended their exercises, Apess believed, something evident in their minister's sermons, for he spoke with authority derived from experience and not book learning.

Then at one meeting when the minister preached on the text *"Behold the Lamb of God, that taketh away the sins of the world,"* Apess understood that Christ had indeed died for all mankind. "Age, sect, colour, country, or situation, made no difference," he realized; and thus he was convinced that, "with all [his Native] brethren," he was "included in the plan of redemption." The power of this experience removed every excuse Apess had to not seek salvation; but, ironically, it led not only to prayer and soul-searching but also to sleepless nights filled with tears and anguish as Apess frequently awoke frightened by visions of his own death and yearning for reassurance that he deserved God's love (37–42).

Apess endured such extreme psychological disruption for almost two months. Then, "on the fifteenth day of March, in the year of our Lord eighteen hundred and thirteen," at work in the garden, he heard a voice say, *"Arise, thy sins which were many are all forgiven thee, go in peace and sin no more!"* Apess's heart "melted into tenderness" and his soul filled with love for God and all mankind. "There was not only a change in my heart but in every thing around me," he recalled (45). Christ had accepted him, poor and despised as the fifteen-year-old thought he was.

Apess's discovery of Methodism coincided with this denomination's remarkable growth through large-scale revival meetings, the most famous of which had been the interdenominational gathering of thousands at Cane Ridge, Kentucky, in 1801. Within a few years, Methodism had spread to western New York state and rural New England. In no small measure, this was due to the influence of its charismatic itinerants. Indefatigable in their efforts, ministers like Lorenzo Dow and his followers literally knocked on doors to rally people to their outdoor meetings, many of which lasted for days at extensive campgrounds on the outskirts of towns.[55]

Although highly centralized under the direction of regional bishops, the Methodist Episcopal Church (its formal name) also decentralized authority below that level by naming lay class leaders and exhorters as well as ordained clergy who traveled to Sabbath services on "circuits," that is, on a regular basis. Coupled with Methodist doctrine's compatibility with the country's nascent democratic culture—the denomination welcomed people of any social station—clergy conferred on converts a dignity and sense of belonging that their custom of calling each other "brother" and "sister" outwardly marked.[56] Not surprisingly, many of the converts came from the lower classes and people of color.[57]

The Methodists' message gave young Apess solace, even if he found it difficult to practice his faith consistently. For one thing, General Williams continued to discourage attendance at the weekly class meetings Apess so much enjoyed, telling his charge that he was deluded to think that such "sectarian nonsense" could save one's soul. To his unsympathetic neighbors, Apess became "like a partridge upon the mountain, a mark for them all to shoot at, and hiss at, and quack at," that is, to ridicule.[58] And attending meetings in spite of such discouragement and humiliation, he frequently returned to severe floggings. Even his peers joined in this petty persecution: on one occasion, a chambermaid pushed him down a flight of stairs and severely injured him, because he was a Methodist. Unsurprisingly, Apess again decided to run away, this time with John Miner, a poor white friend his own age (46–48).[59]

This plan soon enough assumed more importance to Apess than his religion, and he again began to backslide. For his travels, he surreptitiously charged a new pair of shoes on General Williams's store account and bought rum as well, which he and his comrade drank as the young runaways made their way away from the farm. They headed for Colchester, about fourteen miles away, and then visited Apess's father, who had returned to the area to visit other Natives, who presumably had alerted his son to his presence. As he had done previously when Apess had visited him in Colrain, he begged his son to reconsider and return to his master, which, perhaps surprisingly, Apess promised. Later, he remembered how his parent had watched him for a long time as he and his friend departed. But, despite Apess's obvious affection for his father, as soon as the boys were out of the elder man's sight, they changed direction. Apess did not see his parent for eight more years (48–50).

The runaways made their way to Hartford, using a ruse fellow runaway John concocted: they gulled people along the route, telling the sad tale of how a British privateer had captured them off New York City—this was at the beginning of the War of 1812, which was, above all else a naval war—and had later released them near New London. They were making their way back to the city to see their parents, they said; and through this tale they often got free meals and lodgings. They had almost reached New York when the captain of one coasting vessel on which they had hitched a ride began to suspect them—John had told an absurd story of how their captors had served them bread mixed with ground glass—and threatened to return them for reward. Apess blunted the captain's enthusiasm by saying that General Williams had been glad to be rid of him and had thus insultingly offered only a one-cent reward. This put off the captain for a while, and as the vessel neared the New York City, both boys slipped away (50–52).

They found rooms in working-class quarters in Cherry Street, near Pearl and Catherine Streets in lower Manhattan, for two dollars a week, and worked for sixty-two cents a day, unskilled laborer's wages. All went well until Apess learned that Williams in fact had posted a fifteen dollar reward for him, and he rightly suspected that this sizable sum would encourage the suspicious boat captain or others to search for him. He considered flight further down the coast, to Philadelphia. But John instead urged Apess to join him in going to sea, a common escape for runaways. Apess refused and soon found himself alone in New York City (53).

TWO

War, Wandering, and Home
{ 1812-1829 }

The War of 1812 necessitated the recruitment of considerable soldiery, and it is not surprising that shortly after his arrival in New York Apess encountered a sergeant and a few of his men trying to convince volunteers to enlist to fight the British. They considered the young man a likely prospect and plied him with alcohol and stories of what good times soldiers had. They subsequently flattered him by affixing a cockade to his cap and gave him money to procure a uniform. The fifteen-year-old Apess—hazel-eyed, with dark complexion and black hair, five feet two inches tall—was in fact too young to enlist (though he gave his age as seventeen), but the recruiters, eager for more bodies for the front, told him that he could serve as a drum corpsman rather than an artilleryman.[1]

Before he knew it, Apess was on Governor's Island in New York harbor, site of a U.S. Army post since 1783. The island contained two main fortifications, Fort Columbus, built on the site of an earlier eighteenth-century redoubt, and the recently completed Castle Williams, an impressive circular edifice with over one hundred cannons positioned on three levels as well as on its roof, able to marshal weaponry in a 220-degree arc. At this military bastion, Apess seemed to fit right in: he played cards and drank rum as much as any of his fellow enlistees. But in recounting the experience in his autobiography, he had his readers believe that he never forgot his conversion at the Methodists' hands nor escaped the guilt and anguish some of his debauchery caused him (54–55).

Apess had not been there long before he learned about the violent world he had just entered, for with the rest of the enlistees he witnessed the execution of several troops for mutiny. "I cannot tell how I felt," he later wrote, "when I saw the soldiers parade, and the condemned[,] clothed in white with bibles in their hands, come forward." The post's band played the "dead march" as they accompanied the men to the place of their exe-cution, where they were forced to kneel on their coffins alongside newly dug graves. The chaplain spoke with them, caps were pulled over their eyes and then one soldier was separated some distance from the others. Using his handkerchief, the commanding office gave three signals in se-quence—to prepare to fire, to aim, and to shoot at the kneeling soldiers. "Death never seemed so awful," Apess remembered, and even more so for the poor wretch who was led aside and without foreknowledge spared from execution. The man was completely overcome from his close brush with death. He wept like a child and needed help to return to his quarters. "To me," Apess recalled, it was "an awful day" (56–57).

Such scenes were frequently repeated during the War of 1812, often precisely in the way Apess recorded, with soldiers—usually deserters at the front—either summarily executed or brought to the brink of death and saved as a frightening object lesson to themselves and others. The accused might be told that one of the guns held a blank, making them hope for fortune's favor; at other times, without the condemned men's knowledge, all the muskets fired blanks. When they heard the percussion, some of the guilty fainted and had to be revived, to learn that they had been pardoned only this once.[2] Punishment for desertion was draconian because disci-pline was so poor: during the war at least 5,000 American troops deserted, around 13 percent of the recruits. In contrast, one historian has noted, only 3 percent died in combat and 8 percent from disease.[3]

Why this high number of deserters? The war in which Apess had so readily enlisted in fact was very unpopular, nowhere more so than in his home state of Connecticut and in the Northeast generally, where citizens resisted the notion that outright warfare with the British was inevitable. But some "War Hawks" saw increasing evidence of Great Britain's con-tempt of the United States' hard-won sovereignty and urged immediate and sharp response to any challenge, intended or not.[4]

One particularly thorny issue related to the boundary between the United States and Canada. The lands from upper New York state west along Lakes Erie and Ontario to the fort at Detroit remained contested ground, hitherto controlled by Native Americans, who now frequently allied with the British to limit further American encroachment from the south and east. In this region, border skirmishes were frequent and a de-cided impediment to American expansion to the Mississippi River.[5]

Given this tense situation, land-hungry Americans pressed for the conquest and incorporation of Canada into the new nation. Complicat-ing matters, after the Revolution many Loyalists had moved into Upper

Canada, their allegiance now torn between Great Britain and the United States, where many had left behind friends and relatives. As a result, the most important battles in the war occurred on the Great Lakes between hastily assembled and deployed navies.

Kentucky senator Henry Clay, however, observed, that "Canada was not the end but the means" of the war. Its real object was "the redress of injuries," and Canada was the "instrument" by which that redress was to be obtained.[6] Widespread lack of support for the war consequently affected the number and caliber of the troops and contributed to the high percentage of desertions. At the beginning of 1812, for example, Congress had authorized a force of 35,000 men but a year later had raised only a little more than half that number, helping to explain the New York recruitment party's pressure on Apess. But bounties for enlistment and soldiers' pay were low, with sixteen dollars given on enlistment and a promise of five dollars per month, below half of what a day laborer in New York earned.

By the time the sergeant convinced Apess to enlist, Congress had sweetened the pot: forty dollars on enlistment and a promise of eight dollars a month, for a year's commitment. Originally Congress had required recruits to serve for five years, but by 1813, in its desperation to fill the ranks, it had reduced the term.[7] And still recruitment lagged, even with Congress's offer of 160 acres of land per soldier after the war. Most recruits, however, seemed more interested in the monthly stipend, which unfortunately was not forthcoming on any regular basis and by the end of the war was frequently six to twelve months in arrears.[8]

Adding to the field commanders' difficulties were the troops' general lack of training and supplies. Many of the enlistees were intractable, not responsive to discipline, and with short tempers and obstreperous behavior as a result of the prolonged discomfort they endured. Marching much more than fighting, the men soon enough realized how little glory "war" really entailed. In addition to muskets or rifles (or in Apess's case, a drum), troops carried forty- to fifty-pound packs, and often on muddy roads and through swollen streams in the frigid Adirondack winter. In all weather, they camped on the ground and often had to wait for long periods for resupply of food and other necessities. Warm fires were one of the few comforts, but soldiers frequently did without because the light could betray their positions.[9] Excessive use of alcohol was a constant temptation, with daily rations given to help the troops cope with the manifold discomforts of service. Predictably, there was hoarding and stealing, and drunkenness on duty was an infraction officers commonly had to address.[10] Apess was

War, Wandering, and Home

no more immune to drink's supposed pleasures than anyone else and admitted to frequent abuse of alcohol during his period of enlistment.

OFF TO CANADA

After a short time on Governor's Island, Apess and his cohort were ordered to Staten Island, where they waited two weeks before beginning their advance on Canada. They had been mustered to the war's northeastern front, along the St. Lawrence River, and traveled by sloop up the Hudson River to Albany and thence to quarters in nearby Greenbush. To Apess's surprise, he soon was transferred to infantry and provided with a musket, his age now less important than another weapon at the front. He disliked his new duties, particularly night watch, and thought that his reassignment was "contrary to law" because on enlistment he had been promised that he would be a music corpsman, presumably a relatively safe job.

Wishing to see his father again, Apess took his reassignment to infantry to mean that the government had broken their agreement with him, and he simply left camp, not realizing the army's unequivocal claim on him. Soon enough he was recaptured, brought back to camp and charged with desertion, and placed under guard. On the subsequent march north to join other troops at Plattsburgh, New York, on Lake Champlain, the officers continually tormented him. In an unambiguous insult to his background, they repeatedly told him that they intended to stick his skin full of pine splinters and, after "having an Indian pow wow" over him, then light the wood and burn him to death, clear reference to one of the ways that whites believed Natives tortured their captives (57–58).[11]

Late in 1813, Apess's unit went into winter quarters at Plattsburgh, New York, the site of a large American encampment. The conditions were intolerable, even by early nineteenth-century standards. In that frigid season, the troops had only straw to lie on and hardly ever drew full rations. Officers were fed first, and the enlisted men were given what (if anything) remained: raw corn, unleavened bread made from flour they pooled together from their rations, and anything "eatable that fell in their way." The troops also found that any ground they gained had little strategic value, for the British burned everything upon retreat, so that even the army's horses—Apess had again been reassigned, now to units hauling heavy artillery behind these animals—could not find forage. In short, the soldiers' conditions were "indescribable."

Finally, on October 26, the American troops, numbering several thousand and having followed the Chateaugay River north under General Wade Hampton's command, faced off against a force of Canadians and Abenaki Indians one-tenth their size and led by Lieutenant Colonel Charles de Salaberry. Making a terrific din with bugles and shouts, the enemy persuaded Hampton that they were an overwhelming force. After some hours of fighting in swampy land in a cold, heavy rain, Hampton grew disheartened and ordered a full retreat—he did not "fancy the smell of gunpowder," Apess wryly remarked, even as, lacking a sense of indigenous geography and intertribal relations, he failed to mention that he had had to fight against other Natives. Having lost the Battle of Chateaugay even though their numbers were greatly superior, the Americans withdrew to Plattsburgh to wait out the winter of 1813–14 (59–60).

The loss was a disaster, for Hampton's advance had been planned as part of a pincer movement to secure Montreal. General James Wilkinson, head of the American troops at Sackett's Harbor to the west, was to have led his men down the St. Lawrence and approach the city from the west, to join Hampton, a Virginian new to the command, coming from the south. To complicate the comedy of errors, Wilkinson and his immediate subordinate, General John P. Boyd, failed to carry out their part, too. Even more bad news came on November 11, 1813, when the American troops were defeated at the Battle of Chrysler's Farm, essentially forcing them to abort the march on Canada.[12]

In the spring, Apess's unit received orders to join Wilkinson's forces in an attempt to subdue Montreal. The troops crossed into Lower Canadian territory at Odletown, where British soldiers first met them and then retreated to an old, well-fortified mill. From there, they fired a seemingly "incessant cannonade" against the Americans. Apess, in charge of the twelve-pound cannon at the head of the invaders, was shocked at the carnage. "The horribly disfigured bodies of the dead," he wrote, "the piercing groans of the wounded and the dying—the cries of help and succour from those who could not help themselves," appalled him. "I can never forget it." At sundown, the Americans retreated. Even more disheartening, later, as they were pitching their tents, they received the shocking news of the siege of Washington and the burning of the U.S. Capitol (61–63).

In the late summer of 1814, Apess and his cohort again were on the march, this time to help hold Plattsburgh, for the Americans had received word that the British planned a major attack on that strategic town on Lake Champlain. Standing on a height of land at the mouth of the Saranac River, Plattsburgh was fortified with three strong redoubts, but even so the Americans were at considerable disadvantage in terms of manpower. At first, they had over 7,000 troops in the area under the charge of Major General George Izard, who had relieved Wilkinson. But Secretary of War John Armstrong ordered Izard to move 4,000 of them to counter a supposed British buildup near Sackets Harbor on the eastern end of Lake Ontario, another strategic position. That left the defense of Plattsburgh in the hands of Izard's subordinate, General Alexander Macomb, who commanded a force of only 3,400 soldiers.

To complicate the Americans' situation, on the European front of the war British forces recently had defeated Napoleon, freeing thousands of crack British troops for redeployment across the Atlantic. The British commander in Canada, Sir George Prévost, thus had assembled over 10,000 men, including seasoned veterans of the Duke of Wellington's Peninsular Campaign in Iberia, for an all-out assault on the strategically located American encampment.

Prévost also had at his command a formidable flotilla: the *Confiance*, a frigate of thirty-eight guns; a brig with sixteen cannon; two sloops with eleven each; and twelve gunboats with one or two guns apiece, all commanded by Captain George Downie. To fend off this fleet, the U.S. naval forces, under the command of Lieutenant Thomas Macdonough, had the frigate *Saratoga*, with twenty-six guns; the schooner *Ticonderoga*, with seventeen; and a sloop with seven; in addition, there were ten gunboats.[13]

Fighting on land began on September 6, 1814, with the two armies facing off on different sides of the Saranac River. "Congreve rockets [a recently developed propelled explosive device], bomb shells, and cannon balls, poured upon us like a hailstorm," Apess recalled. American troops did not leave their guns for six days and nights, during which Apess commanded a small magazine. Then, on September 11, the British began a full assault on the town, to coincide with their fleet's arrival in the harbor. "The work of death and carnage commenced," Apess remembered. For hours, clouds of smoke from the endless fusillades hid the sun, and a continuous roar from hundreds of cannons echoed off the lake (63–65).

Luck favored the Americans. Under the command of Macdonough, the naval forces prevailed, with a loss of only 52 men to the British side's 200, with Downie one of the casualties. The battle on land also eventually turned in the Americans' favor after Prévost received word that a contingent of 2,500 Vermont militia from Burlington, Vermont, and another 800 from New York were on their way to reinforce the U.S. troops. When Prévost learned of his navy's defeat, he lost his nerve and retreated. Overall, the British lost 2,000 men; the Americans lost only 150. The U.S. forces had won the decisive Battle of Plattsburgh and ended any threat of British invasion from the north.[14]

One day before Christmas, 1814, England and the United States signed the Treaty of Ghent, ending a war that led to few meaningful changes in relations between the countries. Both consented to evacuate territories that they had secured during the warfare and without confiscation of any property; prisoners were returned; and both sides were to make peace with Natives and restore their rights and possessions (even as the United States squeezed them onto ever-smaller tribal lands).[15] Future bilateral commissions were to resolve ongoing disputes over the boundary between the two countries.[16] Like many enlistees, Apess considered his service over, and he left camp on September 14, 1815.

VAGABONDAGE

His unit had not been disbanded, however, and having learned his lesson from earlier in the war when he had tried to leave to see his father, Apess claimed to have sought and obtained a discharge.[17] Entitled to forty dollars bounty money, 160 acres of land, and fifteen-months' salary, Apess never saw any of it. Nor was he alone, for "hundreds [of soldiers] were served in the same manner." The experience bred a mistrust of government that he would feel over and over again, even when he was in a more settled state.

This initiated a liminal period in Apess's life when he wandered through the region penniless and dependent on peoples' charity. He made his way to where some of his "brethren" (that is, other Natives) lived and where he tarried before setting off for Montreal. When he arrived, he was fortunate enough to be hired by a baker, work that he enjoyed but that he admitted he jeopardized by what now was an addiction to "drinking rum." He received a few warnings about his intoxication but finally lost this job after an encounter in a tavern with one of the "king's soldiers," whom he abused and beat, in the process breaking a jug for which he had to pay. Stealing some of his master's money to make reparation, he was caught and summarily fired (66–68).

Apess then held a succession of odd jobs. He hired himself to a farmer for four dollars a month, stayed but two, and with his pay bought better clothes. He worked as a servant; but this did not suit him, probably because the work was too confining. He traveled up the St. Lawrence River to Kingston, where he was hired for twelve dollars a month to cook on

War, Wandering, and Home

board a sloop. He stayed several months but was angry to find that, when it was time "to settle accounts," the captain cheated him of a month's pay. Apess then went "into the country"—presumably to the backcountry, away from more populous settlements—to work for a merchant. His employer gave him a pint of rum a day, as he did each of his employees, presumably to keep them contented. As happened more and more often when liquor was available, Apess neglected his work and soon left his job (68–69).

He continued his odyssey through Upper Canada, again striking off "into the country," this time near the Bay of Quinty (Quinte), on the northern shore of Lake Ontario, near the head of the St. Lawrence River and 250 miles west of Montreal. He stayed there through the winter of 1816 with a Dutch farmer, for whom he primarily gathered firewood. Here he encountered many Haudenosaunees, primarily Mohawks and Mississauga Ojibwes—his "brethren were all around him," and it "seemed like home," he remembered—and he even joined them on hunting expeditions, for in that region they often supplemented their diet with game and as well exchanged skins for goods or cash.[18]

Further north, the forest was even more "alive with its sons and daughters," in whose dwellings he felt welcome and comfortable. He remembered a telling contrast between their encampments and the surrounding British settlements, for the latter had been set up haphazardly, their inhabitants more interested in economic gain than in establishing and maintaining community. In contrast, the Natives kept their encampments "in the utmost order and regularity" and "held all things in common," that is, shared their goods with each other, remaining wary of the kind of division of land often urged on them by Christian missionaries or those who worked for rapacious land companies for whom privatization of tribal land made its later acquisition easier.[19]

When spring arrived, Apess's employer tapped maple trees to gather sap to boil down to sugar. Apess waxed eloquent about the beauty of this season. He continued to spend much time with the Haudenosaunees, who also were "very cheerful on account of [spring's] return, and enjoyed themselves in hunting, fishing, basket making, &c." While among these Natives—about 250 Tyendinaga Mohawks also lived in this area—Apess resisted the vices, particularly excessive drinking, that had dogged him since his early teens.[20]

He was traveling among these tribes during the last years of the great Seneca prophet Handsome Lake (Gos-kuk-ke-wa-na-kon-ne-di-yu), who himself had undergone a remarkable personal transformation. The half brother of Cornplanter, a tribal war chief, Handsome Lake had progressively become alcoholic, so much so that by the end of the eighteenth century even his comrades regarded him as a drunkard, and as sunken into poverty and humiliation. From 1799 to 1801, however, virtually in delirium tremens, he experienced a series of prophetic visions that he subsequently related to his countrymen. At first eschatological in nature and then increasingly proscriptive, his dreams revealed that in order to survive as a people, the Senecas had to reverse their headlong tumble into sin and dissipation, and particularly to renounce both the use of alcohol and the practice of witchcraft, which, fueled by some of the members' increasingly desperate personal situations (attributable to drink and poverty), had spread widely. This came at a critical moment for indigenous revival, for Tecumseh and Tenskwatawa (the "Shawnee Prophet") recently had offered similar prescriptions as well as calls to resist the encroachment of white settlers, and Apess's time among the Senecas thus may have helped to expose him to a broader, more radical form of Native American identity.[21]

Until his death in 1815, Handsome Lake advocated a social gospel—the "Gaiwiio" or "Good Word"—in which, in addition to abstinence, he counseled a rejection of promiscuity and a domestic economy that honored the sanctity of family and tribe. Also, recognizing that Europeans were there to stay, he championed syncretism between traditional Native beliefs and Christianity, and, thus, peaceful coexistence with whites.[22]

Handsome Lake's ethic met resistance during his lifetime, particularly because of his severe denunciation of Native spiritual practices and its rejection by a faction of Senecas around Buffalo Creek in western New York (led by his nephew Red Jacket), who rejected assimilation to white society and led Seneca attempts to resist white settlers' attempts to buy Seneca lands and remove the Natives.[23] In 1826, these efforts culminated in the federal government's support for the Ogden Land Company's plan to sell lands on the Buffalo Creek reservation, and within a year, white settlers were purchasing parcels of the rich farmland.[24]

Despite such resistance, however, after Handsome Lake's death, his ethic spread widely among the Iroquois, particularly those in the middle and eastern parts of their lands, the very areas that Apess visited after the war. This powerful spiritual "renaissance," a mixture of Native American and Christian piety, was part and parcel of what came to be known as the Second Great Awakening. Such an unexpected interest in religion buoyed Christian missionaries—particularly Quakers—who in the 1820s and 1830s redoubled efforts to bring more Natives into the Christian fold.[25]

There are tantalizing clues that Apess knew of Handsome Lake and

War, Wandering, and Home

his important work among the New York tribes, and that, in turn, by the 1840s some of the Haudenosaunees involved in the challenge to the Buffalo Creek Treaty were aware of Apess's writings. William Parker, for example, whose wife, Elizabeth Johnson, was the daughter of Jimmy Johnson, Handsome Lake's successor, had fought in the same part of western New York as Apess. One of Elizabeth and William's sons, Ely Parker, was instrumental in continuing to promulgate Handsome Lake's ethic, translating some of his ancestor's visionary materials for the pioneering anthropologist Lewis Henry Morgan, who subsequently published them as the "Code of Handsome Lake." In the 1840s, Ely had used, without attribution, parts of Apess's *Eulogy on King Philip* (1836) in some of his lectures. Similarly, in some of his extant school papers, Parker's younger brother, Nicholson, also referred to the *Eulogy*.[26]

Most suggestively, toward the end of Apess's career, after he had returned to New York City and begun to lecture on Native history and culture, newspapers reported that one "Gos-kuk-wa-na-kon-ne-di-yu" would deliver these talks, printing virtually the same name (save for the absence of one syllable) traditionally used for Handsome Lake, whose influence by that time was widely discussed in the period's missionary publications.[27]

LONG JOURNEY HOME

Although one cannot say with certainty what Apess took away from his time among the Haudenosaunees, one suspects that his exposure to those who knew firsthand the Seneca revival and the beginnings of the tribe's battles for sovereignty of their lands was crucial to his subsequent career.[28] Apess's experience in Canada and New York later would combine potently with his discovery through Methodism of Christianity's egalitarian message to give rise to his extraordinary self-expression and mantle of leadership among New England Natives.

In the late winter of 1816, when maple sugaring was done, though, Apess again felt wanderlust. He told his employer, the Dutch farmer, that he wished to see his "friends in the east" (that is, the Pequots in Connecticut) from whom he now had been absent about three years. With some regret, the farmer paid Apess his wages, and he began to make his way toward Kingston, Ontario. Predictably, as he got farther from his "brethren" and their lifestyle and closer to this large town where temptations abounded, Apess again fell in "with bad company" (69–74).

Along the way, a Native family—he did not say of what tribe—took him in, but Apess found drink there, too, discovering that there was "much trouble in the wigwam" because of his host's wife's intemperance, a situation that soon split apart the couple. The ensuing acrimony again sent Apess on the road, where he fell in with others as destitute as himself who now urged him to get by through theft. Fortunately, Apess resisted, but for the wrong reason: these men were not his "brethren," but were "whites," and so only were "pretended friends" whose advice he did not trust (74–75).

Throughout these periods of temptations, Apess did not forget his religion. One day, on his way home, he wandered into a church service, where the sermon moved him; and later, sitting in the sun meditating on his future course, he serendipitously met four white "fishermen"—today we would term them sportsmen—who hired him on the spot to accompany them into the backwoods. The party fished and hunted deer for a month in the Adirondack wilderness of northern New York, and Apess impressed them so much that, this outing ended, they wanted to take him to meet their families.

Thankful for their trust and kindness but still yearning to rejoin his family and friends among the Pequots, Apess took his wages, spent most of the money on new clothes, and moved on to Utica, New York. He worked aboard a merchant's boat in exchange for passage down the Mohawk River and then made his way on foot toward Albany, either ignored or "blackguarded" because he was an "Indian." Virtually destitute, when Apess heard meetinghouse bells ring for a man who recently had been struck dead by lightning—it was customary to toll the deceased's age—he reflected on the fragility of his own life and thanked God that he was still alive (76–78).

He then crossed the Hudson River at Troy and went over the mountains to Hoosick, New York, now only a hundred miles from his home. He worked on another farm for a month to get money for clothes, moved on to "Old Hartford," in Connecticut (during the War of 1812 he had traveled by "new" Hartford, near Glens Falls, New York), where he ran into a "ruff," intemperate bunch, who convinced him to accompany them to sea. Whether Apess sought out such company or frequently found himself among it because of his own impoverished circumstances is unclear. Fortunately, this time he steered clear of the rogues, worked in the area through the winter, and in the following spring of 1817, finally reached people he knew in Groton, Connecticut. They greeted him as "one risen from the dead" (78–79).

For the next year, Apess worked as a day laborer for a Mr. Geers, who when the time came to pay Apess, tried to cheat him and physically

War, Wandering, and Home

threatened him "as he would a degraded African slave." Thereupon Apess picked up a "cart-stake," confronted Geers and forced him to put down his weapon, and drew his salary. Apess was still only nineteen years old (79–80).

BY THE GRACE OF GOD

In the autumn of 1818, Apess began to live a "steady" life, self-conscious about the ways in which his moods vacillated from the heights of religious fervor and ecstasy to the sloughs of despond and neglect. He recalled how God often had called him, and how for a while he had eagerly answered, only to tumble back to sinfulness. Shame and guilt weighed him down, and he begged for forgiveness, but now the Spirit did not answer.

Apess became depressed, could scarcely eat or sleep, and was too weak to work. He confronted the "unpardonable sin," despair, and one day, when he was angry and frustrated, uttered a "horrid" oath. At that instant, he heard his heart beat "like the pendulum of a clock." His conscience "roared despair like thunder," and he thought that he was going to hell immediately. Thereafter, whenever he asked God's pardon, the Devil tried to persuade him that his efforts were fruitless, given Apess's blasphemy (80–82).

His despair continued, even though every Sunday he walked seven miles each way to attend services. Then, one weekend, Apess attended a Methodist "camp meeting."[29] A contemporary, Catherine Williams, a writer from Providence, Rhode Island, attended one such meeting in nearby Smithfield at about the same time. She admittedly went from curiosity and was repelled by what she saw. The "free intermingling of society" at such protracted events—the one she attended lasted a week—disgusted her, she wrote. Moreover, she noted that such camp meetings clearly drew many nonbelievers, who were more interested in the flesh than the Spirit. The meeting grounds, she reported, "swarmed with drunkards and gamblers, and horse jockies [sic] and pickpockets, and offenders of every other description." She several times mentioned the presence of African Americans, even passing an "African tent" filled with "coloured people."[30] Apess, though, was bowled over by his experience at similar services. The participants' prayers greatly moved him, as did their songs of praise. He was so overwhelmed that he gazed at the scene "like a brainless clown." Posthaste, he united with a local Methodist society and began what members termed a six-month "trial."

The first time that Apess was called on to pray out loud (as was the Methodists' custom), though, he was terrified, embarrassed by what he believed was his inadequacy. Fellow attendees counseled, however, not to try to please others or himself, but God, and after uttering a halting prayer he felt relieved and buoyed. But, predictably, given the stigma under which Methodists labored, Apess met only ridicule when he reported his newfound joy to his employer and his family. They derided the Methodists as "deluded" (83–84).

Fortunately, Apess was able to keep up his newfound faith even after he rejoined the Pequots in the Groton area. Here he spent time with his aunt, Sally George, a pious widow who supported herself by renting her portion of tribal lands to whites. She was at the center of a group of Methodists from Stonington and parts of western Rhode Island as well as from the Groton lands who held monthly meetings, often three days long. Having no meetinghouse, they met outdoors, and always "in perfect love and friendship" (85).

Sally George (1799–1824) provided Apess with both religious instruction and a powerful model of living faith. She had encountered Christian teaching at an early age and been particularly guided by women—as she put it, she had some "precious privileges," that is, she had "good advice from those who were mothers of Israel."[31] In her early teens, she, like Apess to that point in his life, had been almost overcome with despair and planned to drown herself in a deep brook. But before she carried out her plan, she dropped to the ground, prayed for deliverance, and was thereupon "translated into the kingdom of God." "When I came to myself," she told Apess, "I was praising God; there was a change in everything around me, the glory of the Lord shone around, all creation praised God, my burden and my fears were gone, the tempter had fled, and I was clothed, and in my right mind, sitting at the feet of Jesus."[32]

Sally George eventually became a central religious presence for her people, who "counted [her as] almost a preacher." Her language in prayer and exhortation "was free, lively, and animating," and she ministered to the physical as well as the spiritual needs of her neighbors, often "doctoring the sick."[33] When in good health, Sally George thought nothing of walking twenty miles to meeting, a distance she covered, Apess reported, in a mere three and a half hours, a journey and pace that he struggled to keep up with. Not the least significant, when she died, in her mid-forties, both Natives and whites attended her funeral, so deeply had she touched the inhabitants of the surrounding region (85).

Not long after Apess listened to Aunt Sally George's teachings, he had a conversion experience similar to hers. At another lengthy camp meeting, he felt "moved to rise and speak" and found a powerful eloquence.

War, Wandering, and Home

He was in his "proper element," he wrote, "harnessed" for God's work. After this meeting, which brought over a hundred new believers into the fold, Apess requested baptism by immersion, and in December 1818, in a nearby New London County town called Bozrah (near Norwich), a Reverend Mr. Barnes dipped him and three others in the frigid Thames River (88–89).

Soon wishing to revisit his father and other relatives but not being willing to miss church services, Apess obtained a certificate of good standing from his local Methodist society and made his way to Colrain, where his father again was living. There, Apess joined a small band of Methodists, who allowed him to exhort. During this visit, his father taught him shoemaking, but Apess now believed that his true work was to preach the Gospel. Word of the new preacher traveled quickly through the area, and Apess's next meeting drew a large crowd, though some were curiosity seekers who "had come out to hear the Indian preach." Some tried to disrupt the service, showering Apess with old hats and sticks, but he persisted. Over the next few months, he continued to exhort "wherever the door was opened" and was gratified with his success (90–96). Apess had found his vocation.

A SEARCH FOR LEGITIMACY

As the examples of Apess and Aunt Sally George suggest, at this point in New England Methodist history the denomination welcomed all members of society, including African Americans, Native Americans, and the working poor—particularly factory operatives, men in the sailing trades, and others on the margins of respectable society. Apess seemed a natural to work among such people.

As the next ministerial conference in the area approached, though, one of the circuit preachers counseled Apess to desist temporarily from exhorting because he lacked a formal license to do so. Some might think it presumptuous to do so without approbation, this man confided, and this might damage his chances when he applied formally to the conference for the privilege. For a while Apess heeded this advice, but he soon returned to his lay exhorting. When the presiding elder for the area heard of this, he censured Apess and asked him to admit his error, but Apess refused. Summarily cast from the church, he was livid. What had he done, he later asked, but try to preach *"Christ Jesus, and Him crucified"*? He resented the elder's suggestion that one's fitness for the ministry depended on other men's approbation rather than on a call from God (96–97).

George A. Spywood, another New England Native, had a comparable experience in his attempts to preach for the Methodists.[34] Born in Warwick, Rhode Island, in 1801, to a father from the "Pumham" tribe (that is, a Narragansett, over whom Pomham had been chief) and a mother who was a Mashpee, Spywood early on lost track of his parents and was bound out to different white residents. When he was fifteen, he saw his first Methodist revival, but his master—like Apess's a Presbyterian—discouraged his attendance at meetings. Spywood went to sea, traveled through the Caribbean and to different ports in Europe, and finally, several years later, returned to Providence. There he attended class meetings and then a camp meeting in Woodstock, Connecticut, where he was converted.

Spywood applied for an exhorter's license but during his examination learned that, even if approved, he would not be able to preach to white people. "I now began to see the cruel spirit of prejudice in the Christian church," he observed, and "wanted no such license." He withdrew his application, and when he realized how white Methodist clergy neglected "the situation of [his] colored brethren," he decided to devote all his efforts to them. He had found his vocation, though he was deeply disappointed in his white brothers' seeming rejection of the fact that Christ was no respecter of persons.[35]

Despite the prejudice that Apess and Spywood found in this otherwise democratically inclined denomination, they also encountered Methodists who were genuinely trying to reach a wide variety of converts in a remarkable number of ways. Once awakened, a convert sought out a nearby "society," within which he heard Sabbath sermons when a circuit-riding minister came to the area. Methodists also scheduled larger meetings, called "conferences," to which clergy traveled to decide important matters, particularly the licensing of ministers and the assignment of preaching "circuits." This church hierarchy also worked downward, for each society was divided into "classes" of ten to twenty people who met for religious edification weekly and were overseen by a class leader, a layman who monitored the faith of members and reported the same to the circuit rider. Such classes were themselves further broken into small "bands" of three or four people, of the same sex and general social class, who also met regularly for prayer and discussion.[36] Apess had proved himself effective at all these lower levels and now sought entry into the regular ministry, that is, to his own circuit.

His initial censure in this regard lessened his enthusiasm; but, moved by the Spirit, he continued his lay exhorting. Some good unexpectedly came of all this, for in Saybrook, Connecticut, where he preached to a few "coloured people" who regularly met for worship, he met Mary Wood, a woman ten years older than he, "of nearly the same colour," and who shared his Christian devotion. Wood was born in Lyme, Connecticut, on January 3, 1788. Her father was either—she did not know which for sure—a descendant of one of the "Spanish islands" in the West Indies or a native of Spain. Her mother was a white woman from Lyme, Connecticut.[37] Wood's father had died when she was young, and when she was only six her mother placed her with a family that unfortunately proved "haughty" and "blasphemous." Wood stayed with them until she was twelve and then was bound out to Daniel Ely in Lyme. The Elys were Presbyterians and regularly took Mary to services, but she learned little of religion. She also came to fear and resent both church members and clergy because they gave the impression of being "a better people than others." She began to shed her resistance to the Gospel, however, when she was fourteen and a missionary named Bushnell visited the area and moved her with his message (97).

After she left the Elys, Mary Wood went to Hartford, where she frequently attended music and parties, but she found her conscience pricked and her spiritual state unsettled. At last, at the age of twenty-one and back with her mother, she began to attend Methodist meetings and found at them a concern for the downtrodden that spoke to her own condition and experience as a poor, mixed-race person. Three years later, attending a sick woman, she suddenly "viewed Jesus in the flesh, while upon earth, going about doing good, . . . and sinners falling at his feet, crying for mercy—and Jesus saying, 'Sons, daughters, go in peace and sin no more; for thy sins, which are many, are all forgiven thee.'"

Following this conversion experience, in June 1813 Wood formally joined a Methodist society. In July, Elder Joel Winch of Salem, Connecticut, baptized her and three others by immersion. This ceremony sealed Wood's commitment, even as she knew of the opprobrium that would follow her for having joined the Methodists. This did not dissuade her, though, and like many others in the denomination, once converted, she often traveled to attend camp meetings, once as far as Wilbraham, Massachusetts, where a particularly large one was held.[38] She and Apess crossed paths shortly thereafter and were married on December 16, 1821.

PROVIDENCE, RHODE ISLAND

Apess's means of earning a living remained problematic. Shortly after he was married, he went to Middletown, Connecticut, and worked for a tavern keeper. He next moved to Gloucester, Connecticut, and worked for a farmer who, as part of payment, offered his workers a half pint of liquor each day. At the cost of much derision from his fellow workers, Apess now refused the "bonus." When he left the job, his master paid him extra to make up for what Apess had not drunk. Recalling this episode, he noted what a curse alcohol was to "individuals, to families, to communities," and vowed someday to publish an "Essay on Intemperance," if God would spare him for such work (98–99).

Even though he was now married, Apess continued his peripatetic ways, next going to Hartford to work for a month and then spending a week near Ledyard. In the winter of 1825, with his wife and two children, he moved to Providence, where a sister of his lived. He "follow[ed] trucking [that is, worked at loading, unloading, and pushing carts] for a living" but encountered virulent racial prejudice, for Providence was still feeling the effects of a racially motivated riot. The previous October, white citizens, angered over a purported slight against them by some of the city's African Americans, who had refused to get out of a white person's way on a city street, as custom demanded, attacked and burned the Hard Scrabble neighborhood. William J. Brown, a free African American who lived in Providence at the time, identified the underlying reason for the violence as "our [that is, African Americans'] condition, not having the means to raise [ourselves] in the scale of wealth and affluence."[39]

The Hard Scrabble neighborhood rampage followed other political upheaval in the city, for less than a week earlier a state constitutional amendment to extend the franchise had been defeated, exacerbating social divisions in a community in which, because of stringent property requirements, only half the adult men could vote and where all people of color, no matter how much property they owned, were excluded from the right by a law that had been passed in 1822. Further complicating the situation, after the white assailants and arsonists involved in the Hard Scrabble riot were acquitted, many local people of color faced the added indignity of being driven from town as not being suitable inhabitants, this according to a law carried over from the colonial period.[40] Aimed primarily at African Americans, whom the town fathers increasingly viewed as morally corrosive, the law also applied to Native Americans—in short, to anyone who was "colored."[41]

A contemporary census of tenements and boardinghouses ordered by the town fathers to discover and "warn out Strangers" not considered legally settled described Apess as precisely that, a "Collourd [*sic*] man," residing in a property owned by a local justice of the peace, at 221 North

War, Wandering, and Home

Main Street, adjacent to the Hard Scrabble neighborhood.[42] But Providence also was segregated according to class, and this part of town was home to a motley assemblage of lower-class working people, white, African American, and Native.

Brown later recalled the area as home to "a great many colored people," some of whom owned their own small homes but more who resided in boardinghouses kept by white landlords who rented "to any one, white or colored, at low rates and short terms." Sailors, too, frequented the area seeking all sorts of recreation after months or years at sea, adding to the neighborhood's reputation for moral disorder. "Some of these places had bar-rooms," Brown recalled, "where liquors were dealt-out, and places where they sold cakes, pies and doughnuts." Of more concern to the white middle class, there also were houses where "dancing and fiddling were the order of the day."[43] And some were "disorderly houses," a euphemism for brothels, where patrons found both white and "colored" women. "In these houses," one petitioner complained to the state legislature, "blacks & whites mingle in promiscuous debauching, profanity & intoxication & the whole street is frequently the scene of their criminal exercises."[44]

Providence thus introduced Apess to a complex social world where prejudice, humiliation, and disenfranchisement reigned but also where there was a rapidly growing consciousness among people of color of the injustice of such prejudice and attempts to thread a way through its psychological maze. Here, for example, Apess found an "African Union Church," an ecumenical institution founded in 1820 and not defined by specific doctrine, as well as an African American Masonic lodge founded in 1800. One of the African Union Church's prime movers was the Reverend Nathaniel Paul, brother of the Baptist minister Thomas Paul of Boston, who in 1815 had traveled to London with Prince Saunders, Apess's first teacher in Colchester.[45]

Another important African American preacher whose path may have crossed Apess's in Providence was Hosea Easton. He was born in nearby Middleborough, Massachusetts, of free parents of color—probably of mixed race, for several generations of Wampanoag Indians and African Americans had intermarried in the area. By 1828, Easton was pastor of the West Centre Street Church on Beacon Hill in Boston and one of the most articulate African American voices for abolition, soliciting support for *Freedom's Journal*, an early African American newspaper. Easton also worked with the city's black Methodists, raising funds to pay off the mortgage on their meetinghouse. Later, in 1833, he moved to Hartford and ministered to the Colored Methodist Episcopal Church.[46]

Visiting Providence in 1828, Easton delivered an important thanksgiving address, which Apess may have heard.[47] Easton sharply contrasted the sacred liberty that patriots had secured in 1776 with the current restrictions on people of color in the home of the free, North or South, a direct reference to the state's recently passed law restricting voting rights. After remarking on the pitiable plight of his enslaved brethren in the South, he asked members of his audience, because they were "part of the number who are said to be free," how far their liberty extended. The question was rhetorical, for, he explained, "everything is withheld from us that is calculated to promote the aggrandizement and popularity of that part of the community who are said to be descendants of Africa." Even though blacks had made great strides in education, racial prejudice still kept them from many meaningful positions. "Their minds being expanded, their perception brightened, their zeal ardent for promotion," now they find that "custom cuts them off from all advantages," Easton observed.

In an example that may have deeply affected Apess, Easton recounted the disparagement of the African American ministry. No matter their levels of skill or degrees of spirituality, as often as not they could not get any permanent place and had "to appeal to day labour for support." The best appointment a clergyman of color could hope for when he entered a strange city, Easton noted, even if he was credentialed, was "at a private house on a week day," precisely what Apess was experiencing. Dismissing the colonization movement as only another ploy by whites to rid themselves of people of color, Easton urged his brethren to education and uplift so that they could lay claim to the same opportunities granted whites. He ended with a prophecy. He waited for the day, he said, when the glorious sun of liberty would "burst those fetters with which we are bound, and unlock the prison doors of prejudice," granting people of color "Liberty to enjoy the blessings of life like other men."[48]

After spending five months in this cauldron of race and contested citizenship, Apess decided to make Providence his place of residence. He joined the Methodist group, which shortly thereafter, recognizing his skill as an exhorter, appointed him their class leader.[49] He next obtained verbal permission to "appoint" meetings and finally applied for a license to exhort. This seemed like a logical request, but it was denied because a few people objected that Apess had not yet lived among them long enough for them to support his appointment, even though thirty members endorsed him. When it became clear that if the prohibition stood, the church would fracture, Apess finally was approved.

War, Wandering, and Home

Apess supported his family by becoming a colporteur of religious books, work that allowed him to travel and to preach the Word along his given route. His itinerancy took him from Long Island, through New York City, and then up the Hudson River to Albany. In 1826, he twice fell seriously ill, but fortunately newfound friends nursed him through periods of "fever and ague." At Arbor Hill, near Albany, where he preached particularly effectively, he organized a new Methodist class of about thirty members. At several other stops, he added members to local membership roles, even as he also peddled Methodist tracts (101–3).

After six months on the road and a two-week respite in Colchester, Apess was off to Boston, where he spent two more months (possibly crossing paths with Thomas Paul and some of his parishioners); he then went on to New Bedford, the islands of Martha's Vineyard and Nantucket (which still had significant Native populations), and Salem and Newburyport on Massachusetts's North Shore. In this last place, one Brother Otheman, a Methodist preacher whose associate, John Foster, was ill, asked Apess to preach with him. In a foreshadowing of difficulties, Apess would encounter with other Methodist brethren, however, he and Foster soon disagreed over theology—Foster's was "highly tinctured with Calvinism" while Apess stressed the role of man's free will in seeking salvation. He honestly sought reconciliation with Foster but was unsuccessful, even though some of Foster's own flock criticized Foster's rigid position. Apess decided that rather than accepting the "appointments"—opportunities to preach—that Foster's absence from the circuit offered, he would evangelize in people's houses (105).

This seemingly local conflict dogged Apess. After visiting Portland, Maine, he returned to Providence, where, recommendation in hand, he asked the minister in charge to certify his membership. This individual knew that Apess's letter was valid, but because he had heard "evil reports" about him, he decided that before approving Apess for regular membership, he should inquire further into the dispute with Foster. In the interim, Apess retraced his circuit from Long Island through New York to Albany, where he had many friends. While there, he finally received a certificate from the Providence group and applied for a formal license to preach. But now the quarterly conference denied his request, presumably because of his difficulties in Newburyport (106–7).

Elsewhere Apess was received more positively. Methodists in the

Albany area—specifically, the Watervliet circuit—thought highly of his sermons and asked him to preach there regularly so that they could derive benefits from his "talents and usefulness." Large crowds began to attend his sermons, some people "to *hear* the truth" but others admittedly merely "to *see* the Indian." Because his position there was slightly more permanent, Apess brought his wife and young son; previously when he traveled to other communities, his family had boarded with church families in the Watervliet area.

Usually these families had offered pleasant if not luxurious accommodations, but after Apess's return from one trip, to nearby Hudson, New York, he was distressed to find Mary very ill and then learned that "the treatment she had received [where she was boarding] was very unkind, if not cruel—not fit for a dog," and this from a professing Methodist family. Her hosts purportedly had denied her a light in her room, for example, and when she needed medicine, they had made her take it without any sweetening to make it palatable. Apess thereupon removed his family to nearby Troy, where he preached in a schoolhouse to a group of "coloured" people (107–8). With Mary and their child comfortably resettled, Apess left for a three-week trip to the Utica region.

He returned on April 11, 1827, to attend the regional conference meeting, a particularly important one, for his request for regular preaching was on the docket. As was customary, the presiding elder asked him how he had received his call to the ministry and examined him on points of faith. Anyone else in attendance could interrogate him, but he was asked only one question—how long he had been converted. Apess left them to their deliberations in the belief that all had gone very well. He was shocked to learn that they had rejected his request and instead urged him simply to renew his exhorter's license. They did not know enough about his character to make the appointment, they explained, even though no one had raised this at the examination.

Apess was incensed. He had presented both a certificate of good standing from the Providence church and several recommendations from well-known itinerant ministers in the "connexion." It was baffling to him, he later wrote bitterly, "that men who had thrown open their doors to the poor Indian, and had often sat with apparent profit under his ministry," would now oppose him and say, "We do not know you." More ironically, despite their reservations about his "character," they still approved the renewal of his license to exhort.

This setback highlighted what had become a serious problem for Apess, acceptance of Methodist Episcopal discipline. He had received enough slights at the hierarchy's hands to believe that something other than his "character" was involved; the color of his skin was the issue. On his return to Watervliet, he told friends that he was leaving the *"Episcopal Methodists"* for the *"Methodist Society."*[50]

What precisely did Apess mean? By the 1820s, American Methodism was splintering into various factions. The denomination had emerged in England in the 1740s in the wake of widespread religious revivals led by John and Charles Wesley and other evangelical ministers. Breaking from the Church of England over the issues of one's assurance of salvation and the degree of one's free will, early Methodists chiefly appealed to the laboring classes—factory operatives, coal miners, and the like—and, when they crossed the Atlantic, to Native Americans, Africans, and African Americans as well as to those marginalized economically. Under the influence of Bishop Francis Asbury, American Methodists, as one historian has written, "pursued converts wherever they could be found, opened leadership to all, and allowed popular idioms to color worship and preaching."[51]

Oral performance of the sort that appealed to Apess was central to the denomination's message. Methodist services, sometimes prolonged over days into camp meetings, comprised extemporaneous prayer and exhortation as well as hymn singing.[52] Spilling into print in such forms as lay conversion narratives, accounts of the camp meetings, and the personal journals of itinerant clergy, the denomination's chief message concerned the dignity and worth before Christ of each soul, no matter what his or her background. Historian Russell Richey summarizes it best. Methodism, he writes, was a movement of "preaching, singing, testifying, praying, shouting, crying, and arguing." In this faith, he continues, "people found their voice," and their various kinds of meetings "permitted the most outcast of society" to speak "their inner concerns to God in the supporting presence of peers."[53]

Challenging the Anglican Church in England, and in the United States, the Congregational and Presbyterian Churches, Methodism had an ecumenical and egalitarian message that liberated and empowered many individuals long estranged from power and influence. Its program of cottage meetings and lay exhorting offered, historian David Hempton writes, "a communal and participatory form of popular religion that Anglicanism, with its singular emphases on church, parson, and parish, could not emulate."[54] The Methodist faith, it seems, was tailor-made for the republican ideology that the American Revolution unleashed.

But, ironically, Methodism's promise of spiritual liberation and empowerment—like many others, Apess found its emphasis on free will central to his sense of self-worth—went hand in hand with a virtual obsession with form and discipline. The faith's anti-elitism, for example, was linked to a strong ethic of sobriety, industry, and frugality, virtues central to emergent market culture.[55] These virtues eventually brought it a respectability that worked against its roots among the dispossessed; as its members succeeded economically as well as spiritually, they were removed from their roots among the marginal classes.[56]

This is what Apess objected to when he foreswore the Watervliet circuit, for by the 1820s the Methodist Episcopal Church's concern for larger spiritual harvests in New York and New England began to blunt its once-radical message and eventually even prompted general agreement with southern members' apologies for and defense of slavery. Ironically, though, even as Methodism's leaders were turning it in more sober, stable directions, the denomination in general could not shake its radical origins and remained the target of other denominations that vociferously criticized its purportedly unlearned and manipulative clergy, histrionic camp meetings, and overt emotionalism at the expense of reasoned debate.

In New York City, this internal conflict became public in 1819 when the Reverend Nathan Bangs of the John Street Church, the chief house of worship for the denomination in the city, succeeded Bishop Francis Asbury, well advanced in age. A seemingly minor matter over redecoration of the building—curtains, as an example, and a new carpet for the altar—resulted in full-blown schism. One group, including trustees as well as Bangs's conference supporters, favored such modernization, while many lay members (including a significant number of African Americans) opposed it as unnecessary and smelling of luxury.[57]

Bangs had come on the scene as Methodism was growing in power and influence and garnering a certain degree of respectability, upon which he wished to build. He thus urged more order and less emotion in church services, opposed prolonged camp meetings, and urged stricter enforcement of discipline. No reconciliation was reached between his supporters and those Methodists still wedded to an earlier, more democratic identity. Finally, one of the New York clergy, William Stilwell, led a faction of about 300 that withdrew to form the Methodist Society in the City of New York.

At about the same time, African Americans established the African Methodist Episcopal Zion Church. The underlying issue in their conflict with the John Street Church was illegitimate authority, pure and simple, an overstepping of the sort that Apess had resented in his treatment in upstate New York. Implicit, however, was the denomination's increasing marginalization of the poor and disenfranchised—women and people of

War, Wandering, and Home

color—as Methodists became less the outsiders and more the exponents of a middle-class culture of market and sentiment. Originally a way to bring disparate peoples together, the Methodists' once-constitutive and liberating discipline had become a tool of homogenization and repression.[58]

When Apess rejected the Albany conference's offer to renew his license as an exhorter, he joined this new Methodist Society. He told his friend Brother Covell that there was too much "oppression" in the Methodist Episcopal Church, where there prevailed a disposition "to keep the local preachers down." He also was surprised and disturbed to learn that in the meeting in Albany in which members discussed his candidacy, someone mentioned that his wife had supposedly told another, "in a *hasty way*, or unguarded moment," that she would "expose" her husband, making them think she knew something about his character that he had not shared. Mary Apess denied that she had ever said such a thing; and on further investigation, Apess learned that the rumor's source was the same woman in Hudson who had treated his wife so cruelly during her illness.

Friends urged Apess to remain with the original church, but he had made up his mind. "I feel a great deal happier in the *new* than in the *old* church," he said, for "the government of the first is founded on *republican*, while that of the latter is founded on *monarchical* principles." He rejoiced, he explained, in the spread of the principles of "civil and religious liberty," for sectarian conflict would end only when all views were respected (113–15).[59]

In 1829, without any difficulty, Apess received his preaching license from New York's Methodist Society and became active in the church's affairs. His own conversion had been emotion-filled, and he had no problem associating with this more affective body of American Methodists.[60] He was thirty-two years old and lived now in New York City, where the 1830 census placed him and his wife and two children—a boy and a girl—on King Street, near Varick Street in lower Manhattan.[61]

With God so near, Apess yearned to spread the Word. As he began to do so, however, he completed a remarkable task. He wrote and published the story of his life.[62]

THREE

Interlude
A Methodist Life Composed
{1829-1831}

On July 25, 1829, the clerk of court for the Southern District of New York registered to William Apess the copyright for *A Son of the Forest: The Experience of William Apes, A Native of the Forest. Comprising a Notice of the Pequod Tribe of Indians. Written by Himself.* Inspired by his recent affiliation with the reformist Methodist Society, he wrote his life story to that point and then, with "liberal patronage bestowed upon [the book]," brought it to an unnamed printer in New York.[1] The small volume, issued "for the Author," is considered the first bona fide Native American autobiography and in recent decades has found justly deserved fame for this primacy as well as for its contents. Upon publication, however, the 210-page, octavo-sized book received no known public notice. *A Son of the Forest* sank like a stone in the sea of publications that marked the contemporary proliferation of print culture.

The manner in which Apess issued *A Son of the Forest* pointed to the Methodist Society's lack of any book publication program comparable to that of the Methodist Episcopal Church. By the 1830s, for example, the Methodist Book Concern had churned out tens of thousands of tracts for its multitude of circuit riders to distribute as far west as the Mississippi River.[2] In contrast, Apess, himself a colporteur, sold *A Son of the Forest* along with other religious tracts, as he made his circuits, and for his effort made only a miniscule profit—he sold the book for fifty cents a copy.[3]

Undeterred by the seeming lack of response to his story, in 1831 he revised *A Son of the Forest* and had it printed by G. F. Bunce, a New York job printer. Bunce produced this edition with more care and on better paper than had its predecessor. The book also carried a lithographed frontispiece of Apess engraved by the firm of (Thomas) Illman & (Edward) Pilbrow after a painting by John Paradise (1809–62), a well-regarded artist and engraver whose work frequently appeared in Nathan Bangs's *Methodist Magazine* and other publications.[4] Given the appearance of Paradise's work in such mainstream Methodist publications, Apess's patronage of him—or more likely, that of someone in the Methodist hierarchy who thought that an engraved portrait from such a painting should grace Apess's publication—parallels Apess's more forgiving tone toward the Methodist Episcopal Church in this edition.

This new edition of *A Son of the Forest* was advertised in newspapers from Maine to Maryland and was occasionally noticed by reviewers, if not often treated at length. The most substantive notice came from Samuel Gardner Drake (1798–1875), a well-known Boston antiquarian bookseller and author; his *Indian Biography* (1832) and *The Book of the Indian* (1833) both went through several editions. In the *American Monthly Review*, Drake correctly identified Apess as "a Methodist of the independent order" but quarreled with the author's characterization of King Philip (Metacom) as "King of the Pequot tribe of Indians" rather than of the Wampanoag. Drake thereupon urged Apess to "great diligence, discrimination, and accuracy" if he wanted to avoid being termed ignorant of history. He must not allow himself, Drake lectured, "to be carried away, by every slight and imperfect tradition." "In this way," the historian concluded, "from the other advantages of [Apess's] situation, being *native to the question*, he will make an authentic and valuable book."[5]

In "revis[ing] and correct[ing]" the second edition, Apess removed his criticism of and reasons for withdrawal from the Methodist Episcopal Church. He also claimed to have "improved" the book's style and arrangement, which resulted in an odd mélange, for Apess borrowed from the common rhetoric of spiritual conversion and warnings against intemperance even as he broke new ground in his description of the white man's physical and psychological abuse of Native Americans, documented through his personal experience.

A Son of the Forest's mixture of genres and purposes raises the question of why Apess wrote and published it and precisely for whom. One impetus, perhaps the most important to him in his early thirties, was to document and share the particulars of his religious pilgrimage, a story he recently had rehearsed for those who examined his fitness for the ministry. Here he was heir to a tradition of spiritual autobiography that went back at least as far as the rise of Puritanism in England and that had received a particularly strong boost in British North America during the Great Awakening of the eighteenth century. In those years, an explosion of print culture, pro and con, around the revivals encouraged the recording of thousands of such narratives, a significant proportion duly published in books, pamphlets, and the earliest evangelical magazines, like *Christian History* (1743–44), while even more remain in manuscript in church records or private diaries and correspondence.[6]

Methodism sprang from this early eighteenth-century religious renewal, with the Wesley brothers, the denomination's founders, contributing in major ways on both sides of the Atlantic. Unlike in Congregational and Presbyterian Churches, however, in early Methodist publications, individual recounting of one's conversion after the fact was not as significant as descriptions of the extended church meetings themselves, events filled with what adherents believed to be the work of the Spirit but that their opponents regarded as embarrassing "enthusiasm," characteristic of Methodists' frequently lower socioeconomic status.

Then, as Methodism developed in its second and third generations, it became more common to find published "lives" of prominent clergy, usually compiled by acolytes from manuscript journals and letters, as in the case, say, of W. P. Strickland's *Pioneer Bishop: Life and Times of Francis Asbury* (1858) or Abel Stevens's *Life and Times of Nathan Bangs, D. D.* (1863). But if such individualized life stories of significant figures were found among the Methodist Book Concern's imprints, an account of a still little-known preacher of a different race was sui generis.

In the late 1820s, Apess decided (or perhaps was convinced by "liberal patrons") to write and publish his life story. Any number of Methodist converts might have described comparable spiritual journeys from abject poverty and abuse to effective soldiery in Christ's army, but none were Native Americans as well as ordained clergy. Thus, with the book's first edition, Apess may have wished to expose what he considered to be the growing hypocrisy in the Methodist denomination's ranks. His story, that is, implicitly testified to the Methodist Society's openness to people of any class or race, and by implication, to the Methodist Episcopal Church's increasing segregation of its membership as it gained public acceptance and respectability. (This attempt at self-respectability became even more evident in the next few decades as many Methodists joined the ranks of slavery's apologists.) Finally, one should not discount Apess's undisputed novelty—recall that some people came to his services primarily "to *see* the Indian"—so he may have considered that his book might provide a much-needed financial windfall. He could add to his meager income when he packed it along with other religious tracts that he carried for sale on his travels in New England and New York.

Structuring *A Son of the Forest* as a Christian conversion narrative, Apess followed certain well-established signposts for the genre. Of course, by 1829, there were other ways to tell one's life story, most famously in the pattern established by Benjamin Franklin in his *Autobiography* (1790), which focused on the cultivation of good habits to ensure economic success. Indeed, Apess had a copy of this popular work in his library.[7] Then, too, there was a growing genre of rogue narratives, typified by impostor and counterfeiter Stephen Burroughs's often-reprinted *Memoirs* (1798), in which Benjamin Franklin is stood on his head, as vice proves the more interesting course, if not always as fruitful to success.[8]

But Apess chose the spiritual autobiography. As historian David Hempton puts it, the centerpiece of such narratives among nineteenth-century Methodists was "the drama of the second birth as a means of escaping a world of sin and licentiousness, and of entering a world of faith and godly discipline." Other common elements included the contribution of prayer and class meetings as well as of clergy to one's spiritual progress; spiritual knowledge based directly in personal experience rather than in books or learning; and a fear of backsliding accompanying a desire not only for usefulness as one of God's instruments but complete sanctification (Methodist "perfection").[9]

Apess's story includes all these and thus offered guidance to any troubled soul. What makes his publication unique, however, is that the reader encountered such things in the life of a Pequot. Thus, the most important thing that he offered in his autobiography was an account of his gradually increasing realization of how Christianity provided Native Americans a set of arguments through which to criticize American society. He would continue to build on that structure.

The chief details of Apess's spiritual pilgrimage as he recorded them formed the substance of the previous chapter, but a word remains about his revisions for the book's second edition. In the book's earlier incarnation, for example, Apess included more details of his experience with the Furman family, but the omission of this material did not change the narrative's general thrust. More substantively, in the 1831 edition he eliminated many of the details—particularly the names of those who made his attempt to be regularized in the ministry difficult—of his prejudicial mistreatment at the hands of the Methodist Episcopal Church, facts he previously had clearly sought to make public. For example, he excised the entire episode describing the conference meeting at which he was interrogated and in which he inveighed against the increasingly "monarchical" principles of that group, even as he praised the "republican" ones of the Protestant Methodists (as he calls it, the "Methodist Society"), who later ordained him without hesitation.

Similarly, in the second edition, he omitted passages in which he described the callousness of the family with whom Mary Apess and her child were boarding when she fell ill during Apess's ministry to other groups around Hudson, New York.[10] A reader of the 1829 edition would have linked these episodes to Apess's larger indictment of white society's prejudice against Native Americans and people of color generally. This makes all the more confusing his decision to omit the evidence that supported his decision to leave the mainstream Methodist group.

Apess closed the narrative of his experience the same way in each edition, though, and this signals another of his motives. Addressing who he assumed would primarily be white readers, he declared that he could "truly say that the spirit of prejudice" was no longer "an inmate of [his] bosom," for "the sun of consolation" had warmed his heart. He wanted now only to "sound the trump of the Gospel" to call upon men "to turn and live." In this, he sounded quite conventional, a repentant and now saved sinner giving all glory to God, the kind of message still offered years later by such Native American writers as Peter Jones (Kahkewaquonaby), an Ojibwe and Methodist preacher who in his *Life and Journals* (1860) similarly testified to his thankfulness at having received the Gospel.[11]

But then Apess turned in a new and different direction. "Look brethren," he urged, "at the natives of the forest" like himself who were coming to Christ from all directions. "They come, notwithstanding you call them 'savage,'" and would "occupy seats in the kingdom of heaven before you." Here is Apess's testimony to the saving power of Christianity in his life, and potentially in the lives of both Native and white readers, if they practiced the Christianity of Christ rather than sacrificing its most precious tenets to the false god of white supremacy, a theme he would revisit with even more effectiveness within a few years.

He also wanted readers to see vividly his own example, for when he contrasted his situation with that of the rest of his family or "many of [his] tribe," he was "lost in astonishment at the long forbearance and the unmerited mercy of God." Despite his many "misdeeds and wanderings," he appeared before his audience as "a monument to [God's] unfailing good-

Interlude

ness" in saving the lowest of sinners, a "son of the forest," a mere "savage" in the eyes of white society (115–16).

But Apess was not quite finished, for he added an appendix fully as long again as his autobiography, in which he offered "some general observations on the origin and character of the Indians, as a nation," and thus made clear that he understood that his experience was representative in a hitherto little understood away. He did this, he continued, believing that it would be acceptable to "the numerous and highly respectable persons" who had lent their patronage to his work, which suggests, too, that both he and these unnamed persons believed that his story would carry more weight if he situated himself directly in *Native* history as well as in Methodism (121). Apess thus linked his progress in Christianity as a "civilized son of the forest" to the ongoing national struggle of the tribes against white discrimination and oppression, in the southeastern states as well as in the parts of New York that he had just seen firsthand.[12]

Despite Apess's claim that he had used the diary of the eighteenth-century missionary David Brainerd (edited by Jonathan Edwards in 1749) and Cadwallader Colden's *The History of the Five Indian Nations* (1747), most of this lengthy appendix is borrowed verbatim from Elias Boudinot's *A Star in the West; or, An Humble Attempt to Discover the Long Lost Tribes of Israel, Preparatory to Their Return to Their Beloved City, Jerusalem* (1816).

Boudinot's book joined others of the period such as the Reverend Ethan Smith's *Views of the Hebrews* (1823), whose authors "prove" that Native Americans were the descendants of one of the Ten Lost Tribes of Israel dispersed after the Assyrian conquest of the "Northern Kingdom" in 720 B.C. and who must, like other Jews, return to Jerusalem before Christ's Second Coming, a proposition more famously promulgated a few years later by Joseph Smith (no relation) in the Book of Mormon.[13] Given *A Star in the West*'s publication in Trenton, New Jersey, one presumes that Apess had it called to his attention—he depends on no other such works— by one of his patrons.

Boudinot (1740–1821) was a prominent New Jersey attorney and statesman, a delegate to the Continental Congress, for which he served a term as president, and subsequently a member of the U.S. House of Representatives from his home state. In 1795, President George Washington made him director of the U.S. Mint, a position he held for a decade. Boudinot was a devout Presbyterian, serving as president of the American Bible Society and as a trustee of the College of New Jersey (later, Princeton). He took a particular interest in the rights of African Americans and Native Americans. One of the latter, a young Cherokee named Gallegina Watie, whom he met when the young boy was on his way to the Foreign Mission School in Cornwall, Connecticut, later adopted his new friend and, later, patron's name, and became famous in his own right as a spokesman for his tribe.[14]

Boudinot's book offered an introduction to Native American history and culture that furthered the young Apess's journey on a path from being a lowly Methodist convert to becoming a fiery Native activist. In the very first pages, for example, Boudinot (in words that Apess borrows almost verbatim at the beginning of his Appendix but does not set off in quotation marks) observes that for more than two centuries the "aborigines of America have engaged the avarice and contempt" of Western nations, who call themselves "enlightened." Natives had been "defrauded" of their lands, subjected to warfare, and destroyed by the thousands "with ardent spirits and fatal disorders [diseases] unknown to them before." Boudinot's countrymen believed, openly or otherwise, that such things were part of God's will, moving the tribes further toward extinction as Christianity triumphed. But he rejected this narrative. Boudinot wanted Native Americans treated as human beings and as Christians, not as expendable pawns in a political board game. He warned his countrymen that future generations would either "turn with horror and incredulity" or "blush with indignation" at the "dark story of their wrongs and wretchedness—should [one] tell how they were invaded, corrupted, despoiled—driven from their native abodes and the sepulchers of their fathers—hunted like wild beasts about the earth—and sent down in violence and butchery to the grave."[15]

Boudinot's larger purpose was clear. Euro-Americans should value and support the tribes because, if in fact they were Jacob's descendants, theirs was a special role in Christian history. A reader of scripture, Apess recognized himself in this story; but given the conditions of his upbringing and the prejudice he had encountered, he identified more with Boudinot's litany of the outrages visited on Native peoples than with a triumphant return to Jerusalem.

Most important, the book's range and detail—Boudinot drew from several score histories and travel accounts that treated North American tribes, including those of the Pacific coast—reinforced Apess's sense of connection to an immense "nation" of people. What he had experienced at the hands of whites, he read, had been and still remained the rule over vast expanses of American territory. Differ as he might, as a Pequot, from members of the hundreds of other sovereign tribes, being Native made him their brother. This was Boudinot's signal lesson as Apess began to preach as an approved Methodist clergyman and to consider why white Christians insisted that they were more favored in God's eyes than His red or black children.

FOUR

Evangelist and Organizer
{1831-1833}

In the early summer of 1830, Apess was one of three preachers at a fund-raiser for the Associated Methodist Church at the corner of Frankfort and William Streets in New York City, closing a bill that included William Summersides and Thomas Morris, representatives of the Primitive Methodist Connexion, a sister group across the Atlantic whose organizers criticized the Methodist Episcopal Church on the same grounds as the dissident American Methodists were.[1] In another cross-fertilization, a recent visit from Lorenzo Dow, eccentric and charismatic first-generation American Methodist itinerant, had significantly influenced this English group. Dow—known as the "Cosmopolite"—was notorious for protracted, emotional meetings (filled with bodily "jerkings"), which were the sorts of activities from which the now more-conservative Methodist Episcopal Church wished to distance itself.[2] Apess, though, felt welcome among such evangelists. In 1831, when the New York Annual Conference of the Methodist Protestant Church approved him to preach among the Pequots in Connecticut, he was excited to take this version of the Gospel to his people.

There are tantalizing clues to Apess's whereabouts and activities at this time. The same year in which he issued the revised version of his autobiography, for example, G. F. Bunce, the printer on Cherry Street in New York City who issued this work, also brought out Apess's only published sermon, *The Increase of the Kingdom of Christ*. It included an appendix of sorts, "The Indians, the Ten Lost Tribes," and was bound in wrappers that prominently advertised the *Monthly Repository and Library of Entertaining Knowledge*, a nondenominational general-interest magazine intended for both youth and "those more advanced in years" who "may not have the means to procure, or leisure to peruse, more elaborate works." Edited by Francis B. Wiggins, this periodical, too, came from Bunce's press.

Apess's sermon was on the prophesied accelerating growth of the Church through temporal history, an unexceptional topic in its day but one that he imbued with concerns already aired in his *Son of the Forest*. One was the need for sincere Christians to welcome men and women of all races into Christ's work. The kingdom of Christ, he wrote, is "righteousness" in which "the noble of the earth" are equal to "the poor and humble," and where there are "no distinctions of birth, except that of being born again." Under the saving influence of the Gospel, he continued, the white man, "who has most cruelly oppressed his red brother," would pour out "unavailing tears over the wasted generations of the mighty forest hunters" whom he did not bring to Christ and whose descendants (like Apess) now knew "a suffering and risen Savior" (102). Linking his rhetoric to that of Boudinot in *A Star in the West*, Apess also asked whether, if the Native Americans were part of the Ten Lost Tribes of Israel, their treatment at the hands of white people might not bring upon these callous souls "swift judgments of heaven" for their "nameless cruelties, extortions, and exterminations." Such behavior was a "national sin," he proclaimed, that "lies at the doors of the American people" and would be a "terrible one to balance in the chancery of heaven" (106–7).

In his coda, Apess pushed this argument even more forcefully. Often asked if he did not believe that God had more respect for the white man than for "the untutored son of the forest," Apess was adamant: the Indian's soul, too, is immortal, and God is no respecter of persons. Further, white settlers had grossly misrepresented and misunderstood the Natives' character. When the continent had been discovered, its inhabitants had been a "harmless inoffensive, obliging people," only later turned to violence by the colonists' increasing oppression. Naively, sons and daughters of the forest had placed confidence in their visitors but had been traduced. "Hundreds of thousands [of Indians] perished before the face of the white man," he reminded his readers, but the few, "the remnant of multitudes long gathered to their fathers," now were on "their march to eternity," hastening the second coming of Christ (113–15).

Whatever Apess's ambition for this piece, it was not much noticed. Moreover, for the next several years, his ministry unfolded beyond the borders of New York City proper, for he now returned as a missionary among the Pequots in Connecticut. From this base, he traveled throughout southern New England, preaching and soliciting funds for the tribe's spiritual welfare, not, it is important to note, for Natives in general. The Pequots trusted and respected him, evidence of which came in April 1831 when they named him their delegate to the Annual Conference of the Methodist Protestant Church near Albany.

A few more clues to Apess's whereabouts surface from the custom of announcing in local newspapers that travelers had general delivery letters awaiting them at local post offices in the region where a particular news-paper circulated. In the fall of 1831, for example, mail awaited him at New London and, later, in Portland, Maine.[3] Newspapers offered other clues, too. Earlier that year, a brief notice in the *Mutual Rights and Methodist Protestant* mentioned that Apess was traveling to preach on Cape Cod, an indication of when he may have made contact with the Mashpee tribe in whose history he soon would figure so prominently.[4]

More surprisingly, given his hitherto circumscribed radius, early in March 1831 Apess also traveled at least as far south as Baltimore (where the *Mutual Rights and Methodist Protestant* originated), for a local journal announced his preaching in that city in St. John's Church, Liberty Street. On this trip, Apess proselytized for Pequot rights as well as for Method-ism: the notice promised that after his sermon proper Apess would "fur-nish some interesting particulars relative to his tribe." Two weeks later, another Baltimore paper listed his *Son of the Forest* available for sale "by John Harrod," a local bookseller.[5]

BOSTON'S AFRICAN AMERICAN COMMUNITY

Later in 1831, Apess also visited Boston, where, because of contact with the city's numerous active antislavery advocates, his views on race assumed a more focused form. Here more than anywhere else he developed his criti-cism of the nation's failure to acknowledge and ameliorate the plight of its Native peoples, even as he began better to understand his own role in securing their God-given rights as well as the very different agenda of the majority of African American reformers.[6]

Boston's free black population then numbered around 2,000 and was centered on the lower slopes of Beacon Hill, which the locals pejoratively termed "Nigger Hill." The adjacent neighborhood, higher on the hill over-looking the Boston Common and the gold-domed State House, housed Boston's wealthy "Brahmin" families, for whom many African Ameri-can women worked as cooks and housekeepers. Their husbands and sons worked as day laborers, chopping wood, doing yard work, or loading carts on the docks; others labored as seamen and still others as carpenters or other skilled tradesmen. A minority, de facto leaders in the African American community, owned small businesses—hairdressing establishments and barbershops, for example, as well as used clothing stores. Living cheek by jowl in two-level attached brick buildings, by 1830 this African American population had expanded into the nearby West End neighborhoods, off Cambridge Street and toward the Charles River.

The more prosperous members of this tightly knit community tended to care for those in less favorable economic or social situations. In particular, after the American Revolution, the city's black population organized around important social and religious institutions, which reached out in various ways to the entire African American community. Prominent among these was the African Society, a mutual aid and charity group founded in 1796 whose members solicited donations for the community's needy. Besides responding to emergencies among the black population—assisting those displaced by fire, say, or families who for one reason or another had lost chief wage earners—its members also found jobs for those in need of employment and provided long-term support for widows, orphans, and the infirm.[7]

Working closely with the community's churches—there were three when Apess arrived in 1831—the African Society insisted that anyone receiving its support live by a strict moral code, eschewing alcohol, for example, and observing sexual propriety. African Society members also worked for the moral improvement of the less fortunate by encouraging habits of industry and thrift and expanded their own intellectual and cultural horizons by attending public addresses and lectures. A natural outgrowth of these last activities was members' engagement with the growing movement for the abolition of slavery.

Another organization central to the cohesion of the city's African Americans was African Masonic Lodge #459, organized in 1787 by Prince Hall (ca. 1737–1807), a Methodist minister and well-respected leader in the community. Hall prided himself on his patriotism, having fought in the American Revolution, and in the 1780s he organized a large volunteer force of African Americans to help suppress Shays' Rebellion (Massachusetts refused their aid). Rebuffed by American Masons in an attempt to charter the new nation's first African American lodge, Hall applied to the Grand Lodge in England and gained approval for what eventually became Prince Hall Lodge. Many of the Boston African American community's businessmen and tradesmen became members and worked alongside those in the African Society to provide their less fortunate brothers' and sisters' material needs. The lodge also joined the African Society in vociferously condemning slavery.

Several neighborhood churches also helped to anchor the city's African American population. Faced with humiliating discrimination in white churches, even after the Revolution, in the first decade of the nineteenth century the city's black population began to establish its own houses of worship. In 1805, Thomas Paul organized the African Baptist Church, which the following year completed what became known as the African Meetinghouse, on Smith Court on Beacon Hill's lower reaches.[8] This edifice served as a meeting place for religious services and community gatherings; its basement eventually housed a schoolroom; and the building even contained an apartment for the minister's use. Despite Paul's well-known support for abolition, he maintained fellowship with the city's two other (white) Baptist congregations and supported the national Baptist Missionary Society. Under his charismatic leadership, by 1829 his church had grown to 140 members.

Other African Americans found a home in the Methodist Church on May Street, founded in 1818 and nominally associated with the white Bromfield Street Methodist Church and which in 1827 had close to a hundred members, or in a second black Methodist Church, on Center Street, established in 1826.[9] Neither of these institutions was yet associated with the African Methodist Episcopal Church, the denomination established by the renowned African American clergyman Richard Allen in 1816 and which was headquartered in Philadelphia, the home of his ministry.

The discrimination that kept African Americans in specified pews in white churches carried over to the public education system and led the community to establish its own schools. After the city twice rejected Prince Hall's and others' petition for a separate school for black children, in 1798 Hall started the African School, which for its first eight years met at the home of his son Primus Hall and after 1806 in the basement of the African Meetinghouse. In 1815, one of its teachers, Prince Saunders (who had taught Apess in the African American school in Colchester, Connecticut), convinced a white merchant, Abel Smith, to leave securities to the city of Boston to support this school and the education of black children generally. Thanks to Smith's support, by 1831 there were as well two other black primary schools in the city.

When Apess arrived, the city was already a hotbed of abolitionist activity. Most prominent among African Americans involved in such reform was David Walker, a free black born in Wilmington, North Carolina, who had moved to Boston from Charleston, South Carolina, after Denmark Vesey's aborted slave rebellion there in 1822.[10] Six-feet tall and with a "slender and well-proportioned physique," Walker was a striking figure who quickly made his mark among Boston's black population.[11] By 1825, he had established a used clothing business in a shop on Dock Square, near Boston's harbor, and quickly emerged as one of the city's chief reformers.

In Charleston, Walker had worshipped in the African Methodist Episcopal Church, which had been central to the elaborate communication network through which Vesey had planned his rebellion. Walker's involvement with this denomination (and this meeting in particular) led him to view the abolition of slavery as a religious imperative, and, after Vesey's betrayal by one of his confederates and the subsequent unraveling of his plot, Walker carried to his new home in the North his fervor for radical change in race relations. He joined the church on May Street, whose leader, the Reverend Samuel Snowdon, was already well known for outspoken antislavery views.

Within a year of his arrival, Walker further cemented his relations in the community through marriage to a black Boston native and by membership in Prince Hall Lodge. In 1829, he purchased a home on Bridge Street, across Cambridge Street from Beacon Hill in the area into which African Americans were beginning to move as residences on Beacon Hill proper became less available. He also involved himself in the abolition movement on the national level, supporting the establishment (in New York in 1827) of and acting as a Boston agent for *Freedom's Journal*, the first national black newspaper, whose editors stridently opposed the growing "colonization" movement—the effort to repatriate blacks to Africa or the Caribbean. Walker also was instrumental in the founding, in 1826, of the General Colored Association of Massachusetts, dedicated to abolition and the improvement of African Americans' general welfare.

DAVID WALKER'S *APPEAL*

But Walker's writing is what catapulted him onto a national stage. In September 1829, he published his *Appeal, in Four Articles . . . to the Coloured Citizens of the World*, in which he urged solidarity among African Americans to recognize, resist, and overcome—even through violent means if necessary—slavery and the racism that underlay it. By the following spring, two more editions of his lengthy pamphlet had appeared, and Walker worked assiduously to circulate it throughout the states, primarily through his contacts in Boston's coastal trade in black churches. Copies soon appeared (and often were confiscated) in Norfolk, Virginia; Wilmington, North Carolina; Charleston, South Carolina; and Savannah, Georgia. From these ports, sympathetic African Americans carried the incendiary pamphlet inland, greatly increasing the white slave owners' already considerable paranoia about large-scale slave uprisings, a fear that would become brutally real with Nat Turner's Rebellion in Southside Virginia in 1831.[12]

Walker aimed his *Appeal* not only at the enslaved but at all blacks, no matter their situation. His was not an incendiary screed but a lengthy, reasoned argument that led the reader inexorably to conclude that African Americans north and south had to unite in their acknowledgment of a common interest in combating racial prejudice, the taproot of the slave system. Walker singled out as most insidious Thomas Jefferson's belief, widely broadcast, in the inherent inferiority of the black race. Walker regretted that the revered former president's remarks about African Americans in his *Notes on the State of Virginia* (1785) and elsewhere had sunk deeply into the hearts of millions of whites and would never be eradicated unless African Americans stopped confirming Jefferson's judgment every day by their continued "*groveling submissions* and *treachery*," that is, their complicity in racism by an unwillingness to challenge the lies on which prejudice was based and excused, and their willingness to work within the system for their own benefit, miniscule as it might be.[13]

Walker's underlying message in his *Appeal* was an insistence on the absolute equality of human beings, no matter their skin color. How could Americans in general and preachers in particular believe the Bible and not understand this? Did the Bible teach any distinction on account of a man's color? Could preachers who saw blacks in chains and treated like brutes "appeal unto God, the Maker and Searcher of hearts, and tell him, with the Bible in their hands," that they made "no distinction on account of men's colour"? Was there any "greater absurdity in nature, and particularly in a free republican country," he demanded. "I am awfully afraid," Walker concluded, "that pride, prejudice, avarice and blood, will, before long prove the final ruin of this happy republic, this land of *liberty!!!!!*"[14]

OTHER COMRADES IN ARMS

Apess may never have met Walker, for he died—purportedly of a lung disease that also claimed his young daughter but that some attributed to poisoning—the year after he published his *Appeal*; but his arguments

Evangelist and Organizer

circulated widely in New England's free black communities. His was not the only radical African American voice in Boston in the late 1820s and early 1830s. Another leader among the city's black reformers active during Apess's time there was Maria W. Stewart (1803–80), child of free African Americans who had been orphaned at five and then widowed in her twenties. She was Walker's friend and fellow parishioner at Thomas Paul's church, and Walker's death the year after her husband's precipitated her own activism. She began to speak out in public for the rights of African Americans (particularly women) and between 1831 and 1833 published several works that, while not as militant as *Walker's Appeal*, similarly called for African American moral and educational uplift.

Realizing that her job as a domestic had prevented her from improving her social and economic circumstances, Stewart became a teacher and urged friends and neighbors to comparable ambition: to lay claim to an improved life based in the same ethic of self-reliance responsible for the economic success of white Bostonians. To do this meant to challenge long-accepted habits among her people. Nothing, for example, would so much raise the race's respectability, Stewart wrote in *An Address Delivered at the African Masonic Hall*, add to its "peace and happiness, and reflect so much honor" upon it as taking the money that African American men profligately spent on such vices as "gambling and dancing" and using it for "mental and moral improvement," particularly to support "schools and seminaries of learning for our children and youth."[15]

Citing herself as an example, she wrote that she knew of none who had "enriched themselves by spending their lives as house-domestics, washing windows, shaking carpets, brushing boots, or tending upon gentlemen's tables."[16] African Americans best served themselves when they aspired to economic independence and the middle-class culture it made possible, a message not as threatening as Walker's but that still brought opprobrium on her for her presumption in advocating it publicly and to "promiscuous"—that is, of both men and women and racially mixed—audiences.

More painful to hear was Stewart's claim that African Americans seemed willingly complicit in their degradation. Blacks were "despised above all the nations upon earth," Stewart explained, not because of how God had created them but because of how they had dealt "treacherously with each other." She was particularly distressed that many of them "now possess[ed] that envious and malicious disposition, that [they] would rather die than see each other rise an inch above a beggar."[17] This psychological disposition, historically formed, had to be eliminated.

In 1833, Stewart moved to New York, where she taught and remained active in the abolition movement. Later, she moved on to Washington, D.C., and became head matron at the Freedmen's Hospital and Asylum (later part of Howard University). Even while she was still in Boston, though, Hosea Easton (1798–1837), a financially successful Middleborough, Massachusetts, blacksmith and, after he moved to Boston in 1828, minister to the black Methodist Church on Centre Street, seconded her calls for racial uplift. Believing like Stewart that blacks needed more and different economic opportunities before they could advance socially and culturally, he opened his metalworking shop to aspiring youth and essentially ran a training school for those who sought to enter his trade.

With his friend James Walker, Easton developed arguments against racism, which he published in 1837 as *A Treatise on the Intellectual Character, and Civil and Political Condition of the Colored People of the U. States; And the Prejudice Exercised Towards Them*. He also vociferously opposed the colonization movement and was profoundly upset by the virulent racial prejudice surrounding him in Boston, where people were assaulted daily by "cuts and placards descriptive of the negroe's deformity" and bookstore windows and barroom walls were lined with such offensive material.[18] Easton argued against Thomas Jefferson's notion of intrinsic racial characteristics and claimed that prejudice originated in culture and economics: white people had been *taught* to think of blacks as inferior, not the least because it was economically profitable for them to do so. Thus, white people's belief that African Americans were inferior was based in history, not in heredity; the causes for it were "casual or accidental," not divinely decreed.[19] Although God had created variety in the human species, He never intended that one race should dominate another; all, regardless of skin color, sat at His table as souls equal in their common humanity. Easton also knew firsthand that such prejudice extended to all people of color, not just to African Americans; he was married to Sarah Dunbar, whose own mixed ancestry included Native Americans.

Like Stewart, Easton left Boston in 1833, in his case, for Hartford, where he became associated with the African Methodist Episcopal Zion Church and continued vociferously to oppose the colonization movement. Despite his and Stewart's departures from Boston and Walker's untimely death, others, including whites, continued their attempts to ameliorate the condition of African Americans, north and south.

Most notable was abolitionist William Lloyd Garrison, who had founded his influential journal, the *Liberator*, in the same year in which Apess came to the city. Garrison had arrived in Boston in 1830, intent on starting a weekly abolitionist paper; realizing that much of his initial read-

Evangelist and Organizer

ership would come from African Americans, he assiduously solicited their aid and support. Garrison promulgated a philosophy of nonviolence and moral suasion, but he also was an "immediatist," calling for slavery's immediate end, because he lacked any faith in the political process to bring about that end.

Like Walker, he rejected the American Colonization Society's agenda in favor of urging immediate emancipation, for he wished blacks to have the rights of full American citizens.[20] Realizing the importance of Walker's voice in the black community even as he disavowed his call for violence if necessary, Garrison gave Walker's ideas plenty of press—nine articles in one six-month period in 1831—and also published Stewart's first effort, written shortly after Walker's death.[21] Garrison also served the local community in other, more mundane ways by printing obituaries, announcements of political and social events of potential interest to African Americans, and advertisements for those who sought work or lodging, all of which contributed to a sense of larger community. Also, early in 1832 he helped found the New England Anti-Slavery Society, pledged to not only abolition but also the improvement of African Americans' general welfare. Unsurprisingly, because its founders wished to cement bonds between the city's black and white abolitionists, the Society held its organizational meeting in the basement of Boston's African Meetinghouse.[22]

A NATIVE AMERICAN AMONG BOSTON'S ABOLITIONISTS

More than debates over colonization and abolition greeted Apess shortly after his arrival in Boston in the early 1830s. The passage in 1830 of the Indian Removal Act, which gave President Andrew Jackson the authority to negotiate treaties with the Indians for their removal from ancestral lands sought by white settlers in exchange for territory west of the Mississippi River, incensed many of the city's inhabitants. And most recently, the U.S. Supreme Court, under Chief Justice John Marshall, had heard two important cases involving Native rights, *Cherokee Nation v. Georgia* (1831) and *Worcester v. Georgia* (1832), which were attempts to clarify the Cherokee tribal status vis-à-vis the federal government.[23]

In the first case, the Cherokees contended that they were a sovereign political entity that had existed through time, a condition that the U.S. government had recognized when it entered into treaty relations with them. On the other side, the state of Georgia countered that as a sovereign state, it had full jurisdiction over the tribe and its lands within state borders. Here the Court finessed the main issue by deciding not to rule on the case's merits, with Marshall notably declaring that the Cherokee tribe was not the same as other foreign powers but instead was a "domestic dependent nation." In so declaring, the Court sidestepped the thorny question of the state's rights in the matter. But the implication was clear: although Georgia had no right to Native Americans' lands without consent of the tribes, given the permanent condition of "pupilage" to the American government of the Cherokees, Native people sooner or later would realize the futility of fighting the settlers' encroachment, and thus it benefited them to exchange contested lands for those offered them in the West.

The following year, the Supreme Court again confronted the matter of state jurisdiction in Indian affairs in *Worcester v. Georgia*. This case involved a Georgia statute that required non-Natives on Cherokee land to have state-issued licenses (and to swear an oath of allegiance to the state) if they wished to remain for any length of time. Samuel Worcester and other white missionaries to the tribe refused to recognize the law, arguing that the state could not pass laws that affected sovereign Indian nations. Complicating matters, Worcester was the postmaster at New Echota, the seat of Cherokee government, and contended that in his capacity as an agent of the *federal* government, he was immune from state law. For the majority, Chief Justice Marshall wrote that, after the American Revolution, the United States had assumed the same role toward Indian tribes as England had had—that is, as a party that entered into treaty relations—and thus ruled in favor of the plaintiffs because Georgia's law usurped federal authority over the tribes.

But the state of Georgia did not release Worcester and an associate who also was jailed. For his part, President Jackson, architect of the plans for Indian removal from eastern lands, believed that because the federal government itself had not been party to the case, he had no obligation to force Georgia to act on the ruling, effectively leaving the pair in prison. In 1833, the newly elected Georgia governor, Wilson Lumpkin, finally issued an order to release the missionaries, but not before their plight had been widely publicized throughout the nation and roundly criticized by many citizens, including Boston's abolitionist community, which drew the obvious analogy between the president's wish to remove Cherokees to western territory and the American Colonization Society's plans to repatriate blacks to Africa or the Caribbean.

In the heat of such debates over Native American rights, Apess began to preach and lecture in the Boston area. In April 1832, a local newspaper announced that "Rev. Wm Apess of the Pequot tribe of Indians" would speak at Boylston Hall, one of the largest such venues in the city, on the third floor of Boylston Market, an elegant building designed by the prominent architect Samuel Bulfinch that occupied the corner of Boylston and Washington Streets, the heart of the city.[24] In the first of many editions of his popular *Indian Biography*, Boston antiquarian Samuel Drake also noted Apess's presence, observing that "if Indian tradition does not err, some of the blood of the immortal [King] Philip" recently circulated in the city in the veins of "the Rev. Wm. Apes, of the independent Methodist order, a Pequot who claimed to be a descendant of the great warrior" and who had been "preaching occasionally among us."[25]

Before long, William Lloyd Garrison, in his *Liberator*, took note of Apess, even having a "short interview" with this "member of the Pequod tribe of Indians," from which he emerged with "a favorable opinion of his talents and piety." Apess, Garrison added, would soon preach in Jefferson Hall in Green Street, and he planned to be there. This sermon was evidently a success; Apess spoke there again the following week and continued public appearances through July.[26] On June 9, 1832, he preached in both the afternoon and the evening at Franklin Hall, at 16 Franklin Street, across the street from the headquarters of the New England Anti-Slavery Society. Situated where Franklin and Washington Streets cross, one of the city's main thoroughfares, this building had a third-floor assembly room where the society held its monthly meetings and which was also used for other public assemblies, an ideal location for Apess's lectures and sermons.[27]

That Apess spoke and was mentioned positively in the *Liberator* indicates his growing connections to the city's radical reformers. He even got caught up in the abolitionist tenor of the city, for in Franklin Hall he gave an "Address on the Subject of Slavery." Garrison reminded readers that the seats were free, "with the exception of a contribution." A week later, Apess returned to more religious subjects, speaking first on "the purity of the Gospel" and in the evening on "the judgment of the great day."[28] The week of April 25 he had lectured at Boylston Hall, another choice venue in the city, which could seat 1,000 people.[29] Three days later, he lectured again, at the Federal Street Church, one of Boston's best-known houses of worship and home to the Reverend William Ellery Channing, the nation's most famous Unitarian divine.

APESS AT THE ROSTRUM

The *Liberator* did not report the substance of any of Apess's remarks, but there exists a remarkable first-person account of this last appearance, which may have provided the occasion for Garrison's meeting with him. On April 29, thirty-year-old Louisa Jane Park Hall wrote her stepmother about an event she and some friends had attended in Federal Street. Louisa was the daughter of Dr. John Park (1775–1852), a Newburyport native who had practiced medicine and then in 1811 had switched careers to found the Boston Lyceum for Young Ladies, to ensure that women received the same education in the classics as men. He and his second wife had recently moved to Worcester, and their spinster daughter, Louisa, was in Boston after an extended visit with them; she filled her missive with the minutiae of her reentry into the city's social whirl.[30]

Halfway through her breezy letter, she exclaimed, "Now for the Cherokees!" and there followed an account of going one evening to the Federal Street Church. Louisa was referring to the appearance of Elias Boudinot (1802–39), not the same man who wrote *A Star in the West* (but named for him), a native Cherokee spokesperson who was in New England to raise funds for the *Cherokee Phoenix*, a newspaper he edited. An even-better-known tribal leader, John Ridge, had been with him but had recently returned south.

While on this tour, Boudinot had learned of the Supreme Court's decision in the case of his associate (and the *Phoenix's* printer) Samuel Worcester against the state of Georgia and of President Jackson's refusal to enforce the ruling. Soon enough Boudinot, believing that it was in the tribe's best interest, would advocate acceptance of the land swap Jackson offered and thus head up what was termed the Cherokee "Treaty Party," violently opposed by Ridge and others who took a harder line against the federal government. At this point, however, Boudinot was still radicalized, irate at the president's refusal to act to free Worcester from prison and intent on raising awareness of Georgia's continuing attempts to appropriate Cherokee land.

Boudinot's venue, as well as his companions on the dais that evening, marked the significance of his visit. Designed by Thomas Bulfinch and crowned by a beautiful Gothic steeple, the imposing Federal Street Church had been built in 1809 and, under Channing's leadership, had become a center of the city's reform activity. Appropriately, the chair of the proceedings that evening was the redoubtable Samuel Hoar (1778–1856) of Concord, an attorney and state senator and an anti-Jackson man who in a few years would be elected to the Twenty-fourth Congress. Hoar subsequently became a leader, first of the emergent Whig Party and then in the 1850s of the newly constituted Republican Party. One of the state's most prominent antislavery advocates, his sympathy extended to the mistreatment of the Cherokees.

When Louisa Park and her party arrived, they found the church already so crowded (making one wonder if perhaps Ridge, too, had originally been on the bill) that they felt fortunate to find seats, even if in the back of the building. The meeting got under way when, in his "strong, harsh voice, and in the most *deliberate* manner," Hoar briefly explained its object. He introduced Edward Everett (1794–1865), formerly professor of Greek at Harvard College but now in the midst of serving five terms in Congress as a representative of what (in 1834) became the Whig Party; later, he would serve several terms as governor of Massachusetts. Everett was without peer as a public speaker, considered the finest orator of his generation, and his presence electrified the crowd. Twenty years later, he would be the featured speaker at the dedication of the Civil War cemetery at Gettysburg, where his two-hour oration was overshadowed by President Lincoln's much briefer remarks.

Given Everett's reputation, Louisa's response to his words was amusing. At first, she wrote her mother, the "great man set all [her] teeth on edge, for he hissed like a serpent, every s told." Then, too, though admittedly drawn into his argument, she became annoyed by his "ungracefulness and sameness of gesticulation," for he "perpetually waived his right arm on high, and brought it down with a rat-tat-tat" upon his paper. "He must have been brought up to the trade of a single-handed drummer," she quipped. But soon Everett's voice began to work its magic. She forgot his mannerisms and was swept away by his undeniable eloquence on behalf of the "poor Cherokees," words that would "melt a heart of stone," even if not those of "the state authorities of Georgia," which, Everett claimed, were made of "adamant." He also cited scripture to great effect and took pains to convey (often with such irony that it amounted to "severe invective") the substance of recent communications between the federal government and the tribe. When Everett concluded with a description of the Cherokees being forced from their lands and a prophetic prediction that many would die before they reached their new home across the Mississippi, "the house was still as a tomb" and many eyes, including Louisa's own, "filled with tears." "The manner, you know, is a great deal to these things," she added, and by the end of Everett's appeal, the crowd's "feelings" had been greatly "wrought up."

Next appeared Boudinot, a speaker who some of the assembly clearly had come to hear out of curiosity tainted with a racism whose virulent

contagion even northerners did not escape. He was "a swarthy indepen-
dent-looking gentleman," Louisa wrote, but "to the great astonishment
and disappointment" of her friend Caroline Knowles and others of her
companions, was "drest like *other* [that is, white] *people*." "Little Charlotte
Coolidge," Louisa continued, felt that she had been "imposed upon" and
declared that she "would not have stirred a step" if she had known that
she would not see "a wild Indian with his hair streaming down his back,
a tomahawk in his hand, and a wampum belt, making a speech to us in
Cherokee." Boudinot, Louisa was compelled to explain to her, was a Yale
graduate, editor of the *Cherokee Phoenix*, and, with "a fine command of
language," talked "like a man of sense and education." But unlike Everett's
speech, Louisa admitted, Boudinot's contained nothing "figurative" and,
being terribly long, was disappointing and finally "dry and uninteresting."

The party—and presumably most in the house—had not heard of the
next speaker, William Apess, another Native but not a Cherokee. He was
unannounced on the bill and may have been a late substitute for Ridge.
Although Apess was new to the crowd, Louisa thought that he "hit the
taste of the audience more decidedly" than Boudinot had. He too dressed
like a white man, she dutifully observed, and spoke effectively, even if he
was not quite so well educated or as *"civilized"* as Boudinot. "We had a few
tropes and metaphors," Louisa reported, "which never failed of applause,"
even if some were "manifestly claptraps."

But Louisa particularly noticed and admired Apess's evident forthright-
ness: he possessed more "native eloquence" and his carriage was more
"sincere." In him, she "felt the difference between hearing an actor on the
stage, or even a lawyer defending his client—and listening to a patriot engaged bona fide, with all his heart and soul." She also recalled his invective
against President Jackson, whom Apess gave some "side-knocks." In short,
the unknown speaker made a strong impression, enough, one supposes, to
bring him to Garrison's attention.

Before the audience dispersed, they also were privileged to hear the
Reverend Dr. Lyman Beecher, pastor of the nearby Park Street Church, an
orthodox Congregational bastion, presumably invited to show ecumenical support for the Natives' cause. But, Louisa admitted, this illustrious
clergyman shed no new light on the evening's topic. Good liberal Christian
that she was, Louisa was suspicious of the orthodox minister's motives and
speculated that Beecher's purpose may have been more self-serving than
sincere: if the Cherokees were to be a nation, she speculated, he wanted
them to "remember that the champion of orthodoxy came forward as their
champion in the dark days of trouble." Predictably, too, the hall presum-

ably contained many more Unitarians than conventional Christians, for after Beecher's address, Louisa heard "a hiss of disapprobation" along with polite applause. The next day, a friend reported that "the Doctor" had been "'quite distressed' by this ebullition of public admiration," an account that probably met with Louisa's approving smile.

<hr />

FALSE LIBEL

Not all of Apess's appearances carried so high a profile. More often, he pursued his agenda as Methodist missionary raising money to improve the lot of the Pequots, and he did not expect such efforts to bring him the kind of public notice he had received after the Federal Street Church meeting. Unfortunately, some of his wider notice was not complimentary. His solicitation of funds for "the completion of a House of Worship and School for the use of his people" became controversial when an ex-associate accused him of misusing some of the money so gathered.

In the fall of 1832, the *Newburyport Herald* (reprinting a recent piece from the *Boston Atlas*) reported that one John Reynolds, a Methodist clergyman, recently had been arraigned in municipal court on an indictment for a libel upon "William Apes, a colored man, professing to be a minister of the same church." Apess had brought the suit after Reynolds was cited in another Boston paper, the *Commercial Gazette*, as alleging that Apess was an impostor, "guilty of crimes and offences, and of buying Lottery tickets and misappropriating money collected by him from religious persons for charitable purposes."[31]

These unsubstantiated charges continued to circulate even after Apess initiated the proceedings against Reynolds. Early in 1833, the *Norwich Courier* carried a lengthy article about a "young man of the Pequot tribe of Indians by the name of William Apes" who traveled about the country "preaching and soliciting charity for the ostensible purpose of building a Church upon the Pequot Reservation." A "very respected [though unnamed] woman of the tribe" had asked the editors to caution the public "against any impositions" that Apess might "practice upon their generosity." He had done nothing toward the erection of any such building, she claimed, and had refused to give any account of his use of money that he had already collected; a "white man from the same neighborhood" corroborated her story.

The editors admitted that they had no further knowledge of the matter, but because these two people told a "consistent tale," the paper thought a public warning was warranted so that "no one should be taxed for a benevolent object, and be disappointed by a perversion of their bounty." The Pequots very much needed a church, they continued, and they urged anyone who felt so disposed to give toward it. They urged caution. "The young man alluded to may have correct intentions," but if so, "he should lose no time in making satisfactory explanations."[32]

Reynolds's charge was specious and had its origins in personal pique, for he was angry with Apess for his having refused to support Reynolds's application for ordination as a Methodist elder. Indeed, Reynolds had served two terms (for a total of sixteen years) in Vermont's state prison before joining the Methodist Episcopal Church, in which he had been licensed as a local preacher in Windsor, Connecticut. Later, a clergyman in southern New Hampshire for whom Reynolds was substituting discovered that he had pursued "a course that rendered him worthy of censure" and moved to bar him from further preaching.

Reynolds then applied to the Protestant Methodist Church, where Apess opposed him because he considered it a "dishonor to sit by his side." Reynolds countered by publishing things he presumably concocted with "the aid of certain of [Apess's] enemies in New York," namely, Joseph Snelling, G. Thomas, and Thomas F. Norris, Methodist Episcopal Church members who had opposed his own, earlier application to preach (242–45). Although Reynolds pled not guilty and gained a continuance until the next municipal court session, the court eventually settled in Apess's favor. Unfortunately, these and other imputations acquired a second life, Apess later claimed, in response to his increasingly visible activities as a spokesperson for the Mashpee tribe on Cape Cod.

A "LOOKING-GLASS FOR THE WHITE MAN"

One result of Apess's circulation among Boston's abolitionists was the publication in the early spring of 1833 of his *Experiences of Five Christian Indians of the Pequot Tribe*, a pamphlet to which he appended a brief essay, "An Indian's Looking-Glass for the White Man," intended for the self-reflection that its title indicates.[33] The five Natives about whom Apess offered personal religious narratives were his wife, Mary; Hannah Caleb; his aunt on his father's side, Sally George; Anne Wampy; and himself. In his own account, Apess reprised the story he had related at greater length in *A Son of the Forest*; his wife's narrative is in her own voice. The other three narratives are "as-told-to" accounts; Apess had interviewed the women and redacted their words.

Emphasizing these individuals' spiritual progress, the pamphlet as a

Evangelist and Organizer

whole—but especially the "Looking-Glass"—displayed a radicalization of Apess's rhetoric that owed much to his exposure to Boston's African American and abolitionist circles. In the account of his own conversion, Apess related some of the chief episodes that he had discussed in more detail in *A Son of the Forest*, reemphasizing how the Methodists' message of Christian brotherhood had moved him. "I felt convinced," he said of listening to the preaching of one "Brother Hill," "that Christ had died for all mankind; that age, sect, color, country, or situation made no difference" (127). Not only had his own heart changed, he recalled, but everything around him had too. Apess had a compelling desire to press any human near him "to his bosom," he wrote, for his love now embraced the entire human family (129). He also voiced the complaint that he had deemphasized in the second edition of *A Son of the Forest*: after about four years, he had joined the Protestant Methodists rather than remain among the Episcopal Methodists because it had become clear that the latter's "government was not republican" (133).[34] This was his polite way of saying that the Episcopal Methodists no longer shared his views of the dignity of each individual and, thus, of mankind's final unity.

Mary Apess's experience took the form of more mystical devotion. She did not appreciate Methodism's egalitarian emphasis as much as the spiritual peace it brought her: at camp meetings she thought that she had arrived in "the suburbs of glory," so much did God's love sweep her away (142). Hannah Caleb, on the other hand, remembered bitterly the racial prejudice that she had experienced before she found her faith. Her husband's death while fighting with the French army in Canada and then that of all of their children, who had succumbed to one illness or another, had brought her to the brink of despair.

At first, religion offered Hannah no solace because, although the Christians she knew "openly professed to love one another . . . and every people of all nations whom God hath made," they would "backbite each other, and quarrel with one another, and would not so much as eat and drink together." Worse still, the "poor Indians, the poor Indians, the people to whom [she] was wedded by the common ties of nature, were set at naught by those noble professors of grace, merely because [they] were Indians" (145). After experiencing a striking conversion in which "the heavens seemed to descend, and with them an innumerable company of angels," she joined a Free-Will Baptist Church and found the love and respect she sought. Hannah Caleb, Apess added, found her Christian work in teaching young Native children to read and spreading the Gospel to any who would listen (147–48).

Apess's next example of true piety was his Aunt Sally George of Groton, Connecticut, another who found solace in the Baptist faith. This remarkable woman "was counted almost a preacher" as well as a healer, and when she died at the age of forty-five, all who knew her remembered how remarkably "useful" she had been to all with whom she came into contact (150). Finally, there was Anne Wampy, a Pequot who was "not able to speak plain English" and for a long while had derided and rejected anything said to her about salvation. With the help of other Native women who had become Christians (including "Sister Apess"), at the age of seventy through the love of Jesus, Anne Wampy was able to rid herself of her hatred for "everybody." Like the other exemplary Christians in this pamphlet, Anne Wampy found self-worth, as well as connection to others, through sincere Christian devotion (151–52).

These accounts were prefatory to what in the Puritan era would have been termed the "application" of Apess's texts, specifically, how they served as "looking-glasses" or mirrors for white people to see themselves as they were. Look at the "reservations" in the New England states, Apess commanded, home to "the most mean, abject, miserable race of beings in the world," places of "prodigality and prostitution" where rum corroded the inhabitants' moral fiber, and sexual exploitation often was the result. "Agents" or overseers appointed by the state offered no help and often participated in the Natives' exploitation, neglecting to educate them as the law required and helping themselves to wood and other cash crops on tribal lands. And why? It was because of racial prejudice, whites' unwillingness to acknowledge the simple humanity of the Indians. "I would ask," Apess wrote, "if there cannot be as good feelings and principles under a red skin as there can be under a white" (155–56).

His recent experience in Boston had confirmed Apess in this realization: there reigned in the breasts of many whites, including their leaders, "a most unrighteous, unbecoming, and impure black principle," the use of skin color "as a pretext to keep us from our unalienable rights." And yet herein lay a "black inconsistency," for "if black or red skins or any other skin of color is disgraceful to God," He had disgraced himself a great deal, "for he has made fifteen colored people to one white and placed them here upon the earth" (156–57). "Assemble all nations together in your imaginations," Apess suggested, and "let the whites be seated among them." "I doubt not it would be hard finding them," he observed wryly, for they made up so small a part of total humanity. Yet this minority had brazenly robbed "a nation almost of their whole continent," murdered their women and children, and deprived them of the "remainder of their lawful rights."

Did Christ, Apess asked, ever teach his disciples that they ought to despise someone because his skin was different from theirs? (157–58). Indeed, he continued, Christ was a Jew, and Jews were "colored people, especially those living in the East," where he had been born. Would he, too, be shut out from rights and privileges in the United States? (160).

Buttressing such pointed observations and arguments with scriptural texts, Apess broached an even more sensitive matter: interracial marriage.[35] He condemned a recent law passed by the Massachusetts legislature that levied a fine upon any clergyman or justice of the peace who "dare[d] to encourage the laws of God and nature by a legitimate union in holy wedlock between Indians and whites" (159). How many of his readers, Apess asked sarcastically, were blushing because they themselves had married someone of another color? Whites had taken the liberty, he continued, to choose Natives, "hundreds and thousands of them, as partners in life," so why did they not have as much right to choose their wives from among whites, if they wished? In light of such legal and moral inconsistencies, people had to uproot the "tree of distinction" between races and tear "the mantle of prejudice . . . from every American heart" (160–61).

Apess chose his trope of the "looking-glass" from his own experience with racial prejudice and linked it to that of nonwhite people in general. He thus began to realize more fully that the physical and psychological oppression he knew linked him to all Native Americans, to the Cherokee, say, so much in the news. But even more, he realized that racial discrimination was part of an extensive, interconnected ideological system through which whites rationalized and justified their cupidity toward other peoples, including African Americans, whose paths he crossed in Boston. He still framed his criticism of racism as well as his hope for its elimination in scripture, but he recognized that prejudice was as much institutional as it was moral obliquity. Racism, as crusaders like and James Walker and William Lloyd Garrison knew, was not just a matter of temperament but of law and politics. In Massachusetts, all three came together in the plight of the Mashpee tribe.

MASHPEE HISTORY

Apess learned this firsthand, for he next traveled to southeastern Massachusetts, where he had proselytized since the late 1820s. This time, however, he went with a new and very specific purpose, to look into and assist the Mashpee Indians in their difficulties with state-appointed overseers and an unpopular minister chosen without their input. While Apess was lecturing and preaching in Boston, tribal representatives had arrived to seek to regain control of the tribe's meetinghouse and the adjacent parsonage, as well as to end their white overseers' illegal profit taking (to which Apess had alluded in his "Looking-Glass") from the pitch pine and oak forest on their lands.

As early as 1827, members of the tribe had filed a formal complaint with the state legislature and shortly thereafter, with the state's tacit approval and on their own initiative, had begun to reorganize their tribal governance. This action, through which they essentially assumed powers of self-government, had been a long time coming and was in response to the progressive diminution of sovereignty that other eastern tribes had experienced through the late colonial and early national periods. As a consequence, the Mashpees' actions, while not yet providing the relief they sought from untoward intrusions, brought them into new and more threatening relationships with the Massachusetts authorities.

The local press picked up on the controversy. The southeastern Massachusetts *Taunton Sun* reported, a bit histrionically, the "rumor" that "the miserable *Aborigines* now residing in Massachusetts, intend to bring their case before the Supreme Court of the United States, in order to obtain exemption from the state laws by which they are degraded and oppressed, and deprived of all those rights which are considered as belonging to human beings." Other papers borrowed such reports for their own issues, as was the case here with the *Boston Investigator*, which broadcast the "rumor" in a much larger area.[36]

Like the Pequots, the Mashpees were among the six recognizable tribes that the European explorers and settlers encountered in southeastern New England in the early seventeenth century. First known as the Pokanoket or Wampanoag, the Mashpees (again, like the Pequots) spoke a dialect of the Algonquian language and followed a lifestyle that Apess found familiar, moving about their lands seasonally to harvest or catch their food and supplementing their small income through the sale of lumber or handcrafts.[37] These Wampanoags, however, though ravaged like all New World natives by European diseases to which they had no immunity, never experienced the catastrophic warfare with settlers that decimated the Pequots. As a result, their community on lower Cape Cod had retained greater coherence than what, as a child in Connecticut, Apess had known of his tribe.[38]

Control of forestland was at the root of the Mashpee conflict with the Massachusetts authorities. In the early nineteenth century, lumber for building and firewood had become ever more scarce on Cape Cod's sandy

Evangelist and Organizer

soil. Comprising about 10,500 acres (then worth about five dollars per acre) situated on the widest part (between the elbow and the shoulder) of Cape Cod's armlike geography, bordered on the west by Falmouth, on the north by Sandwich, on the east by Barnstable, and on the south by Popponessett Bay and Vineyard Sound, the Mashpee holdings contained some of the last sizable stands of pitch pine and oak in a region with too little wood for the white settlers' needs.[39]

In addition, the Mashpee land was well watered, with Marshpee Pond, in the northern portion and near where many of the Natives lived, covering almost 400 acres, and with nearby Wakeby Pond adding 375 more. In addition, the Marshpee River ran from the larger pond to Popponessett Bay at the south, and the Quashnet River fed into Waquoit Bay to the southwest; both streams were well known for alewife runs in spawning season. Thus, although for two centuries the Mashpee lands were relatively isolated—the Cape's main east-west road was laid out to the north, closer to Massachusetts Bay over a ridge of low hills in Sandwich and Barnstable—as time passed, white settlers coveted the tribe's resources.

For centuries, the Mashpees had depended for their subsistence on the nearby ocean and these ponds, rivers, and forests, even as the Europeans began to encircle them. In the late 1650s, for example, English settler Richard Bourne began missionary work among them: given their fierce attachment to the land, the Mashpees had never been dispersed as other New England tribes had been and thus offered the opportunity for the Puritans to make good on their promise to convert Natives. In 1670, Bourne established a church among these "South Sea Indians," as they were then called, and helped construct a system of local government that conformed to that in other of New England's "praying towns." For their part, the Mashpees swore allegiance to the laws of Plymouth Colony and, isolated as they were from other Native groups, thankfully remained neutral during the upheaval of King Philip's War.

Bourne served as well as a broker between the Mashpees and the other colonists, particularly as the latter began to have designs on Native forests. To end such tensions, in 1685 the General Court confirmed in perpetuity the tribe's ownership of lands in Mashpee and nearby Cotuit, with no part of them "to be granted or to be purchased by any Englishmen whatsoever, by the Court's allowance, without the consent of all the said Indians."[40] After Bourne's death that same year, the Mashpee Simon Popmonit, the first of many Native ministers from the tribe, became responsible for the spiritual welfare of his brethren, who in 1698 comprised a total population of 263 persons over the age of ten, in fifty-seven families.[41]

After the Province of Massachusetts Bay absorbed Plymouth Colony in 1691, the Mashpees became subject to the General Court in Boston. In the early 1720s, they changed their system of internal government to conform to how Native Americans historically had understood land usage, electing overseers to ensure that all tribe members—"proprietors"—had an equitable share and no more. Lands so granted could be improved and left to one's children; but if a proprietor died without heirs, his share reverted to the tribe.[42]

In 1746, however, the General Court made a change in oversight of the Mashpees that set the stage for new conflict: it passed a law providing for the appointment of three guardians for each Indian settlement in the province, who could distribute a tribe's lands to best accord with what they regarded as the lands' "particular improvement." Practically speaking, this meant that these white guardians could lease tribal lands to other Englishmen without the Mashpees' permission as long as income from such rental went into tribal coffers.[43]

The Mashpees objected but got nowhere. Then, in the late 1750s, they sent a representative, Reuben Cognehew, across the Atlantic to petition the king directly, complaining that the Massachusetts General Court had not taken requisite steps to protect their land and rights. After a remarkable journey, which sent him against his will to the West Indies, where he was shipwrecked on Hispaniola and then impressed on an English ship based in Jamaica, Cognehew finally made it to London, where he received a sympathetic hearing. As a result, in 1763, Massachusetts made Mashpee a self-governing district and placed over it a board of five elected overseers, only two of which were Englishmen. These individuals could allot land, regulate fishing, and lease any surplus lands to outsiders.

Importantly, the province also gave the Mashpees permission to admit "other Indians or mulattos to be inhabitants and proprietors."[44] This set the stage for African Americans to marry into the tribe and to improve and pass on land (even though they could not vote on internal affairs), benefits that took on particular importance after the Revolutionary War when the number of Mashpee men of marital age was greatly reduced because of their significant losses in fighting on the patriot side. In the early nineteenth century, the pool of eligible men shrank even more because many Natives entered the sailing trades, particularly whaling.[45]

By 1820, the Mashpee population had grown to about 320. Some were farmers, and many others worked in the fishing or whaling industries, which further reduced the already small number of males available for marriage. Thus, only 50 or 60 were "pure-blooded," the rest having mar-

Evangelist and Organizer

ried African Americans or, in a few cases, Hessian mercenaries who had remained among them after the Revolutionary War.[46] Beginning in 1811, Phineas Fish, a Congregational minister (Harvard, 1808) who was paid through an endowment that Daniel Williams left to Harvard College in 1711 for the support of "the blessed work of *converting the poor Indians*" in New England, was charged with the oversight of the Mashpees' spiritual welfare but made little effort to connect with or assist the tribe. Also, though nominally a Congregationalist, his own faith tended toward the liberal Christianity soon called Unitarianism, a faith based in intellect rather than emotion, and as such, he was unlikely to appeal to his charges, who had been accustomed to Fish's predecessor's Calvinist principles.[47] Adding to his difficulties in winning over the tribe, Fish had competition from a Baptist preacher, Joseph ("Blind Joe") Amos, whose sermons and willingness to treat the Natives as equals found eager followers.

In 1822, in response to questions from the Reverend Jedediah Morse, a prominent Massachusetts Congregationalist minister whom President James Monroe had appointed to review the status of Natives in the United States, Fish reported that the Mashpees had "altogether adopted the habits of civilized life" and had "forgotten their ancient names, and indeed their language also," with the exception of a very few individuals who retained a slight knowledge of it. Addressing Morse's inquiry about whether the Mashpees might be enticed to exchange increasingly valuable land for comparable amounts in the West, Fish expressed doubt. "Their local attachments [are] strong" and they were "tenacious of their lands," he wrote, and thus any attempts to remove them would prove unpopular. Besides, he observed, the Mashpees were of some "public utility" on Cape Cod, contributing to the economy "as expert whalemen and manufacturers of various light articles," by which he probably meant woven baskets and brooms.[48]

In the next decade, many members of the tribe grew frustrated with and complained to the Massachusetts legislature about what they regarded as the overseers' continued disregard for their concerns. In particular, these Mashpees objected that the overseers permitted outsiders to harvest wood and hay from their lands; that the state provided too little support for adequate schooling, with a resultant low literacy rate; and that the Reverend Fish did little to address their spiritual needs. Not receiving any response to their complaints, the tribe took matters into its own hands and developed a new system of internal tribal government. As a state legislative committee's report in 1827 put it, the Mashpees had "assumed the business of self-government," holding town meetings in which they chose such offices as clerks and overseers of the poor and otherwise taking care of municipal concerns. In a few years, the overseers, who for decades had essentially neglected or abused their charges, finally became enough concerned about this new attempt at independence to decide to reassert their control.

The Mashpees countered with a formal petition to the Massachusetts governor, Levi Lincoln, that they couched in the language of liberty derived from the Founding Fathers. "We as a tribe," they declared, "will rule ourselves, and have the right so to do for all men are born free and Equal says the Constitution of the Country." Angry that the overseers continued to allow outsiders to harvest wood and hay from tribal lands, they issued an ultimatum: after July 1, 1833, they would not permit any white man to come onto their lands for that purpose without their express permission, and they would deal with any trespassers "by binding and throwing them from the Plantation."[49] No fewer than 102 members of the tribe signed the document, which got the legislature's attention.

Soon enough the governor sent a representative, Josiah Fiske, to look into and report on the matter. Aware of increasing tensions with the Cherokees in Georgia and the Seminoles in Florida, the Massachusetts government knew that the tribe had ignited a potentially dangerous spark. But they were not yet aware of the degree to which William Apess was acting as an accelerant on these long-smoldering coals. He was the source of the new, highly incendiary rhetoric through which the Mashpees expressed their frustration.

FIVE

The Mashpee Revolt
{1833-1834}

WILLIAM APESS, PEQUOT AND MASHPEE

While he was preaching in Scituate and Kingston on the South Shore of Massachusetts, Apess heard conflicting accounts of the Mashpees' situation. Some evidently were content with the government-appointed overseers' protection of their tribal rights, while others vehemently opposed the paternalism and corruption that such oversight encouraged. Apess knew of the tribe's various petitions to the Massachusetts legislature, for the Mashpees' case had been front and center while he was lecturing in Boston. Indeed, in his recent *Experiences of Five Christian Indians*, he had alluded to overseers' appropriation of wood from Indian lands, one of the Mashpees' chief complaints. In May 1833, Apess traveled to Cape Cod to learn more about this situation as well as to preach to them, for they also objected to having non-Native, unsympathetic clergy presiding over their worship.

On his way from Boston, Apess stopped in Plymouth and preached for the Reverend Doctor James Kendall, who welcomed him warmly and provided a letter of introduction to Phineas Fish, the current minister assigned to the Mashpees. At Sandwich, adjacent to Mashpee, the Reverend Asahel Cobb, another Congregationalist, similarly offered Apess Christian fellowship. Serendipitously, the following Sunday, Cobb was scheduled to exchange pulpits with Fish, but now, unable to meet the commitment, he offered to ask Fish if Apess could substitute for him. It was precisely the opening that Apess sought. Traveling to Mashpee, he met Fish and gained his consent, fully expecting to preach to "some hundreds of the tribe" the next day.

Apess and Fish, who for some reason rearranged his schedule to appear with his new acquaintance, drove together the two and a half miles to the Mashpee meetinghouse. The building was already venerable, having been

{ 77 }

built around 1684 and moved to its current location in 1717. It stood "in the midst of a noble forest" and beside a "delightful brook," and its double doors led through a small entry into a large room, above which was a small gallery. The tribal burial ground, overgrown with pines, stood adjacent; it dated to the late eighteenth century, its graves arranged north and south, according to the tribe's custom (170).

What Apess next saw, however, surprised him. Expecting Mashpees to fill the pews, he was "astonished" to find hardly any in the crowd. Controlling his emotions, he preached a "humble" but not particularly effective sermon. After the service, he visited the Sabbath School and found a similar demographic: a Mashpee child here and there but many more whites, whom the teachers clearly favored, even having supplied them with books sent for the benefit of the Native students, who still went without. When worship resumed in the afternoon, Apess decided to deal more "plain[ly]" with his audience, pointedly asking where the Mashpees were. Predictably, most of the audience found his words "disagreeable" (171). It was clear to Apess that the Reverend Fish and the area's white residents had essentially appropriated the meetinghouse.

Apess soon learned that the majority of the tribe's parishioners met in another part of town, where Blind Joe Amos, a twenty-eight-year-old Wampanoag and regularly ordained Baptist minister, instructed them. Amos spent some of his time ministering to a flock on Martha's Vineyard, where he was also renowned as a musician—he played the accordion and violin and "possess[ed] an excellent voice" for everything "from spirituals to cheerful airs." His brother Daniel was a leader among the Mashpees, and his home was "the social and political center" of the Cape Cod community.[1] When Apess inquired why Fish did not invite Amos to use the Indian meetinghouse, Fish replied that, although Amos was an Indian, he did the flock "more harm than good," because he was impaired (as his name suggested), and he had "educated himself by his ear and his memory" and thus was not "qualified" to preach.[2]

Apess realized that Amos's Mashpee congregation was the one that he had come to find, and he arranged to visit them the next afternoon. He preached on temperance and education, topics he considered particularly important because whites had promoted the impression that the Mashpees' "general disposition [was] to be idle, not to hoe the cornfields they planted, to take no care for their hay after mowing it, and to lie drunken under their fences" (171). At the service, Apess also prayed that God might relieve the Mashpees of "the oppressions under which they labored," clear reference to their difficulties with their overseers and Fish; the latter subsequently cautioned him to avoid the subject in the future lest he stir up discontent. The Mashpees had "liberty enough," Fish explained, and if it were increased by the removal of the overseers' supervision, the tribe might soon "part from all their lands" (that is, sell them off), soon enough leaving them as wards of the state. Apess coolly urged Fish to spend more time learning about their true needs and not avoid the tribe's "worldly concerns" (172).

Apess was to preach again to the Mashpees the following Wednesday, and in the interim he traveled to "Great Marshes" (Eastham) with a letter of introduction to the Reverend Enoch Pratt. There he spoke on the subject of "Indian degradation" at the hands of the white man, but the audience did not warm to the topic.[3] He traveled back up Cape Cod as far as Hyannis, just east of Mashpee, where he spoke on the same "soul-harrowing" subject and received a better reception, although, he subsequently noted, his words still offended "some illiberal minds," as truth always does "when it speaks in condemnation" of some evil (172).

Prior to his scheduled sermon in Mashpee, Apess had decided to query the Native community concerning their difficulties so that he might preach appropriately. He knew, however, that they might not immediately confide in him because they "had been taught to be sectarians rather than Christians, to love their own sect [the Baptists] and to hate others." To his surprise, they received him warmly. He even read to them from a "small pamphlet that contained a sketch of the history of the Indians of New England" (what this was remains unclear), and this openly moved them, with one auditor immediately clapping his hands and shouting, "Truth, truth!" This display of emotion opened the floodgates to much discussion and confession, which Apess found "truly heartrending," as he heard firsthand how the Mashpees had suffered at the hands of their white neighbors. At their invitation, he set several more such discussion meetings, "to hear their whole story and to [see if he could] help them."

Apess so energized the Mashpees that they scheduled a council of the whole tribe. Just prior to that date, May 21, 1833, he preached in nearby Falmouth at the invitation of the Reverend Benjamin Woodbury, again on "the civil and religious rights of the Indians." Again his message met resistance, from people "who apparently thought that charity was due to themselves but not to the red men." Probably as a response to his treatment of such touchy subjects, hostile reports of Apess's recent activities began to surface in local newspapers, particularly the *Barnstable Patriot*, questioning Apess's intentions and potential effect on public order.

Sylvanus Bourne Phinney, the twenty-five-year-old editor of the recently founded *Patriot*, had reported the missionary's "cool reception" in the village of Barnstable on his way to Sandwich and warned his readers of Apess's growing reputation as a rabble-rouser.[4] The recent appearance in Boston of captured Sauk chief Black Hawk, whom the U.S. government triumphantly paraded through different eastern cities, served as the occasion for Phinney's indictment, for he slyly compared Apess to this fomenter of the Black Hawk War in Illinois.[5] "If we are not misinformed," Phinney wrote, Apess's teachings were calculated to excite the distrust and jealousy of the Mashpees toward their present guardians and minister. Given the tribe's "ill-prepared state for such preaching," Apess's words could make them "ten times more turbulent, uncomfortable, unmanageable and unhappy" than they already were, something Phinney clearly deplored. Given the incendiary character of Apess's sermons and lectures, Phinney hoped that "a little of the spirit shown by the authorities of Georgia in a somewhat similar instance will be exercised towards him," an allusion to the missionary Samuel Worcester's treatment there even after the Supreme Court had recently adjudicated in his favor.[6]

Both Apess and the Mashpees, however, ignored such inflammatory rhetoric and continued to discuss what they regarded as the tribe's untenable situation. At the council on May 21, Apess suggested that to assist the Mashpees as effectively as he could and to give him legal standing to press their case before the Massachusetts legislature, they should adopt him into the tribe. Ebenezer Attaquin, one of the tribe's leaders who supported this idea, added that it would help further if Apess actually moved onto the tribal lands, and he persuaded the others to offer the missionary a house and whatever they could raise for his support. In response to this generous offer, Apess assured them that he "could dig, and fish, and chop wood, and was willing to do what [he] could" for himself. As a result, the tribe formally adopted him, along with his wife and children (then waiting in Essex on the state's North Shore), as well as any of "his descendants." To allay the fears of any who had appreciated Amos's preaching and might view Apess's actions as a usurpation of the other's ministry, Apess declared his willingness to share instructional labors, "as there was plenty of work" for both of them (174).

Apess's encouragement of this course, which promised a degree of security to someone whose life had been constantly peripatetic, had its practical side. It also indicated his growing awareness of and willingness to identify with Native causes other than those in his immediate sphere of experience. The anti-Mashpee *Barnstable Patriot*, though, saw his adop-

The Mashpee Revolt

tion into the tribe as trouble. A recent packet-ship from Boston, editor Sylvanus Phinney opined, came "freighted" with Apess's "implements of housekeeping," and people saw him "wending his way, with bag and baggage, squaw and papooses," to his new home.

With Apess's assistance, the Mashpees drafted a memorial to the governor in which, among other things, they expressed the wish to rule themselves. Concomitantly, they prohibited any white man from cutting or carrying off "wood or hay or any other article" from their lands without their expressed permission, a resolution they intended to enforce beginning on the first of July; the tribe would enforce this injunction by "binding and throwing" trespassers from their lands.[7] This veritable declaration of independence, prepared at the "National Assembly of the Marshpee Tribe," had no fewer than 102 signatories, including Blind Joe Amos. A comparable number supported a contemporaneous petition to the Corporation of Harvard College to dismiss Reverend Fish and use the funds from the Williams bequest to support a minister of their choice. Presumably, this could be Apess.

After this momentous meeting, Apess again took to the road, this time to New Bedford, preaching or lecturing on "Indian affairs" at several places along the way. His reception remained predictably mixed. Many who "advocate[d] the general oppression of Native peoples" became "clamorous, on hearing the truth from a simple Indian's lips," Apess recalled, while others approved his analysis. (One of these may have been the prominent New Bedford resident Richard Johnson, an African American merchant to whom Apess later mortgaged his home and belongings). Some feared outright insurrection and called Apess an "impostor" only intent on aggrandizing himself, while Quakers, "whose generous good will toward colored people of all races" was long established, supported him (177–78).

A LOAD OF WOOD

After Apess had returned to Mashpee and joined Blind Joe Amos at services to the tribe, these two accompanied a delegation of tribal members to Boston to deliver and wait on the Mashpee petition. Because Governor Levi Lincoln was at his family home in Worcester, the Natives presented their request to the lieutenant governor, Samuel T. Armstrong, who immediately questioned its wisdom and asked if duplicitous white residents who wished to set up the tribe for governmental reprisal had persuaded the Mashpees to issue it. Assured that this was not the case, Armstrong had their petitions referred to the secretary of state, whose job it was to route them to appropriate committees at the commencement of the legislative session.

Apess then traveled to Essex to gather up his wife and two daughters, and in late June he returned to Cape Cod (prompting Phinney's sarcastic remarks), where they found tensions heightened by the Mashpees' actions.[8] Stopping for the night in Barnstable, the Apess family was refused decent lodging (even though one of their party was ill), and they were reduced to paying to sleep in a stable. "We regarded ourselves, in some sort," Apess later wrote, "as a tribe of Israelites suffering under the rod of despotic pharaohs" (179).

Several weeks later, the Mashpees still had received no word from Boston, prompting them to more action. On June 25, 1833, their revolt went in a yet more radical direction, for they voted to form a government "suited to the spirit and capacity of freeborn sons of the forest, after the pattern of our white brethren," with but one exception: under their laws, "*All* who dwelt in [their] precincts were to be held free and equal *in truth*, as well as in letter," rhetoric probably suggested by Apess. As July 1 approached, the Mashpees posted notices in surrounding communities as fair warning of their intentions to prohibit unlawful trespass on their lands. More inflammatory, they peremptorily dismissed their state-appointed white overseers and demanded that they turn over all monies due the tribe.

They also revoked the Reverend Fish's tenure, and ordered him to move from the parsonage and surrender the keys to the "Indian" meetinghouse. Although Fish had been among them twenty years, they explained, he had done little for their spiritual welfare—indeed, they "seldom" saw him "upon [their] plantation." But more important to matters of sovereignty, they were never "consulted as to his settlement over [them], as a people" and "never gave [their] vote or voice, as a tribe," to his appointment, even though by state law they had "the right to do so."

The Mashpees believed their demands were reasonable and constitutional. "Perhaps you have heard of the oppression of the Cherokees and lamented over them much," the petition read, "and thought the Georgians were hard and cruel creatures." But had the administrators of the funds from the Williams bequest "ever heard of the poor, oppressed and degraded Marshpee Indians on Massachusetts, and lament[ed] over them?" (175–77). "We desire," they wrote directly to Fish, "to be men in this business and not savages."[9]

When the tribe's state-appointed guardians realized that the Mashpees were not bluffing, they dispatched well-known local resident Gideon

Hawley (the son of a long-time minister to the Mashpees who had preceded Fish) to Governor Lincoln's family residence in Worcester with a letter from Fish in which he detailed what he viewed as the increasingly untenable situation. Fish made the exaggerated claim, for example, that "the Indians were in open rebellion and that blood was likely to be shed." Even more inflammatory and exaggerated rumors about the contents of Fish's missive circulated in Mashpee, to the effect that he had told the governor that the Mashpees were armed "and were prepared to carry all before [them] with tomahawk and scalping knife." "Death and destruction, and all the horrors of a savage war," Fish supposedly had warned, "were impending" (180–81).

Word of the Mashpee Revolt spread as far as Washington, where the *Globe* reported that "a little band of Indians . . . encouraged by the declamations about the rights of the Cherokees which they heard all around them, and instigated it seems by their missionary [Apess]" had begun a rebellion, a comment that fueled fears of Pan-Indian revolt, which remained fresh throughout this period.[10] The paper wondered "that no more ha[d] been made of this affair," for it certainly was "as fine a topic for declamation about the natural and original rights of the ancient natives as the case of the Georgia Indians."[11]

Fish's letter to the governor provoked a quick response. Two days after Levi Lincoln received it, he dispatched a troubleshooter, Josiah Fiske, to investigate the escalating crisis. He told Fiske to convey respectfully "the parental feelings and regard of the Commonwealth" toward the Mashpee tribe but also to remind them that the state had not imposed guardianship upon them; earlier in their history they had requested it. Because the legislature had approved this arrangement, now only its action could amend it. Finally, Fiske was to warn them firmly that "should there be any seditious or riotous proceedings," its instigators would be "arrested and delivered over to the civil powers."[12] Fiske was hardly an impartial emissary, though, for he already was on record as suspicious of Apess's role in the situation. The Pequot is "unquestionably a false and dangerous man & ought not to be permitted to have a resting place any longer upon the plantation," Fiske wrote Governor Lincoln from Mashpee, even before he had heard Apess out.[13]

Massachusetts did not have long to wait to see its will tested, for on the day set for the enforcement of the Mashpees' newly declared authority over their property, two Sampson family brothers came onto tribal land and began to haul away a cartload of wood. Apess himself discovered them and ordered them to stop. He explained that the Mashpees were awaiting a response to their petition and that they had requested a new arrangement with the overseers concerning the use of their lands.

The Sampsons were unmoved: "They knew what they were about and were resolved to load their teams." Before anything was settled, the Mashpees who owned that particular parcel of land arrived. When the Sampsons still would not return the wood, the Natives themselves unloaded the wagon, even as one of the brothers, a justice of the peace, threatened to prosecute them for taking *his* property! Throughout this encounter, Apess insisted, "the Mashpee uttered neither a threat nor an unkind word," even when the thieving teamsters verbally abused them (181).

When Fiske arrived shortly thereafter, he summarily ordered the Mashpee leaders to meet him at Ezra Crocker's tavern, a demand that they rejected as high-handed and disrespectful. Instead, they asked Fiske to meet *them* the following day (July 4, the symbolism of which was not lost on Apess) at the meetinghouse. When the Mashpees learned that their state-appointed white overseers did not plan on attending the meeting, they had them sent for. In a tiff, they arrived, bringing with them no other than the Honorable John Reed of Yarmouth, "the high sheriff of Barnstable County," and some other whites. Fiske and these visitors got an earful, for the Mashpees kept them the entire day while they detailed the wrongs they had suffered at the hands of overseers and neighbors and from the minister's neglect of their spiritual welfare. Understandably, Fiske and the others were uneasy—they frequently left the meetinghouse to consult among themselves—and it did little to calm them when they realized that several of the Mashpees had guns with them. Their presumption that things would turn violent, however, was humorously erroneous, for, as Apess later explained, these men carried rifles only because they had come to the meeting directly from hunting (183).

After the Mashpees had had their say, Justice of the Peace Reed reminded them that "merely declaring a law to be oppressive could not abrogate it" and that, "as good citizens whom the government was disposed to treat well," they should calm down and await the next session of the legislature, when their petition would be examined and discussed. Apess, however, acting as moderator in the meeting, observed that the Mashpees never had been true "citizens, from [the signing of] the Declaration of Independence" to the recent session of the legislature, and claimed that to any objective observer it was "perfectly manifest" that the tribe had been treated unconstitutionally. Apess evidently spoke with an "energy" that considerably alarmed some of the whites present and did little to calm fears of growing insurrection.

The Mashpee Revolt

But tensions soon became even more heightened, for after Apess's verbal wrangling with Fiske and Reed, someone handed the latter a warrant for Apess's and several others' arrest on charges of "riot, assault, and trespass," after which they were summarily remanded to jail in nearby Cotuit.[14] Apess did not protest, he later said, because he did not wish to give the impression that he had done anything wrong. If he had wished to resist, he explained further, his supporters, numerically superior, could easily have carried the day against the visitors and the local authorities (183–84).

Local feeling against the Natives for their purported insolence now ran high, and a large crowd gathered at Apess's subsequent arraignment. The Sampson brothers testified (now there were four of them, even though only two had been present at the encounter) that Apess had threatened them repeatedly, saying that he would "*cut up a shine with them*" (that is, do them mischief), a locution Apess claimed, in his defense, was not even in his vocabulary (185).

But the trumped-up testimony did its work: Apess was bound over to the Court of Common Pleas for trial. Eventually, he was sentenced to thirty days in jail and fined one hundred dollars, and he had to post bond for another one hundred dollars as a promise "to keep the peace for six months." The sum was considerable, and Apess contacted Lemuel Ewer of Sandwich, a white man who previously had acquitted himself honestly as treasurer for the tribe, who gave surety for Apess's appearance. The crowd was incensed that Ewer had come forward with bail: they "bellowed like mad bulls and spouted like whales gored mortally by the harpoon."

Only two other Mashpees were indicted, Charles De Grasse and Jacob Pockett, both jailed for ten days but with no fines or bond levied. The authorities clearly had wanted to make an example of Apess. Subsequently, he and Fiske, who genuinely wanted to resolve matters peacefully, discussed how to calm the situation, for by then there was, Apess later reported, "a great deal of loose talk and a pretty considerable uproar" (185).

Those unsympathetic to the Mashpees erroneously believed that Apess's indictment would frighten the Indians into compliance, and they continued to malign the tribe. They talked much about the pains they had taken to educate the Natives—a patent lie, because for decades neither Reverend Hawley nor Reverend Fish had supported schools for the Native children—only to have their charges prefer to go "about the country picking berries and basket making."

Neither were the Mashpee youth provided any education, Apess later explained, when they were bound out to white families, as they frequently were. The supposedly charitable Christians (here he remembered his own painful experience as a child) "used them more like dogs than human beings, feeding them scantily, lodging them hard, and clothing them with rags." Apess could barely control his anger. Better should the Natives keep Christmas and July 4 as "days of fasting and lamentation" rather than of celebration, he wrote, that is, as times to "pray to heaven for deliverance from their oppressors," for there was "no joy in these days for the man of color." "Heigh-ho," Apess wrote bitterly. "It is a fine thing to be an Indian. One might almost as well be a slave" (187–88).

Apess continued to negotiate with Fiske, whom he believed to be an honest broker. Aware that Fish was reputed to have Unitarian leanings, Fiske suggested to Apess that the Mashpees should "turn Congregationalists" (that is, rather than Methodist or Baptist), the more effectively to use the Williams fund. Apess replied that he was not interested in denominational politics and "could unite in the worship of God" with any and all "good Christians." For his part, Fiske agreed that for years Fish seemed to have been derelict in his duties toward the Mashpees.

WAITING FOR JUDGMENT

In part due to Apess and Fiske's discussions, on July 6, Daniel and Israel Amos, appointed leaders of the Mashpees, agreed to rescind the tribe's earlier statements about their sovereign rights and to await the next session of the legislature for redress of grievances. Fiske returned to Boston, and for the month before the seating of the legislature, things remained relatively calm on the Native lands. Local newspapers, however, continued to enflame matters, fabricating reports that there were "hostile movements among the Indians at Cape Cod," stories that were then picked up by the newspapers beyond the region.

One report, in the *Boston Daily Advocate* for July 12, even spoke of the "Marshpee nullification," making the analogy to controversies at the national level about the power of the federal government over the state governments, specifically South Carolina's opposition to the Federal Tariff Acts of 1828 and 1832 (189–90).[15] Supported by Senator John C. Calhoun, that state had threatened to withdraw from the Union to demonstrate its continued sovereignty, and then, stepping back from the cliff of secession, argued that the state had the right to nullify a specific act of Congress. Presumably, the *Advocate* viewed the Mashpees as they did the South Carolinians, as wrongly assuming that they could reject a law duly instituted over them.

During this trying period, Apess did not neglect his ministerial duties. In early August, he held a four-day camp meeting at "Great Neck," on Joseph Tobias's farm on the Mashpee lands. "The place is near the water, and pleasant," Apess noted in one advertisement; and in another he noted that "those of our brethren of color coming from Nantucket, New Bedford, and elsewhere, by water," could put in at Oyster Island (in present-day Osterville), from where they would find "ready conveyance to the [camp] ground." "Friends of religion, without regard to color," were invited to attend, for Apess hoped that "colored brethren" would put aside "that bitterness of sectarian spirit which arises in the hearts of some. "Ministers of all order," too, were invited.[16] The revival at Great Neck was successful, for it brought in twelve new Indian converts, which Apess offered as proof that, properly instructed, the Mashpees responded to the Gospel message (191).

Toward the end of the month, however, friction with white neighbors again increased. When the Mashpees harvested their grain and brought it to their granaries, a dispute over ownership of the crop arose between a woman of the tribe—her husband was absent at sea—and some of the overseers, who claimed it as their own. With Apess's help, the tension was defused; but his involvement, he wryly noted, was probably the cause for his later prosecution for trespass, after his horse had bitten off "five or six rye heads in a rye field" of one of the white townspeople. For this infraction, Apess was fined ten dollars, "though the actual damage was not six cents," his prosecution a signal of how vituperative matters in Mashpee had become (191).

An unsigned letter from "Marshpee" in the July 25 *Barnstable Journal* illustrates the sharp rhetoric to which the tribe (presumably under Apess's tutelage) now had recourse. Speaking of the Indians' subjection to unwanted, unnecessary, and oppressive "guardianship," the writer gave his readers a history lesson. He asked the good people of Massachusetts, that "boasted cradle of independence," to remember "the days of their fathers, when they were under the galling yoke of the mother country." When the Crown refused to consider the patriots' petitions, they reverted to other, extralegal means to get the British authorities' attention, specifically, they threw a load of tea into Boston harbor. But the Mashpees, the correspondent explained, had no English tea, so they had had to unload two wagons of wood illegally taken from them. Surely Massachusetts's citizens could appreciate this, particularly when they considered that during the Revolutionary War the "Marshpee furnished them with some of the bravest men" (195).

At this juncture, with the Mashpees more and more buttressing their arguments with reference to the rhetoric of the American Revolution, their cause gained the support of Barnstable native Benjamin Hallett, prominent attorney and editor of the influential *Boston Daily Advocate*. His father, Captain Benjamin Hallett, was a prominent merchant and well-regarded Baptist, the same faith as Blind Joe Amos.[17] His son was a leader of the Massachusetts Anti-Masonic Party, whose platform the *Daily Advocate* actively promoted, and in recent national politics (in the election of 1832), he touted the presidential prospects of William Wirt over those of the eventual nominee of the National Republicans, Henry Clay, not only because the latter was a Mason but because Wirt supported the Cherokees in their contest with Georgia and condemned President Jackson's wider Indian policy.[18]

Hallett extensively covered the situation in Mashpee, writing editorials to support the Indians' cause, which contained what Apess later termed "a noble spirit of independence and love of right" (195). In early August, for example, Hallett pointedly asked why Massachusetts's citizens displayed such "an overflow of sensibility" toward the Cherokees yet neglected the mistreatment of Natives in their own state. Later that month, he argued that the law that allowed the removal of wood from Indian proprietors was "as unjust and unconstitutional as the Georgia laws that take the gold mines from the Cherokees," an allusion to the fact that in the early nineteenth century, gold had been found in northwest Georgia on tribal land. Simply put, Hallett explained, "it is the interest of too many to keep the Indians degraded." He also reported the injustice of the recent incident at the granary in Mashpee and, given such outrages, praised the Natives' restraint toward their obstreperous white neighbors.

In contrast, the Cape Cod papers continued to condemn the Mashpees' actions and inflamed both sides. In late August, the *Barnstable Journal* referred to Apess and the others' encounter on the woodlot as part of the Indians' "recent revolt" against legitimate authority (199–201). Similarly, Phinney, editor of the *Barnstable Patriot*, complained that Apess had promised the Mashpees that "if they will shake off the yoke, many of them may become as great as 'their brother,' Daniel Webster." Apess wrought them up "to a high pitch of PATRIOTISM," Phinney added, "and so they had concluded to 'secede,'" another blatant reference to the national political arena.[19] Such exaggerated reports circulated as far south as Washington, where the *Globe* copied a report from the *Boston Advocate* in which a friend of the paper who "resided near the seat of the war between the Mashpeeian Indians and the overseers of the plantation" wrote that Apess, "the leader of the Nullifiers in Marshpee," went about the plantation "in full command of all its disposable force and treasure, ordering every white man he meets to quit the territory of his new Republic."[20]

At their trial before the Barnstable Court of Common Pleas and Sessions, the young Bostonian Charles Sumner, a riveting orator and eventually senator from Massachusetts in the Free Soil Party, had "ably" but "futilely" defended Apess and his confederates. News of the conviction soon circulated even as far as "Washington City," the nation's capital, and with this verdict against one of the Mashpees' leaders, Hallett worried that they might not be willing to wait for legislative action and even feared true "acts of violence."[21] He also reported a rumor of jury tampering: "Three individuals, favorable to the Indians, but having formed no opinion in that case," had been excluded from the panel, he claimed, one for saying "he thought the Indians ought to be free."

The Mashpees' opponents took the severity of Apess's sentence as proof that he was at the root of the hubbub on Cape Cod. One local resident went so far as to tell the Natives, "If you will only get rid of Apess, and drive him off the plantation, we will be your friends" (201–3). Fish, too, lay the blame on Apess. In a letter to Harvard's president, Josiah Quincy, he described Apess as someone who "flatter[ed]" the Mashpees that he could "enlighten & enrich them—that he can break their chains & in a moment exalt them to happiness & direction." He also claimed that the Pequot (Apess) wanted the meetinghouse for himself, promising that he would "occupy it at a certain time" and that he would "exclude myself—church and congregation, & *no white man shall have any connection with Indian affairs.*"[22]

Despite Apess's month-long incarceration, his posting of bond for six months' good behavior, and his having to suffer continued abuse in the press, he remained a force for good among his adopted people. In October, he led a meeting at which he spelled out "the evils that King Alcohol practiced upon [them]," after which forty-two Mashpees established a Temperance Society and elected him its president; various regional newspapers took note of the new organization. At a subsequent meeting, in November, twenty more Natives joined, and the group passed several resolutions, foremost, that they would "not countenance the use of ardent spirits among [them], in any way whatsoever," and that they would meet monthly "to regulate [themselves]," with anyone found to have used alcohol immediately expelled (203–4).

But he continued to focus as well on the heart of the matter. As the legislative session approached, Apess placed "An Indian's Appeal to the White Men of Massachusetts," dated December 19, 1833, in regional newspapers. He again linked the Mashpee case to the controversies over the southeastern tribes, reminding readers that the Mashpees only wished to be as free as "the red men of Georgia." The Mashpees' state-appointed overseers had continually betrayed their charge, and Apess implored citizens to convince their duly elected legislators to hear the Natives' pleas and acknowledge the justness of their claims (205).

Predictably, this did not sway many people from Cape Cod, for when it was time for a member of the House of Representatives from Barnstable County to present the Indians' petition to the legislature, Hallett, their counsel, could not find anyone to do it. Finally, he persuaded Caleb Cushing of Dorchester, near Boston, to read the document, which had been signed by seventy-nine men and ninety-two women on the plantation, as well as seventy-nine more men and thirty-seven more women who had left the lands because they did not wish to live there under present laws.

The tribe had delegated Apess, Daniel Amos, and the deacon in the Mashpee church, Isaac Coombs, to represent it at the proceedings and explain the reasoning behind the "Memorial." The Mashpees, the legislators learned, sought the following: "The privilege to manage their own property"; the abolition of the state-imposed "overseership" and subsequent incorporation as the town of Mashpee, with the right to make municipal regulations like any other Massachusetts community; the appointment of one or more magistrates from among themselves; and the state's repeal of any other laws relating specifically to them, save for the one that prevented their selling tribal lands to outsiders (206).

Hallett explained the convoluted history of the Mashpees' relations with the whites from the period of settlement on, arguments he subsequently printed as *Rights of the Marshpee Indians* (1833). In so doing, he linked the tribe's situation to the U.S. Supreme Court's recent decisions in those cases that concerned Native American tribes. Hallett believed that the Mashpees' right to oversight of their lands was incontestable because they were both U.S. *and* Massachusetts citizens, not in terms of having voting rights or being subject to taxation but by virtue of the fact that, unlike members of some other tribes, they were not subordinate "domestic nations" whose rights were guaranteed by treaties nor hereditary "vassals" made such by "conquest," as people claimed enslaved African Americans were. The state constitution, he explained, defined an "inhabitant" as a person "in that town, district, or *plantation* where he dwelleth or hath his home," making the Mashpees bona fide "citizens."[23] Hallett also pointed out that the Mashpees never challenged the state's ultimate authority over them but merely sought control of lands granted in earlier negotiations

The Mashpee Revolt

but now usurped by corrupt overseers. Neither, too, did male members of the tribe seek the right to vote. They wanted only to protect their resources.[24]

The arrival of the Mashpee petition at the legislature generated heated debate. Predictably, representatives from towns near Cape Cod led the opposition. Hallett's *Boston Advocate* reported the proceedings in detail. At the outset, Mr. Swift of Nantucket simply wanted to table the matter, arguing that, since a response to the Mashpees' complaints was forthcoming from Governor Lincoln, the legislators ought simply to await his directive. A representative from Pembroke, a town near Cape Cod with its own Native population, seconded Swift's suggestion; and a representative from Hingham, on the state's South Shore, agreed. Cushing, though, said that awaiting the governor's reply had nothing to do with a public reading of the document, which had been properly submitted and so should be heard. This only raised the ire of Mr. Lucas of Plymouth, who began to slander Apess even as he bent truth beyond recognition. Lucas claimed that Apess, "an itinerant preacher, who went [to the Mashpees] and urged them to declare their independence," was the cause of all the difficulties there. Lucas had no doubt that the petition before the General Court had originated from the Pequot (that is, Apess), "who had been pouring into their ears discontent until they had a riot," with some Natives having to be imprisoned (207).

Charles Allen of Worcester, Governor Lincoln's hometown, thought that those who opposed the reading in fact hurt their cause; in the public's eyes, their recalcitrance only increased the petition's seeming significance. If the House refused to hear it—something Allen did not remember ever having happened to a "respectful petition," this would become "a subject of much more speculation than if [the matter] took the ordinary course." An H. Lincoln of Boston concurred, arguing that, from respect "to ourselves, and from justice to the petitioners," the petition should find "every favor, which in justice ought to be extended to it." Finally, a Mr. Chapman rose and observed that the petitioners had "a constitutional right to be heard," for of what value was the right to present a petition if the House could refuse to hear it? "They do not ask for action," he observed correctly, but only to be heard, after which the petition could be tabled if the legislature so wished. When the Speaker of the House called the question, mirabile dictu, it passed with only five votes opposed. The legislature then ordered the petition printed, so that the legislators could refer to it later when they debated what action to take in regard to it (207–8).

A subsequent letter to the *Boston Advocate* indicates that the cause was finding a wider audience. Someone—perhaps Hallett, perhaps Apess himself—used the pseudonym "William Penn" (invoking the late Jeremiah Evarts, who before his death in 1831 had used the pseudonym of the great colonial Pennsylvania Quaker in a series of essays in the *Washington National Intelligencer* in support of the Cherokees) to point out the absurdity of the Natives being kept in a condition of essential "vassalage," controlled by pernicious overseers who only had their own interests in mind.[25] Further, because the Mashpee and other tribes were not included within the jurisdiction of any incorporated towns, they essentially were without any policing for their protection, except for that to which the overseers consented. As a consequence, "the Indian grounds are so many *Alsatias*, where the vagrant, the dissipated, and the felonious do congregate," a reference to the region in Europe bordering France and Germany where the population had developed its own language, and whose territory was frequently disputed among European powers.

Massachusetts had "demolished Indian customs" but had not established any "regular administration of municipal laws in their stead." "Penn" pointed to the Indians at Gay Head on Martha's Vineyard as especially marked by the abuses—particularly the effects of liquor—such lack of oversight encouraged (215–16). A letter in a subsequent issue spoke of the fact that, as now established, the laws of the Commonwealth of Massachusetts "almost permit the Overseers, with impunity, to sell the Indians as slaves," binding them out as they wished, doing as they pleased with any contracts made with them, and expelling them from the plantation at will. In short, "the whole system of government [toward them] is wrong."[26]

While Apess and the other Mashpee delegates remained in Boston to await formal legislative action, they continued to publicize their story. On December 22, they spoke in Boylston Hall to a crowded house that listened to them attentively, and they also had held forth in the legislative chambers, with the same effect. In the *Liberator* for January 25, 1834, William Lloyd Garrison gave a lengthy account of this event, for he was "proud to see this spontaneous, earnest, upward movement of our red brethren."[27]

At this meeting, Isaac Coombs spoke first, in a brief but "somewhat indefinite" speech in which he explained that, had he so wished, he might have thrown in his lot with the overseers to advance his own interests but that he preferred to suffer with his own people, on whom the overseers imposed "excessive exactions." Next came Daniel Amos, who in broken English—he admitted he was aware of his "ignorance"—told his life story.

In his youth, he had signed on to a whaling voyage, only to be badly injured and incapacitated from many years' "hard labor." When he returned to Mashpee he encountered the repressive hand of the overseers, who aggrandized themselves at the tribe's expense. He had been "round a large portion of the globe," he continued, and never had been "struck for ill behavior, nor imprisoned for crime or debt; nor was he ashamed to show his face in any place he had visited," his ways of signaling to the audience his belief that the tribe's petition was sound and honest.[28]

Then came Apess, who, Garrison reported, "in a fearless, comprehensive, and eloquent speech, endeavored to prove that, under such laws and overseers, no people could rise from their degradation." Apess repeated his version of the now well-known encounter in the Mashpee woodlot and explained that he and the others had "used no violence; uttered no oaths; made no threats; and took no weapons of defense." Apess demanded to know, Garrison continued, from what derived the state's right to tax the Mashpees without their consent and to subject them to the arbitrary will of the overseers. "It was," he feared, "from the color of their skin."

Garrison clearly was moved. This was the first time, he admitted, that "our attention has been seriously called to the situation of this tribe," and it was not a case to be "treated with contempt, or be disposed of hastily."[29] Garrison did not equate the Mashpees' plight with the "enslavement of "two millions of American people in the South" but believed that Massachusetts was guilty of "a series of petty impositions upon a feeble band" that should not so much excite indignation as "disgust." The Natives' plight resulted from nothing less than blunders of legislation, "philanthropy of prescriptive ignorance," and the "atoning injuries of prejudice rather than deliberate oppression." Theirs was "sedition, it is true," Garrison admitted, but "only the sedition of freedom against oppression; of justice against fraud; of humanity against cruelty." Given the appreciation for freedom in the present legislature, he was confident that "the limb, which is now disjointed and bleeding, will be united to the body politic."[30]

The specter of the Cherokees in Georgia continued to hover over the discussions, particularly because of Governor Lincoln's missive to Fiske upon first commissioning him as emissary to the Mashpees, in which he said that if Fiske found that the Natives indeed were in revolt against the commonwealth, the county sheriff could deputize citizens to quell the matter,; and that, if the troubles grew larger, he, the governor, was willing to make "any military requisitions" necessary to restore order (183). Apess thought this directive ludicrous and, given the peaceful nature of the Mashpee protest, potentially combustive, particularly after equally paranoid (and erroneous) reports circulated in the Boston papers that the Mashpees were dangerous.

In January 1834, for example, the *Boston Courier* reported that when Fiske arrived in Mashpee, he had "found these deluded people in a state of open rebellion against the government of the state" who "threatened violence to all who should attempt to interfere with them." Given such escalation of rhetoric, in his subsequent account of the events, Apess asked sarcastically, "Does it not appear from this, and from his message, that the ex-governor [he had left office early in 1834] is a man of pure republican principles?"[31] He seems to consider, Apess continued (in words dripping with sarcasm), "the Marshpees as strangers and thinks they ought to be driven to the wilds of the Far West, in humble imitation of that wise, learned, and humane politician, Andrew Jackson" (225).

The Mashpees' good friend Hallett agreed about the absurdity of the threat to call out the troops against the tribe, who possessed perhaps twenty firearms among them, and like Garrison, he lambasted his fellow citizens for their concern for the plight of the Cherokees while neglecting a similar situation within their own borders. "When it comes to our own bosoms," he wrote, "when a little handful of red men in our own State, come and ask for permission to manage their own property, under reasonable restrictions, and presume to resolve that all men are free and equal, without regard to complexion," the governor terms this "sedition, the Legislature are exhorted to turn a deaf ear, and the Indians are left to their choice between submission to tyrannical laws, or having the militia called out to shoot them."[32]

In response, the *Barnstable Patriot*, never a friend to the Mashpees, printed a communication from supposed "True Friends of the Indians" that verged on the apoplectic. Its writers repeated the old saw that the troubles on Cape Cod were all Apess's fault and complained about the friendly welcome the *"Mashpee Deputation"* had been receiving when it appeared at this or that hall, with audiences come "to cheer and applaud Apes in his ribaldry, misrepresentations, and nonsense." The Mashpees had been quiet and peaceable, they continued, until "[in came] this intruder, this disturber, this riotous and mischief-making Indian, from the Pequot tribe, in Connecticut." Apess went among the Mashpees, they claimed, "and by all the art of a talented, educated, wily, unprincipled Indian, professing with all, to be an apostle of Christianity," he stirred them "to sedition, riot, *treason!*" He was nothing but an "impostor," the letter writers concluded, who had vilified and abused the "irreproachable pastor of the plantation," flung "his sarcasms and sneers" upon the attorney and jury who had indicted him, and "stigmatiz[e]d and calumniz[ed]" the court that had tried and convicted him.[33] Hallett coolly replied that in fact the Mashpees were not hoodwinked; their enlistment of Apess, "an educated Indian, with Indian sympathies and feelings," was perfectly understandable.[34]

MASHPEE TRIUMPH

That spring, the General Court finally debated the Mashpee petition, even as histrionics against them continued in the newspapers. The legislators' investigative committee consisted of "Messrs. Barton and Strong" of the Senate and Dwight of Stockbridge, Fuller of Springfield, and Lewis of Pepperell from the House. Hallett represented the Indians, whose list of witnesses included Deacon Isaac Coombs, Daniel Amos, Ebenezer Attaquin, Joseph B. (Blind Joe) Amos, and Apess himself from the tribe; and only one white man, Lemuel Ewer of Sandwich. On the other side, Kilburn Whitman of Pembroke served as counsel for the overseers; and J. J. Fiske of Wrentham and Elijah Swift of Falmouth, both on the Governor's Council; the Reverend Fish himself; Judge Marston Nathaniel Hinckley and Charles Marston of Barnstable; Gideon Hawley of Sandwich; Judge Whitman of Boston; and two Mashpees, Nathan Pocknet and William Amos, appeared as the overseers' witnesses. These last two, Apess claimed, were those with whom the overseers had made friends "in order to use them for their own purposes" (228–29).

In subsequently describing Fish's testimony, Apess disputed the clergyman's supposed commitment to his mission. He also ventured onto hitherto unexplored ground, commenting on sexual relations between members of different races because the topic "had been rung in [his] ears by almost every white lecturer [he] ever had the misfortune to meet." Apess doubted that any missionary ever really sought to make "the Indian or African" his equal for precisely that reason: as soon as the issue of equal rights arose, "the cry of amalgamation is set up, as if men of color could not enjoy their natural rights without any necessity for intermarriage between the sons and daughters of the two races." He assured readers that Mashpee men had less inclination to seek the white men's daughters than they did the Indians' own. Returning to rhetoric he had voiced in his "Looking-Glass," Apess asked, "Does the proud white think that a dark skin is less honorable in the sight of God than his own beautiful hide?" It seemed to him, he continued, "that it is more honorable in the two races to intermarry than to act as too many of them do," that is, to consort together outside of marriage. His advice to whites was, "Leave the colored race alone" unless they really did wish to "*marry* our daughters, and [then have] no more ado about amalgamation" (230–31).

Hallett's presentation, befitting an attorney, was thorough, reasoned, and fact filled. After describing the Reverend Fish's dereliction, he praised the recent activities of the Baptist minister, Blind Joe Amos, whose ordination the overseers had not even allowed in the Mashpee meetinghouse; the ceremony had taken place in a private home. Hallett also mentioned the Mashpees' sincere interest in religion, for, in addition to having the benefit of Amos's tutelage, they now also could attend the services of the "Free and United Church" that Apess had started. In fact, he reminded the legislature, in two years Apess and Amos had brought in more church members than Fish had netted in two decades. In addition, the two had started a total abstinence "Temperance Society," which (again without any aid from Fish) already had sixty members (233–34).

After praising the judiciousness of Fiske's report to Governor Lincoln, Hallett pilloried (as Apess had done) the governor's fatuous threat to call out the state militia. "His Excellency," Hallett offered, "seems to have been strangely impressed with the idea of suppressing some rebellion or another Shay's insurrection," a reference to Shays' Rebellion of 1787, when state militia was indeed called up to suppress disgruntled and rebellious backcountry citizens who were marching on the courts in protest of stringent economic measures (237).[35]

The wrangling in the legislature went on into March, but the deliberations ended in full vindication of the Mashpees' political agenda: the General Court granted their request for incorporation as the Marshpee District with the right to govern themselves like any other Massachusetts community. Efforts to get rid of Fish lasted longer, but in 1836 the Mashpees finally secured permission from Harvard (then celebrating its bicentennial) to allot them half the annual amount from the Williams fund to support a clergyman of their choice.

They chose E. G. Perry, an ordained Baptist, to oversee their services and organize their school, freeing Blind Joe Amos, who through these years had maintained a congregation on Martha's Vineyard, to return there. Despite the Mashpees' vote for Fish's dismissal, though, he still refused to relinquish the meetinghouse or even to share it with the Reverend Perry. The Mashpees finally were rid of Fish in 1840 when, after yet more wrangling among him, Harvard, and the state, he agreed to move to

The Mashpee Revolt

a new meetinghouse built for him in the adjoining community of Cotuit.[36] The Mashpees finally had gotten what they sought.

———

PYRRHIC VICTORY

But this was less than Apess wanted. For members of his newly adopted tribe, the issue at debate, as Fiske had noted in his testimony, was whether the "guardianship laws" that had been imposed "by the consent of one generation" should be enforced "against the will of another," that is, about ongoing control of the tribe's land. Phinney, writing in the *Barnstable Patriot*, saw a larger issue. Apess had "wro't [the Mashpees] up into a high pitch of PATRIOTISM," so that they concluded to "secede."[37] But in fact they still considered themselves in a special relationship to the state—the law establishing their incorporation, for example, exempted them from paying taxes to Massachusetts and specified that voting rights for local officers were restricted to descendants of the seventeenth-century proprietors or those who had been granted the right by a vote of the same. Further, the selectmen had to be Natives.[38] The Mashpees were not interested in voting for state officers, and by not requesting this privilege they had forgone political equality with whites. Apess's demands for just that, however, had frightened white citizens who saw the Mashpee "riot" as a harbinger of worse to come.

Thus, even after the legislature had settled the Mashpee claims, Apess remained in the public eye. In his *Indian Nullification of the Unconstitutional Laws of Massachusetts Relative to the Mashpee Tribe; or, The Pretended Riot Explained* (1835), an amalgam of newspaper articles, documents, and his own commentary on the recent events pertaining to his adoptive tribe, he spent several pages detailing how his reputation continued to be maligned, and only because, as he wrote, he cared about "the welfare of [himself] and brethren," and because he would not suffer himself "to be trodden underfoot by people no better than [he]."

Admittedly, some of these slights, real enough, were small. After the Mashpees' success in Boston, for example, the legislature had approved expenses for the Indians who had attended the session, but "the high-minded Senator [Barnabas] Hedge of Plymouth" had succeeded in striking Apess's name from the list of those to be reimbursed, on the basis of his questionable character. The House eventually reinstated his payment, prompting Apess to offer that Hedge must have been "sadly disappointed" that he could not save the state this twenty-three dollars "by his manly efforts to injure the character of a poor Indian." Hedge, Apess added sarcastically, was "a descendant from the pilgrims, whom the Indians protected at Plymouth Rock" (242), "dexterous and pointed remarks," the *Liberator* claimed, that when Apess had voiced them in the legislature, drew considerable applause.[39]

More insidious, however, were reports that continued to circulate in the mid-1830s throughout New England implying that Apess was a charlatan who, under the guise of raising money for his missionary work, used it instead to play at the state lotteries. Apess thought that he had put these accusations to rest by hauling disgruntled Methodist John Reynolds and two others into civil court in the summer of 1833. But in the spring of 1835, Apess was still embroiled in the matter and included in his *Indian Nullification* attestations to his good character from whites and Natives from "the Pequot tribe," in Groton, Connecticut. Apess was their "Agent," the attestation recorded, "to collect subscriptions and monies toward erecting a house of worship," and they had given him permission to subtract from what he solicited an amount sufficient for his own expenses (247).

In the summer of 1834, Apess continued his evangelical outreach, preaching in Lowell, Massachusetts, in the last week of June; in a Baptist meetinghouse one night, where he raised over twenty dollars for his work; and in "the Methodist Chapel on Chestnut Street" another night, where he also took a collection. A report of his first appearance is telling. The reporter heard "the Indian Preacher at the 2nd Baptist Church" and was pleased at Apess's "putting forth of the moral truths of the Gospel in their simplicity, disburthened of the mystic nonsense with which they are clogged by the generality of the clergy." This "son of the forest," he continued, "told many historical truths which could not be very palatable to those who so term themselves." Finally, Apess "spoke charitably, fearlessly, but unfavorably of the conduct of the white missionaries" among the Natives.[40]

Another slight occurred in this period, when the Mashpees were still wrangling with the Reverend Fish over the use of the meetinghouse. Apess sought to have a camp meeting where he previously had held a very successful one. The location was in a pleasant grove on the Mashpee lands, beside the river, and was not even within sight of the meetinghouse. Fish claimed that the land was for his use and refused permission for the gathering. Apess enlisted the Mashpee selectmen to approach Fish, and they explained how the meeting would cause no more disturbance "than people passing in carriages in the main road." "We had no meetinghouse," Apess wrote, "our schoolhouses would not hold the people, and we had no

The Mashpee Revolt

other means but to erect our tents and worship God in the open air." When a white family from Nantucket arrived to start erecting the tent, Fish imperiously ordered them to leave, to which the head of the household replied that if Fish threw them from the land, they would comply but would "publish [Fish's] conduct to the world."

As word of the standoff spread, it became enough of an imbroglio that Fish relented, while making clear that his permission hinged on there being no damage to his property and that "*peace, order, and quietude*" should rule. He also reminded Apess that he granted this license as a one-time "*special favor.*" He did not want the Mashpees to construe his permission as his concession that they had a "*right*" to do on the land what they pleased (255–56).

This and the other episodes of discrimination led Apess directly to his "Concluding Observations." For troubling readers so much with his own affairs, Apess wrote, he offered this excuse. "I have been assailed by the vilest calumnies, represented as an exciter of sedition, a hypocrite, and a gambler," slanders that, though without merit, continued to circulate. But, he continued, "though I am an Indian, I am at least a man, with all the feelings properly to humanity." Most on his mind was the matter of history: It was his duty to his children, and not the least to himself, not to leave behind "the inheritance of a blasted name" (274). In *Indian Nullification*, Apess tried to clear that name, as well as bring dignity and respect to the term "Indian." Leaving Mashpee for Boston and elsewhere, he continued this task.

SIX

King Philip's Heir
{ 1835-1836 }

MORE TROUBLE IN MASHPEE

With the path cleared for Mashpee's incorporation as a state-recognized district if not quite yet a town, the tribe returned to normal business: cultivating the land; fishing in the ponds, rivers, and Nantucket Sound; and harvesting firewood. The group now numbered about five hundred and had about seventy simply constructed houses, "none of which cost more than $100," a contemporary magazine reported. Their holdings of livestock, too, were minimal, with eight teams of horses, thirty cows, and a few sheep, one observer noted. In terms of their education, "about one hundred of the Natives could read" and "half that number [were] able as well to write."[1]

There also were signs of other kinds of enterprise. An article in the *New-York Weekly Mirror* (copied from the *New York Evening Post*) reported that some Mashpees had "built, rigged, and manned a beautiful little sloop, which was launched the other day at Marshpee Harbour," to work in the coastal carrying trade. Five-eighths of the vessel was owned by members of the tribe, the remainder by whites on Nantucket who had bought in to enable the purchase of rigging and sails. "Appropriately," the paper noted, the boat was named the *Native of Marshpee*, and it was commanded by Solomon Attaquan, "a pure Indian." The crew, too, were Mashpees, the writer continued, and the wood was from the tribe's forests. "Success to her!" the writer concluded.[2]

Religious matters, however, still were not settled. The Mashpees continued to be united in their wish that the lackadaisical (and racist) Reverend Fish be removed as their shepherd and the parsonage and meetinghouse restored to their control. And now that Apess was a tribal member with full rights for himself and his descendants, he had reason to think that the way was open for a call from the tribe and thus for his move to

Cape Cod to become permanent. But the invitation did not come. One reason was circumstantial, for under Blind Joe Amos's preaching, many of the tribe had begun to follow Baptist, not Methodist, principles. A few years later, when Harvard gave the Mashpees half the annual allotment from the Williams fund to support a minister of their choice, they selected another Baptist.

But personal matters also were in play. Even though Apess had played so crucial a role in the tribe's challenge to the state's authority, a rift had opened between him and some members of the tribe. As early as December 7, 1833, for example, long before the Mashpees had presented their petition regarding Fish's ministry, that clergyman reported to President Quincy of Harvard that "what was once [Apess's] party are now divided & separated. His *followers* are now reduced (comparatively speaking) to a handful."[3] Later that month, Daniel Amos and a few other Mashpees, perhaps reacting to some of the legislators' belief that Apess was the self-serving instigator in the Mashpee affair, sent a letter to the *Boston Advocate* in which they insisted, "We know something of our own rights without being told by Mr. Apes or any one" else (did they mean Benjamin Hallett?).[4]

Similarly, in 1835, the Reverend James Walker, a well-respected Unitarian minister then serving in Charlestown, Massachusetts, and three years later to become professor of religion and moral philosophy at Harvard, issued a report to President Quincy of Harvard assessing the ongoing difficulties between the Mashpee and Fish. He noted that Apess "was popular among the Indians for a while but is now understood to be rapidly loosing [*sic*] this confidence, & not without good reason."[5] Unfortunately, Walker did not elaborate. His informant probably was Hallett, who, answering Walker's queries, had written him that the Indians were "dissatisfied with Apes" but gave no further explanation.[6]

Later, a visitor to Cape Cod who was writing travel sketches for the *Boston Recorder* evidently had heard enough about such tensions to include them in one of his offerings. Redacting a bit of the Mashpee Revolt's history, he wrote that the tribe's smoldering dissatisfaction at their treatment had been "fanned into a flame by a foreign Indian, who went among them and set himself up as a sort of Moses to deliver them from bondage." But, the writer continued, in fact Apess "has been a great curse to the unsuspecting Indians, on whose wealth, and temporal and spiritual happiness he has been preying." At first Apess had the Mashpees' "almost unbounded confidence and popularity," the reporter concluded, "but his character is now [1838] understood and he is estimated according to his merits."[7]

Fish—he was writing in the early fall of 1835—noted to one correspondent that Apess now was "very frequently absent" from the area. Earlier, in April, for example, billing himself as "an Indian preacher," he had traveled around the state "soliciting contributions for the purpose of building a teacher's house" as well as a school in Mashpee. At these appearances, he shared his "opinion that the American Indians are as capable of intellectual improvement as the whites," and he condemned "[the Natives'] continued ill treatment, and the laws and prejudices of the whites towards them."[8]

Without a regular ministry in Mashpee, Apess also now periodically returned to the Boston area, even as his family remained on Cape Cod.[9] The first matter to which he attended was the publication of his *Indian Nullification of the Unconstitutional Laws of Massachusetts Relative to the Marshpee Tribe; or, The Pretended Riot Explained*, which the Boston printer Jonathan Howe—who also had issued Benjamin Hallett's pamphlet, *The Rights of the Marshpee Indians*—published late in the spring of 1835 and for which Apess retained the copyright. A mélange of documents that was supportive of the Mashpees' cause, by its very title the book conveyed Apess's belief that the conflict in which he had been a spokesperson had larger, constitutional import. It contained Apess's first-person interpolated narrative; excerpts from private letters and reports and from government documents; and newspaper accounts.

The book's publication also kept the now-settled controversy in the public eye, for given their wide coverage of the Mashpee petition, New England newspapers and the periodical press noticed this book more than any of his others. The *Boston Morning Post*'s review was typical. Its reviewer pointed out that beyond a doubt Apess showed how the Mashpees had been "most shamefully abused and neglected" while citizens of Massachusetts instead "weep[ed] over the fate of '*the poor Cherokees*.'"[10] The Unitarian-leaning *New England Magazine*, which published many of the region's emerging literati, agreed, even as it engaged in still-prevalent racism. Its reviewer was surprised that the book was "written far better than could have been expected from an Indian" and well worth reading. For some reason, this journal also pointed out that Apess had received no pay for his ministry to the Mashpees and so had to support himself "by the labor of his hands, and by vending books," suggesting that this work, too, was something of a mendicant's tract. Apess appeared, the reviewer concluded, to have "suffered himself to be exasperated by the persecution he has endured," which suggests that the incendiary tone of some of the book's passages did not escape this reader's notice.[11] Finally, the *Boston Pearl and Literary Gazette* admired the book's "plain, unvarnished, warm style, without hindrance or palpable dullness." "To those interested in the cause of the persecuted Indian," the reviewer continued, "it is a desirable book."[12] The rhetoric in such reviews thus cuts both ways, for praising the surprising quality of the work reinforces the idea that Indians should not be capable of such writing, even as the refrain of the "persecuted" Indians aids in convincing the reader of their "vanishing" from the cultural landscape.

Perhaps the most unusual reaction to *Indian Nullification*, however, came from Samuel Gardner Drake, the well-known Boston antiquary, publisher of much-circulated books about the New England Indians, and proprietor of the "Antiquarian Book-store," the city's first, which he had established in 1830. The store, at 63 Cornhill, had long been a meeting place for the region's serious historians, and his publications had been required reading for them.

An audience with Drake was its own special experience, for to find his place of business one mounted forty steep steps and first entered "a large six-windowed oblong . . . crowded with shelves and cabinets—overflowing with antique books, pamphlets, periodicals, maps, and MSS," all waiting "like learned ghosts for some patron of the arts to lead them to a more commodious and secure asylum." Then one opened "a kind of sesame door" and went up another flight of yet steeper stairs before reaching "the threshold of a long antechamber lighted at either end and bearing a similitude to the cloister of some erudite monk." There, "sitting by a desk near a window one found the learned proprietor."[13]

We know that Apess knew Drake's books, for he quoted from them; and he very likely had met the man himself in his sanctum, for Drake sold tickets to Apess's Boston lectures at his store. The antiquary also had been the one who in one of the few notices of *A Son of the Forest* (in his *Indian Biography* [1832]) had complained that, even though "the blood of the immortal [King] Philip" then circulated in Boston in William Apess, there was reason to question the Native's historical knowledge of the tribes: Drake chided Apess for describing Philip as king of the Pequots when in fact he was a Wampanoag.[14] Someone—most certainly Drake—repeated the same charge in a review in the *American Monthly Review* of *A Son of the Forest*'s second edition and urged Apess to "enlarge the boundaries of his knowledge of Indian history" before he offered any formal history of the tribe, as he evidently had suggested (again, very likely directly to Drake) he might.[15]

Even though through the mid-1830s Drake seemed genuinely interested in Apess, and Apess clearly trusted the bookseller's grasp of history (when he came to speak about King Philip's War, he cited the antiquary directly), Drake inexplicably was responsible for a misattribution of *Indian Nullification*'s authorship that remained uncorrected long after Apess's and his deaths. In Drake's copy of *A Son of the Forest* and in a scrapbook "autographical biography," as he called his elaborate collection of the autographs of prominent contemporaries whose biographies he entered next to an example of their handwriting, he claimed that the traveler William Joseph Snelling wrote *Indian Nullification*, on the surface a plausible claim but patently incorrect.

After a stay in the Minnesota Territory, for example, Snelling had published *Tales of the Northwest* (1830), which included material on the Dakota and Ojibwe Indians he had encountered. On his return to the East, he edited *New England Galaxy*, and in the July 1833 issue, he reprinted "Red Jacket's Reply to Reverend Cram," in which the Seneca spokesperson inveighed against the abuses of Christian missionaries in terms similar to those Apess soon enlisted.[16] Further, Snelling and Apess crossed paths in Boston when the latter was pressing charges for libel against John Reynolds, who had asked Snelling to serve as a character witness *against* Apess. In his account of the matter, Apess writes only that his "friends [stood] by him," leaving it unclear if that meant that Snelling did not support the accusation or whether he in fact did, and that others exonerated Apess in the case he eventually won (244).

Whatever his position in that court proceeding, Snelling clearly intended to establish himself as something of an expert on Native Americans and their writings. In his approving notice in the prestigious *North American Review* of recently captured Sauk leader Black Hawk's autobiography, for example, Snelling dismissed Apess's claim to be a genuinely Native author because he had so assimilated to white culture. Even if Apess had unmixed blood, Snelling wrote, it was more telling that there was no trace of the "wild, unadulterated savage, gall yet fermenting in his veins," as he found in Black Hawk's. "If [Apess] writes," Snelling continued dismissively, "it is in the character of a white man."[17] This does not sound like someone to whom Apess would entrust the assemblage of the Mashpee documents, especially given the fact that by this time Snelling also was commonly known to be an alcoholic, as Drake dutifully noted in his entry on the man in the "autographical biography."[18] Repeated in subsequent bibliographical literature, the attribution now is generally regarded as false; but the question remains, why did Drake say this?[19]

And why did he write in his "autographical biography" that, among other things, Apess was a "Mohegan" who told him that he had fought in the War of 1812 and "came to me begging money to build a church for his tribe"? Later, Drake continued, Apess lived on Cape Cod and became a leader in "the Marshpee war," a history of which was published by "W. J. Snelling."[20] In terming Apess a "Mohegan" when he knew the author called himself a Pequot, Drake simply aligned himself with other Euro-American commentators who accepted the commonly held notion that with the Pequot War the tribe essentially had been exterminated, the only survivors transformed by colonial fiat into Mohegan and Narragansett.

There may be more to Drake's pique, however, for his entry on Apess in the "autographical biography" came after he had delivered in Boston, on two separate occasions, his remarkable, and remarkably iconoclastic, "Eulogy on King Philip." This has prompted one historian to suggest that Drake's subsequent animus toward Apess had as much to do with the content of these lectures as with his part in the Mashpee Revolt.[21] In lecturing and publishing on the figure of King Philip, Apess addressed a subject then being resurrected in popular culture and one that that remained a touchstone for Euro-Americans' understanding of their treatment of Native Americans, and, implicitly, of themselves as settlers in the New World.[22] Sympathetic as the antiquary was to Native causes, in other words, he could not endorse Apess's claim to represent a tribe that all his peers considered long extirpated.

METACOMET MEMORIALIZED

In these years in Boston, for example, audiences thrilled to the wildly popular John Augustus Stone play *Metamora; or, The Last of the Wampanoags*, which starred Edwin Forrest in the title role and was based on King Philip's life.[23] First produced in New York in 1829, the drama remained popular for decades and became one of Forrest's best-known presentations, with several of Metamora's lines falling into popular parlance, including those from his lips as he died: "The curse of Metamora stays with the white man!"[24] Even some Native Americans knew *Metamora*. Forrest's biographer mentions that "many a time delegations of tribes who chanced to be visiting cities where [Forrest] acted this character . . . attended the performance, adding a most picturesque feature by their presence."[25]

The play's origin is interesting. Forrest, eager to promote American arts, had put up a $500 prize for "the best tragedy in five acts, of which the hero, or principle character, shall be an aboriginal of this country," and the selection committee chose Stone's drama.[26] Like other representations of King Philip in the early nineteenth century, it traded in revisionist history, with the Puritans portrayed as cruel and inhumane persecutors of a noble warrior, an interpretation of this character that owed much to Washington Irving's sketch "Philip of Pokanoket," included in his popular *Sketch Book* (1819–20). In Irving's redaction, Philip and his warriors had struggled against an oppressive outside force, much as the Americans had had to defend themselves from the ever-more-greedy English.

At the same time, James Eastburn and Robert Charles Sands collaborated on an epic poem called *Yamoyden, A Tale of the Wars of King Philip: In Six Cantos*, which similarly sang the chief's praises.[27] And in his highly regarded and monumental *History of the United States*, the Romantic historian George Bancroft drew the by-then-expected conclusion when he treated King Philip's War. "Destiny had marked [King Philip] and his tribe," Bancroft wrote in 1837, for the war was "but the storm in which the ancient inhabitants of the land were to vanish away." For them, he concluded, "there was no tomorrow."[28]

How different from this was the seventeenth-century historians' depiction of Philip as little better than the devil's minion who deserved the horrible death he received! Shot by one of his men, who had turned traitor after a colonist lost his opportunity, the mighty warrior lay in the mud and looked like little more than "a doleful, naked dirty beast." Captain Benjamin Church, who was present on the scene and memorialized it, declared that because Philip had "caused many an Englishman's body to be unburied, and to rot above ground," he should not be buried.

Instead, the English summoned an "old Indian executioner," whom they tasked with beheading and drawing and quartering the body. First, though, he spoke derisively over the corpse, crowing that Philip had "been a very great man, and had made many a man afraid of him, but so big as he was, now he would chop his arse for him." Finishing his bloody work, the Indian suspended the four quarters from different trees and presented Philip's head to the Englishmen, who delivered it to Plymouth, where it was mounted on a pole for everyone to see.[29]

A century after Church's publication, however, even the high-minded *North American Review* had joined in Philip's rehabilitation, asking its readers to consider that, even if his defense of his people had been in vain, he had done and endured more than enough "to immortalize him as a warrior [and] a statesman" even if his people's day was done.[30] This was the prevalent view when Apess decided to offer his "Eulogy," even as

King Philip's Heir

he drew very different conclusions from the example of the warrior's life and death.

In the first week of January 1836 Apess began to place advertisements in local newspapers—including the *Liberator* and the *Daily Advocate*— for a lecture he planned to give in Boston.[31] The notice read: "THE INDIAN KING PHILIP.—An Eulogy will be pronounced upon him by an Indian Preacher at the Odeon on Friday Evening next, at 7 o'clock," with the doors to open an hour earlier. Apess even promised to "give a specimen of Philip's language," which suggests that he still could use the Massachusetts tongue.[32] Those interested could purchase tickets—twenty-five cents admission for a gentleman and lady—at such well-known local bookstores as those of Drake, William Ticknor, James Loring, and others.[33]

The recent agitation over the Mashpees had brought Apess enough attention to warrant his speaking in such a prime venue. The Odeon (formally known as the Boston Theater) on Federal Street was elegant and spacious. Named after a Greek building built by Pericles and designed for musical entertainments and other public events, the Odeon provided a home for the Boston Academy of Music and as well offered a dais for popular lecturers, including the Transcendentalist Ralph Waldo Emerson, who there delivered his series on "Representative Men." The building's primary space, illuminated by gaslight, recently had been refurbished to seat 1,500 patrons on red "moreen" seats "arranged in a circular order," and in several "spacious galleries" on the upper level.[34]

The address caught the public's attention, for Apess was asked to repeat it, which he did on January 26 at another choice location, Boylston Hall, on the third floor of Boylston Market, on the corner of Washington and Boylston Streets. This hall, built in 1810 and home to the popular Handel and Haydn Society, was equally commodious, with twenty-four-foot ceilings and a seating capacity of 800.[35] Advertisements for Apess's encore stated that he had "consented to give an Abridgement of [the "Eulogy"] and his full view of the Mission cause—as there was some dissatisfaction with the previous one at the Odeon," an allusion to his claim of Christian missionaries' half-hearted commitment to the tribes, particularly in New York state, a situation that had been widely reported in various denominational journals. Apess also invited debate: "Any gentleman wishing to reply may do so."[36]

A month and a half later, he repeated his presentation in the Hartford, Connecticut, area, where, a local newspaper noted, "AN EULOGY will be pronounced upon this truly noble Son of the forest [King Philip], by an Indian Preacher, who well understands his history" (perhaps a barb at Drake, who, we recall, in his review of *A Son of the Forest*, had urged Apess to learn his Indian history). This time, Apess spoke in Farmington at Union Hall, a site owned by the First Church and used for public meetings and lectures, including by abolitionists. Apess made tickets available at the bookstore of Canfield & Robbins and charged the same admission, a quarter, with "Children half price."[37]

Apess's life and experiences culminated in this "Eulogy," one of the most powerful and radical public pronouncements in a golden age of American oratory. Even among New Englanders who despised and condemned President Jackson's persecution of Native Americans (and who may well have sided with the Mashpees in their recent dispute with Massachusetts and Harvard), the vanishing Indian had become a household trope.[38] Audiences could cheer Forrest's heroic depiction of Metamora because it helped them believe that, despite King Philip's bravery, his day had passed, even as they knew as well that the Cherokees soon enough would. In the face of white Americans' "progress," Native American destiny was assured. Painful as the process was, it was inevitable, part of what a later generation termed the nation's "Manifest Destiny."

CELEBRATING NEW ENGLAND HISTORY

The criticism of missionaries that two weeks earlier had upset some of Apess's audience in the first iteration of the address was only one part of a complex rhetorical performance that included lessons from history, scripture, current events, and autobiography. Coming when commemorations of the bravery and wisdom of the Pilgrim Fathers and the Massachusetts Bay Puritans were commonplace as many Massachusetts communities celebrated their bicentennials, and just a few months after the golden-tongued orator Edward Everett's 160th anniversary "Commemoration of the Fall of the 'Flower of Essex,' at [Bloody Brook], in King Philip's War," a battle in South Deerfield, Massachusetts, in which many militia men from Essex County on the Massachusetts North Shore were killed, Apess's oration drew much attention.[39]

The proximity of the "Eulogy" in time to Everett's "Bloody Brook" speech and Apess's virtually immediate publication of his effort suggests that he intended a corrective if not a direct challenge to the way most New Englanders understood their history and Native American history in general. One of Everett's rhetorical ploys, for example, also used in many of such commemorative speeches, was to excuse whites' past behavior toward and current treatment of Native Americans by proclaiming the superiority of Christian civilization and its eventual and inevitable triumph over that of the sons and daughters of the forest. Unlike in Spanish-controlled Mexico, he wrote, where millions of the population still "subsist in a miserable vassalage," in the United States treaties with the Natives "will be entered into, mutual rights [will be] acknowledged; [and] the artificial relations of independent and allied states will be established." And, because God has so ordained it, "as the civilized race rapidly multiplies, the native tribes will recede, sink into the wilderness, and disappear."[40]

Or at least that was the white citizens' wish or, perhaps better, rationalization for their behavior. Oblivious, like so many New Englanders, to any sense of the importance of the land to Native Americans, Everett thought their removal from ancestral territory would be relatively painless. For the Pequots and Narragansetts, and the Wampanoags and the Nipmucks "who live by hunting and fishing, with scarce any thing that can be called agriculture, and wholly without arts, the removal from one tract of country to another is comparatively easy," he said, and a "change of abode implies no great sacrifice of private interest or social prosperity" (640).

To his credit, Everett acknowledged that both sides were to blame for the level of violence in King Philip's War. "However justly we may defend the memory of our fathers against the charge of wantonly pursuing a policy of extermination," he explained, "it is not the less certain that the march of events was well calculated to excite the jealousy of the native tribes" (643). Everett even repeated the apocryphal tale of King Philip sitting down and weeping when he was told that one of the Natives had been shot because he realized that retaliation then was inevitable, in this case, against the town of Swansea (648). But neither did Everett avoid mentioning the Puritans' remanding of King Philip's wife and young son into West Indian slavery. They allowed "an Indian princess and her child [to be] sold from the cool breezes of Mount Hope, from the wild freedom of a New England forest, to gasp under the lash beneath the blazing sun of the tropics" (660).

Everett insisted, though, that despite such barbarity the Puritans had made "as near an approach to the spirit of the gospel, in their dealings with the Indians, as the frailty of our nature admits, under the circumstances in which they were placed" (664). "The grand design with which America was colonized, and the success with which, under Providence," that design had been "crowned" in the century and a half since the fighting at Bloody Brook mattered more. For all Philip's intelligence and bravery as a leader and warrior, from the day the Pilgrims landed at Plymouth his destiny and that of his people was assured. Everett's commemoration of this signal event, in which scores of white settlers had been killed, was meant for one thing: to make Americans realize that God's hand directed whatever had been and was being done to Native Americans.

The *Liberator* reported that Harriet Martineau, a feisty Englishwoman then visiting the United States, had "boxed [Everett's] ears soundly" for what she took as "his electioneering oration," but her response was mild compared to that of Apess.[41] He did not equivocate about who was to blame for what and assured his audience that he did not "arise to spread before [them] the fame of a noted warrior" like Philip of Greece or Alexander the Great or George Washington, "whose virtues and patriotism [were] graven on the hearts" of his audience. Rather, it was to recall an individual they were not used to considering, someone who was "made by the God of Nature," a warrior and leader without the benefits of what the white settlers deemed "civilization." Apess wanted them to remember someone who was among "the mighty of the earth," a "rude yet accomplished son of the forest, that died a martyr to his cause . . . as glorious as the American Revolution."[42]

Apess's goal was to "melt the prejudice" that existed in the hearts of those who possessed "this soil," and only by the supposed "right of conquest." Sarcastically noting that in the "wisdom of their civilized legislation" whites thought it no crime "to wreak their vengeance upon whole nations and communities, until the fields are covered with blood," he observed that they also found ways to shut their ears to the voices of "the ten thousand Indian children and orphans, who are left to mourn the honorable acts of a few—civilized men." Whites had to realize that the Indians' violent defense was nothing but the same that had been dealt them, a fact that erased any meaningful difference between what the settlers defined as the actions of "civilized" as opposed to "natural" men. "My image is of God," Apess declared; "I am not a beast." He unveiled the violence and hypocrisy that resulted from the whites' belief that they did God's work in "civilizing" the nation, dismissing the Natives' lifestyle as bestial and claiming that all men who were "governed by animal passions" were "void of the true principles of God." The audience too conveniently forgot that the settlers had been so governed when they massacred women and children and forced families and nations from their lands (277–78).

Apess then schooled his audience in some undeniable though little-mentioned facts of American history—how, for example, from the New England settlers' first encounter with the Native peoples in the early seventeenth century, they had shown themselves to be nothing but "hypocritical Christians," drunk on their purported superiority over the tribes. Such power, however, had not been given "to abuse each other," he declared, but was only delegated by God as "a weapon of defense against error and evil." "When abused," it would "turn to [the whites'] destruction" (279).

Starting from this premise, Apess piled example upon example (some drawn from Drake's book) of the colonists' treachery until he reached the time of King Philip of the Wampanoags, he "of cursed memory" in Puritan Increase Mather's account but whose dedication to the defense of his land and people Apess claimed was as admirable and worthy of remembrance and celebration as that of the Revolutionary patriots. Admittedly, from Irving's account of Philip in his *Sketch Book* and Stone's *Metamora* to such scarcely veiled fictional accounts as those of novelists Catharine Maria Sedgwick in her *Hope Leslie* (1827) and James Fenimore Cooper in *The Wept of Wish-Ton-Wish* (1829), whites had granted Philip some admirable virtues, but they always were ones that they presented as identifying a race destined to pass from the newly "civilized" landscape. Now Apess reminded his audience that King Philip's blood still ran in people like him, which thus gave the lie to the white attempt to write this warrior into oblivion.

Asking his audience to consider a different version of the past, Apess spared no sacred cows. "Perhaps if Doctor [Increase Mather] was present," he observed, the good man would realize that "the memory of Philip was as far before his [that is, more famous than he], in the view of sound, judicious men, as the sun is before the stars at noonday." And as for the militia captain Miles Standish, he was "a vile and malicious fellow" who, at the head of a band of "lewd Pilgrims," delighted in massacring Natives—women and children—at midnight. "Do you believe," Apess asked his auditors, "that Indians cannot feel and see, as well as white people"? (284).

Apess also castigated those who praised the settlers for bringing the light of Christianity to the supposedly benighted Indians, reminding them that with the Bible their ancestors also brought "rum and powder and ball, together with all the diseases" to which the Native population succumbed. Apess even suggested that these epidemics, which swept off "thousands and tens of thousands," were "carried among them on purpose to destroy them." In regard to July 4 and December 22 (recognized as the date when the Pilgrims landed at Plymouth), he counseled each auditor on these dates to "wrap himself in mourning," not in celebratory colors, for to Natives these never could be days of joy (285–86).

When Apess turned to contemporary missionaries to the "heathen," he was no less severe. Why must Natives be driven from their lands before they can hear the word of God, he asked, for "if God wants the red men converted," He should be able do it "as well in one place as in another." Moreover, he wanted missionaries to "use the colored people they already have around them like human beings, before they go to convert any more," and urged those in attendance to withhold any donations to missionary societies until their representatives treated Indian converts with the dignity they deserved (287).

Halfway through his oration, having traveled much historical ground, Apess finally rose to his chief subject, "his Majesty, King Philip," whom he termed the "greatest man that ever lived upon the American shores" (289–90). After Philip had attempted to hold off violence as long as he could, when he finally had to defend his lands and people, he uttered these noble words (295):

> Brothers, you see here this vast country before us, which the Great Spirit gave to our fathers and us; you see the buffalo and deer that now are our support. Brothers, you see these little ones, our wives and children, who are looking to us for food and raiment; and now you see the foe before you, that they have grown insolent and bold; that all our ancient customs are disregarded; the treaties made by our fathers and us are broken, and all of us insulted; our council fires disregarded, and all the ancient customs of our fathers; our brothers murdered before our eyes, and their spirits cry to us for revenge. Brothers, these people from the unknown world will cut down our groves, spoil our hunting and planting grounds, and drive us and our children from the graves of our fathers, and our council fires, and enslave our women and children.

This was his moving call to arms, and the result was two years of King Philip's War.

Apess graphically described the last days of that conflict. In swampy lands near Pocasset (Bourne), Massachusetts, where Philip and his men had hidden after a ferocious battle, he managed to escape through the only outlet and retreated to the Connecticut River, a strategic move that Apess claimed to be "equal, if not superior, to that of Washington crossing the Delaware." By such actions, Philip showed himself "as active as the wind, as dexterous as a giant, firm as the pillars of heaven, and fierce as a lion" (296–97).

Apess did not avoid sensitive points. In his discussion of those taken captive by the Indians, like Mary Rowlandson, for example, whose ordeal many contemporary orators invoked, Apess observed that not only had her captors treated her fairly well, all things considered, but all such female captives had been "completely safe, and none of them were violated, as they acknowledged themselves." But was it so, he asked rhetorically, "when the Indian women fell into the hands of the Pilgrims?" No, he answered categorically, connecting such rape to the by-then common stories of what female slaves suffered at the hands of their masters.

Nor did the Natives often get the opportunity (as whites did) to rescue their own people from captivity, for whites usually imprisoned them, sold them into slavery, or simply killed them. Here Apess mentioned how Philip's son was sent into slavery in the West Indies, just as after the Pequot War people from Apess's own tribe had been, in this case to the Spanish in Bermuda. "With shame," Apess said, "I have to notice so much corruption of a people calling themselves Christians" (300–301).

However uneasy the audience was at this point, it soon had even more reason to squirm. Up to this point, Apess had spoken mainly of history, but what of the present? The result of "all the slavery and degradation in the American colonies toward colored people" had led to the current virulent prejudice against Native Americans, which he knew firsthand. He cited several examples from his own experience of white peoples' callousness when he or another Native needed assistance. "Look at the disgraceful laws," he told those in the Odeon, "disenfranchising us as citizens." "Look at the treaties made by Congress," he continued, "all broken." Look at "the deep-rooted plans laid, when a territory becomes a state, that after so many years the laws shall be extended over the Indians that live within their boundaries," a reference to the ongoing experience of the Iroquois in New York (306).

Channeling President Jackson's supporters, Apess explained to the nation's "red children" that whites "have a right to do with you what we please," for "we claim to be your fathers." In this patronizing falsetto, he continued: "We think we do you a great favor, my dear sons and daughters . . . to drive you out, to get you away out of the reach of our civilized people, who are cheating you, for we have no law to reach them." So "it is no use, you need not cry, you must go even if the lions devour you, for we promised the land you have to somebody else long ago, perhaps twenty or thirty years; and we did it without your consent, it is true," but this has been the way "our fathers first brought us up, and it is hard to depart from it" (307). Apess's hard-hitting sarcasm was unrelenting.

Sadly, the prejudice he detailed seemed to have no end, for even as Apess spoke, new offensives against Native peoples were breaking out upon the frontiers. Why? Because "the same spirit reigns there that reigned here in New England; and wherever there are any Indians that spirit still reigns."

So what were enlightened New Englanders to do? "Let every friend of the Indians now seize the mantle of Liberty," Apess urged, and, honoring the courage and spirit of King Philip, "the greatest man that was ever in America," throw it over "those burning elements that has [*sic*] spread with such fearful rapidity, and extinguish them forever." Apess then ended his oration dramatically, surprising the crowd with a recitation of the Lord's Prayer in "[Philip's] language," that is, in Massachusett, something very few (if any) in the audiences had ever heard (307).

Apess then asked his auditors to forgive his "bold and unpolished statements," for he trusted that they now understood that what he had related of white behavior could hardly be excused as "religious." This truth did not merit "any polishing whatsoever"; it was as it was—sinful. Sadly, when one had been deceived as much as Native Americans had—and here Apess referred to his own example—"it spoil[ed] all confidence" in white people. He had had some "dear, good friends among white people," he admitted; but always he "eye[d] them with a jealous eye," for fear that they would "betray" him. "Having been so much deceived by them," he asked plaintively, how could he ever behave otherwise.

The only way to end such prejudice on both sides, Apess concluded, was to have all men "operate under one general law," for whites and Natives. When the audience asked itself, "'What do they, the Indians want?'" they had only to consider the unjust laws made against Natives and say, "'They want what I want,' in order to make men of them, good and wholesome citizens." The nation's racism would end when the Golden Rule became prevalent. Given the history lesson that he offered his audience, Apess trusted them now to understand this.

APESS VERSUS HIS NEIGHBORS

Apess shortly thereafter published two editions of this *Eulogy* as well as a second edition of the *Experiences of Five Christian Indians*, all "for the author." He revised both second editions, shortening the *Eulogy* and eliminating without explanation the "Looking-Glass" from *Experience* (as the title now appeared, without the "s"). He may well have self-published these works to help his deteriorating financial situation, hoping to peddle them for a small profit as he had done the first edition of *A Son of the Forest*, for things began to fall apart for him financially in Mashpee. Apess became involved in several lawsuits for nonpayment of debts, and his recent assistance to the tribe was no guarantee of immunity from the pressures of what quickly was becoming the nation's most severe economic downturn to date, the Panic of 1837.

Early in 1835, for example, Ezra Toby of nearby Sandwich loaned Apess fifty dollars and later one hundred more, but Apess did not begin repayment for over a year and a half (and then only delivered twenty-five dollars). Toby filed a complaint, and the sheriff issued a summons and eventually attached Apess's dwelling house. Toby brought him to court in the spring of 1837 and again in 1838, claiming accumulated damages of three hundred dollars owed to him, but Apess never appeared at any of these proceedings. It is unclear if he ever paid off the original loan.[43]

In another case, brought in April 1836, Phebe Ann Weden, a young Mashpee represented by Isaac Coombs, who had been Apess's fellow petitioner to the General Court, accused him of harvesting and selling 200 oak trees worth ten dollars and 500 pine trees worth fifteen dollars from land she claimed as a proprietor of the tribe. The magistrate found Apess guilty of trespass, a decision he challenged in the October session by an affidavit from Levi Scudder, who claimed that Weden was the illegitimate daughter of Richard Weden of Nantucket with Hetty Kecter, though Weden was at the time of Phebe's birth still married to Hannah Swift. Apess's point was that Weden, acting as her guardian, had indeed given him permission to harvest the wood. The court, however, decided in Phebe's favor. Encouraged, she continued her case against Apess into the April 1837 term in an attempt to recover costs as well. But there the record ends, perhaps because Apess had left the area.[44]

Adding to Apess's immediate difficulties, in the same judicial term, William Pope brought a suit against him, but in that case neither party appeared to speak to the matter.[45] Then, in September 1837, Enos Ames of Barnstable petitioned for reimbursement of $25.75 for work performed for Apess on his property. Again, Apess was delinquent, and court documents indicate that he had left the area. Another Mashpee proprietor, Alvis Simpson, resided on what had been Apess's property.[46]

Earlier, in September 1836, Apess also had obtained a sizable loan—of $1,500—from Richard Johnson of New Bedford and had provided his Mashpee dwelling and household goods as collateral. Apess needed this money to clear some of his other indebtedness, but his activities in the Boston area probably also required capital outlay, namely, for the printing and advertising associated with his "Eulogy," rental fees for lecture halls, and, subsequently, publication of the *Eulogy* in two editions as well as his reprinting of *Experience*, all of which were self-financed.

The record of this transaction with Johnson is remarkable for two reasons. First, supporting documents provide a detailed listing of Apess's personal property and thus of an early nineteenth-century itinerant Methodist minister's lifestyle.[47] One learns, for example, that at Mashpee he and his family lived in a one-and-a-half-story house eighteen feet by thirty-one, "made of good stuff and finished" (which suggests that some of the other Mashpee houses were not), and with a barn seventeen by twenty feet, again with "wall finished." In the barn, he kept a twelve-year-old stoutly built, dark chestnut bay horse, with a white spot on his forehead; a "pleasure wagon" and more primitive farm wagon; and two harnesses. He also owned three axes, two hoes, a shovel and scythe, and three water pails.

The family's rooms were sparsely furnished: a mahogany table with a set of yellow Windsor chairs; two large dish kettles and two pots; and one "field bedstead" with a mattress made of "live[!] goosefeathers," another with "common feathers," and another only illegibly described. For these beds, the family had sheets (ten pair), pillowcases (six pair), a pair of flannel blankets, and four bedspreads. They kept their clothes in two chests and in several trunks—a finer one of mahogany, another for "traveling," and two "common" ones. Their kitchen and dining utensils consisted of a set of silver teaspoons; one carving knife and fork; a set of knives and forks "well finished"; a set of "Liverpool ware" with "tea plates"; a set of tumblers and another of wine glasses; four glass dishes for preserves; and four blue-and-white saltcellars.

Their lighting implements were minimal—a glass lantern and a pair of brass candlesticks and snuffers—and for the fireplace, both brass and iron tongs. The rooms were decorated with a few prints and engravings: a "picture of the Dying Saint" and another of "Adam in the Garden"; "the nations of the world in the 19th century" (probably a map); "Drunkard's Progress," perhaps a version of a lithograph most popular in a later (1846) version by Currier & Ives; and, valued at fifteen dollars, a portrait of Apess, presumably the original oil painting by John Paradise that was copied for the engraved frontispiece of the revised edition of *A Son of the Forest*. Finally, with household goods Apess listed a fifteen-dollar watch and a "white hat," probably dyed beaver.

***

A NATIVE AMERICAN METHODIST'S LIBRARY

Separately on the same document, Apess listed something of even more value to the historian: all of his bound books by title—probably the earliest known description of a Native American's library. Predictably, there were several works of scriptural exegesis and criticism. But he owned other religious books, some by Methodists and others by writers from a range of Protestant denominations, as well as secular works.[48] Not surprisingly, Apess had a copy of Drake's *Book of the Indians* (1833), which he probably used to prepare his lecture on King Philip; Martin Moore's *Memoirs of the Life and Character of Rev. John Eliot, Apostle of the N. A. Indians* (1822); one of the many editions of Benjamin Franklin's *Life* (that is, his *Autobiography*); David Dudley Field and Chester Dewey's *History of the County of Berkshire, Massachusetts, in Two Parts* (1829); and a single copy of his own *Son of the Forest*.

In all, Apess listed forty-one titles, some of them multivolume sets, whose worth he set at $510, a sizable library for a young and still unsettled clergyman. Many of the books—like scriptural commentaries and concordances—were essential to the preparation of his sermons. Others displayed his interest in the Methodist faith. Still others were by that time classics of the Nonconformist tradition, like the English Baptist J. G. Pike's *Persuasives to Early Piety, Interspersed with Suitable Prayers* (1830s) and Nonconformist Philip Doddridge's *Rise and Progress of Religion in the Soul* (1830s), which Apess very likely owned in the inexpensive American Tract Society editions that proliferated in the 1820s and 1830s. He also owned several works of what might be termed controversial literature, that is, books that addressed contemporary theological issues like the manner of baptism and the possibility of universal salvation or that contained arguments against the liberal Christians now known as Unitarians, the faith toward which the Mashpees' minister Phineas Fish had drifted.

By the 1830s, Benjamin Franklin's *Life* already was standard reading for many Americans and particularly useful to young men like Apess who found inspiring Franklin's rise from impoverished candle maker's son to successful printer, statesman, and diplomat. Other of the books are less easily explained. Did Apess have Field's history of Berkshire County in order to read about the early Indian mission in Stockbridge? Why did he, as a Methodist, feel the need to learn Latin, so much associated with an educated, "hireling" ministry? And why did he have a book about Roman Catholicism?

Drake's *Book of the Indians* and Moore's biography of John Eliot, the seventeenth-century Puritan termed the "Apostle" to the Indians, fit with Apess's interest in Native American history; but surprising, given his previous publications, is the absence of Elias Boudinot's *A Star in the West* (1816), the book from which he borrowed liberally in the Appendix to his *Son of the Forest*, and of any other books from which he might have gleaned information about the Pequots or the seventeenth-century New England Indians in general. Presumably, he used Drake's work and the life of Eliot as he prepared his "Eulogy." It is also curious that he did not list any significant number of copies of his own works, either because he had already sold them or was holding them back for future colportage.

NEW BEDFORD'S ABOLITIONIST COMMUNITY

Richard Johnson, the New Bedford resident who accepted the library and Apess's other belongings as collateral for the substantial loan, was one of that seaport's best-known African American citizens, a "trader" who had moved from humble origins as cabin boy to being a prominent business-man who made his living in coastal shipping along Long Island Sound.[49] Around 1825, after the death of his partner, the ex-slave-turned-merchant Alexander Howard, he married Howard's widow, Ruth Cuffe, and thus allied himself with an important local family. She was the sister of Paul Cuffe, part African American (his father was African), part Wampanoag. Cuffe was one of the area's wealthiest merchants and ship owners, an avid abolitionist, and a prime mover in attempts to repatriate freed African Americans to the British colony of Sierra Leone.[50]

Cuffe's many coastal trading voyages to Virginia and the Carolinas had stirred his hatred of the peculiar institution. Given his commitment to "colonization," he assembled a considerable library of antislavery tracts, which he frequently loaned to other African Americans.[51] Cuffe, the John-sons, and a host of other African Americans made New Bedford a beacon of liberty in the 1830s. There, for example, in 1838 the escaped slave Fred-erick Douglass found refuge and work and as well a place where he could bring his wife, a free black from Baltimore whom he recently had married.

In his *The Colored Patriots of the American Revolution* (1855), William C. Nell, who knew Johnson, described him as "distinguished in prudence and sagacity" and "always ready to extend the hand of relief to his enslaved countrymen" and thus "to assist, according to his ability, in the elevation of his people." An early associate of William Lloyd Garrison, Johnson sub-scribed to the *Liberator* and for several years was one of its agents.[52] Nell's testament to Johnson's generosity (as well as his considerable means) ex-plains the sizable loan to Apess, who recently had received much press for what Johnson would have considered a worthwhile cause.

Apess probably had met Johnson during one of his visits to New Bed-ford to preach or lecture, and the trust he received suggests the local abo-

King Philip's Heir

litionist community's embrace of the Native American preacher. When, for example, the *Liberator* ran a notice for a "Temperance Convention of People of Color in New England" to be held in Providence in May 1836, a few months after Apess had delivered his "Eulogy" in Boston, Johnson's name was there, as was that of Apess, the sole signee from Mashpee.[53]

After Cuffe's death in 1817, Johnson assumed a leadership role among New Bedford abolitionists, to which his financial success contributed. By the mid-1830s, he owned shares of the whale ships *Francis* and *Washington*, and he owned the *Rising States* outright. In 1837, the town assessed his wealth at a remarkable $13,800. This was in a community whose "colored" population totaled around 1,500, half of whom owned real estate estimated at a *total* value of only $60,000 and most of whom made their living in one way or another from the sea.

Like Providence and Boston in the late 1820s and early 1830s, New Bedford experienced significant incidents of racial violence, including arson and beatings, in its racially segregated areas, but overall its black population's industry and economic success impressed visitors, even if this did not compensate for severe racial discrimination.[54] The community welcomed lecturers like Apess—he had spoken there during the Mashpee affair. And, in turn, citizens like Johnson were acquainted with movers and shakers in the larger cities like Boston and New York, men like Lewis Tappan, a prominent New York abolitionist, who, with his brother Arthur, had founded the American Anti-Slavery Society in 1833.

Johnson's sizable loan did not persuade Apess to stay in Mashpee, however, for as his nonappearance at court in the fall of 1837 indicates, by that time he seems to have left the area. Further, Apess's domestic situation had changed, for sometime in 1836 he married a woman named Elizabeth, who at the inquest after his death testified that they had been married for three years. Apess's previous wife, Mary, was last noted in Mashpee records in 1834, when she was listed as a "mulatto" age forty-four; her husband was listed as "Indian and white" and a decade younger. Whether she left Apess or died is unknown, as is the fate of a child, listed as "mulatto" and age twelve, in the same listing.[55] Apess himself next surfaced in lower Manhattan, the working-class section of New York City.

SEVEN

Mashpee to Washington Street
{1837-1839}

RETURN TO NEW YORK CITY

The last three years of Apess's life—from the time he left Mashpee until his death at forty-one in a boardinghouse in lower Manhattan—remain clouded. In 1836, he had recharged his career as a lecturer with his inflammatory eulogy on King Philip. Buoyed by the Mashpees' success before the Massachusetts legislature, and perhaps as well by the example of antislavery advocates Sarah and Angelina Grimké and Theodore Dwight Weld, who by the mid-1830s had emerged as major speakers on the lyceum circuit, Apess now chose the rostrum rather than the pulpit from which to sound his message about Native Americans.[1] His frequent and ostensible topic was their history and rights. In addressing these issues, he added his unique voice to others that were probing the open wounds of racial prejudice, which sapped the young nation's energy and centered the cause of Native people in that crucial question.

On his new path, Apess already had supporters among Boston's reform community and an audience primed to hear more about Native Americans. In the wake of the Cherokee removals, editors—for example, William Lloyd Garrison—regularly published notices about the Natives' plight. He included news as well of the Second Seminole War in Florida, where a cadre of runaway blacks, "maroons," had joined the tribe in resisting removal. Garrison also published the full text of Ralph Waldo Emerson's letter to President Martin Van Buren, protesting the treatment of the Cherokees, and poems about the tribes, including one by Lydia Sigourney, one of the nation's best-known poets.[2] Garrison placed notices of Native American issues beside those relating to the antislavery cause, as when he reported that "Mrs. [Angelina] Grimke of South Carolina" gave Governor Everett "a dignified and lady-like but very severe rebuke" in a recent address she gave "in which she made him out to be much more of a despot than Louis Phillippe [Louis Philippe] of France" because of his attempts to dampen public discussions of slavery.[3]

THE REVEREND PETER WILLIAMS CONNECTION

After Apess reissued his *Eulogy* and *Experience(s)* in Boston in 1837, he returned to New York City, where he tried to continue his lecturing. His intermediary may have been Richard Johnson, the person from whom he had received his sizable mortgage and a close associate of the Wampanoags and a friend of Paul Cuffe, supporter of the colonization of freed slaves to Africa. After Cuffe's death, Johnson remained committed to the cause of the nation's people of color and toward that end communicated with important New York associates.[4] One was the Reverend Peter Williams Jr., an African American leader of the Episcopal Church, who later paid tribute to his friend in a *Discourse on the Death of Capt. Paul Cuffee* (1817). Williams (ca. 1780–1840) was the son of Peter Williams, born a slave in New York but who later was freed, and who became, first, a member of the John Street Methodist Church and then a principal founder of a church for "colored Methodists" in the city, the African American Methodist Episcopal Zion Church.[5]

The elder Williams son followed his example but joined the Episcopal Church. In 1810, he was made a lay reader in a church founded a year earlier specifically for people of color, St. Philip's Church on Collect Street (later, Centre Street) in the Five Points neighborhood of Manhattan. Like Apess, Williams had a hard time attaining legitimacy; as a lay reader he led morning and evening prayers and preached, but he could not administer the sacraments, duties that were left to visiting (white) clergy. Williams was made a deacon in 1820 and thus was allowed a little larger part in worship; but even though he was qualified, he was not ordained as a priest until 1826, when Bishop John H. Hobart finally approved and performed the ceremony.[6]

Williams was also active in the American Anti-Slavery Society and known as a powerful speaker for its cause. He was a founder of the New-York African Institution, a benevolent organization for blacks, and co-founder of the first African American newspaper in the United States, *Freedom's Journal*. But he paid a price for his outspokenness.

In 1834, anti-abolition mobs rampaged during four days of civil unrest, known as the Tappan Riots, incited by the antislavery activities of Arthur and Lewis Tappan, brothers and wealthy merchants in the city who were ardently and vocally antislavery. The Tappans had scheduled the annual convention of the American Anti-Slavery Society for July 4 because seven years earlier on that date the state of New York had banned slavery. This year, however, rioters forced the group from its meeting in the Chatham Street Chapel. Fueled by unscrupulous newspaper editors who published the locations of African Americans homes and businesses (and those of abolitionists, including the Tappans) in the city, the rioters began targeting these locations.[7] In Five Points, home to many African Americans, the mobs broke windows and furniture and pulled down walls and roofs.

St. Philip's was only a block from the intersection that gave the area its name, and after a rumor got started that Williams had performed a marriage ceremony for an interracial couple, it became a prime target. Rioters shattered the brick church's stained glass windows; destroyed its curtains, candlesticks, and organ; and broke its altar.[8] With the building enough damaged to force its temporary closure, New York's Episcopal bishop, Benjamin Onderdonk, wishing to calm matters and not drag the entire Episcopal diocese into the turmoil, ordered Williams to resign from his position on the executive committee of the American Anti-Slavery Society and to announce the fact publicly. A good Episcopalian, Williams (with much regret) obeyed his superior and issued a letter to that effect, which was published in many of the city's newspapers.[9]

Williams did not, however, revoke his membership in the group, or condemn the society's general purpose and work, for he was a strong believer in African American uplift. Although earlier he had supported the colonization efforts of Cuffe and others, he came to believe that such repatriation simply avoided the larger, moral question of continued slavery in the United States and also perpetuated blatant racism because of its suggestion that there was no place in the United States for free blacks. In particular, like many others, Williams began to object to being called "African" when he had been born in and considered himself a legitimate citizen of the United States—he cited his father's admirable service in the American Revolution as proof of his family's contribution to the nation.[10]

Williams insisted that, with proper educational and occupational opportunities, African Americans would become important contributors to the American experiment in democratic citizenship. In a Fourth of July address in 1830, for example, he urged his audience, many of whom were white, "to lay aside their prejudices" and grant black people equal rights. Why send freed blacks to Africa, he asked, a place that no longer was home to most of the people who heard him, when it was "nothing but prejudice" that hindered their potential contributions to the United States? "We are

Mashpee to Washington Street

natives of this country," he declared, and "we ask only to be treated as well as foreigners," not as a different class of humanity.[11]

In the 1830s, then, Williams played a central role in the city's African American life. A hastily and informally written letter from Richard Johnson to him on November 18, 1837, suggests a potentially important connection to Apess. Dated "Saturday," it is to "Mr. Williams" and reads: "Please call on Mr. Tappan & explain my wishes & ask him to draw up the deed of emancipation for Marcellus Chason [?] a Boy of Colour & I will pay the cost [?]of writing & acknowledging the deed before the proper officer & the Seal of office & meet me at my room at 4 o'clock or say where I could see him at 4 o'clock[.] I go away Monday morning at 6 o'clock[.] I greatly oblige[,] Richard Johnson."[12] On the reverse is a note: "Get Mr. Birney [Binney?] to draw deed of emancipation[.]" The docket in the same hand (presumably that of one of the Tappans) indicates that the "boy" is someone "who left him [Williams?]" and perhaps became known to Johnson through his mercantile activities. If Apess needed an entrée to New York's reform community, in other words, his creditor Johnson could have expedited it.

INDIANS EVERYWHERE

When Apess returned to New York in 1837, the city was awash in talk of "Indians." In September, the artist George Catlin opened his prodigious Indian Gallery, a collection of several hundred paintings that he had made since the beginning of the decade, as well as original artifacts—weapons, robes, ornaments, and even a full-sized Crow "tipi."[13] Catlin set up this extravaganza, an early and somewhat tamer version of the "Wild West" shows that Buffalo Bill and others mounted later in the century, at Clinton Hall, then located at Nassau and Beekman Streets, and, when he needed a larger space because of the crowds, at the new Stuyvesant Institute on Broadway.[14]

Catlin charged the public admission and through the month of October supplemented his income by giving lectures on Native American culture, using his paintings as illustrative material to show that Indian civilization was much more complex and more intrinsically worthy of interest than easterners thought, even though this implicitly contributed to the myth of the "vanishing Indian." The *New York Morning Herald* testified to his success. "He has opened a new and unexplored mind," the paper gushed redundantly. Catlin has "enriched the field of fine arts, with the study of the savage faces and savage landscape," for every one of his paintings is "fresh from nature" and "taken on the spot."[15]

Catlin personally invited Philip Hone, the former mayor (1826–27) and one of the city's most prominent merchants and social figures, to the exhibition. Hone visited in early December at what, given the guest list, must have been the exhibit's formal opening, which included U.S. senator Daniel Webster of Massachusetts, "some members of the Common [City] Council, the mayor [Aaron Clark]," and some newspaper editors. In his diary, Hone recorded how interesting he had found Catlin's "great collection of paintings, consisting of portraits of Indian chiefs, landscapes, ceremonies, etc. of the Indian tribes, and implements of husbandry and the chase, weapons of war, costumes, etc. which he collected during his travels of five or six years in the great West." For his part, Catlin gave his distinguished guests the full frontier treatment: they enjoyed "a collation of buffaloes' tongues, and venison and the waters of the great spring" and then "smoked the calumet of peace under an Indian tent formed of buffalo skins."

The exhibit stayed open into late December, when Catlin, having learned of the capture of the Seminole chief Osceola and other leaders of the just-ended war in Florida, hustled off to Fort Moultrie in South Carolina, where they were imprisoned. He remained there two weeks to paint them and on his return to New York added their portraits to the exhibit that he had reopened. Osceola's unfortunate death in prison on January 30 made the crowds even more interested in Catlin's exhibit.[16]

Earlier that same fall, Hone and other New Yorkers had been treated to another, different extravaganza, a living tableau of representatives of several western Native tribes that had signed treaties with the U.S. government after Black Hawk's defeat in the war that bears his name. Earlier, in 1833, the city already had seen such a display, in the immediate aftermath of that war when the captured chiefs (including Black Hawk) were paraded through eastern cities, ostensibly to view the might of the country that had defeated them. Ironically, they visited some cities at the same time that President Jackson was embarked on a well-publicized tour of the eastern states.

This led to awkward moments, such as in Baltimore, when the Indian visitors and Jackson both attended the theater, albeit seated in separate boxes but with the crowd gawking to see if they would acknowledge each other. (They did not.) Later, when the president arrived in New York two days ahead of the other party, the crowds voiced disappointment that Black Hawk was not with him.[17] One young New Yorker was right on target: "Black Hawk and his companions," he observed, "now occupy the place in the public curiosity which Gen. Jackson so recently filled."[18]

Now, in 1837, East Coast residents saw chiefs from the Sioux tribe, who had ceded all their lands east of the Mississippi, and as well of the Sauk and Fox, who recently had relinquished hunting grounds between the Mississippi and Missouri Rivers. After the delegates signed treaties in Washington, they and their families toured other cities before returning to the nation's capital and heading west. Coincidentally, Apess was in Washington at the same time (for what reason is unknown) and objected to their being made a public spectacle.

The *Baltimore Sun* reported the incident on December 4, noting that among recent arrivals in Washington was "a delegation of Indians" who had been on "a visit or tour to the North." They did not attract as much "curiosity" as they had done earlier, he continued, speculating that public interest probably would not be revived "until a 'war dance' or some refined exhibition of the sort" was advertised. He then added, "I last night listened to Mr. Apess, an Indian missionary, who resented, in strong language, the treatment of the Indians, taking them out on the common for the gratification of the people." Apess's words had touched a nerve, for the reporter ended with the suggestion that "those who have charge of the Indians would better consult, not only their own propriety, but also that of the citizens of their city, by stopping such exhibitions."[19] Apess's comment is even more powerful, however, when one realizes that he had offered his criticism even though he was financially dependent on the same lecture circuit that produced shows like this one.

Predictably, when this group of Indians arrived in New York in late October, Hone was on the scene. His subsequent diary entry was tainted by the era's pervasive racism. "Broadway in the neighborhood of the City Hotel has been crowded for the last two days by curious spectators," he wrote, who hoped to obtain a glimpse of a large party of Indians who, "after having made a treaty at Washington by which their 'broad lands' are diminished in quantity to the trifling amount of a million and a quarter acres," were now touring "the principal cities." At each stop, he continued, they were showered with "presents" and "stared at for the benefit of theaters, fairs, and lectures." There were about seventy representatives from three tribes, he noted, with the Sauk and Fox ensconced at the City Hotel and the Sioux across the street, at the National Hotel. The two tribes, Hone explained, "are not on a friendly footing," and their "white keepers did not think it expedient to get up a real war fight for the edification of the spectators."

As he would later from Catlin, Hone received a special audience courtesy of Daniel Jackson, "a sort of agent for the tribes." Hone found the whole party—"warriors, squaws, and papooses"—seated or lying on the ground, "opening and dividing sundry pieces of colored cord, such as is used for hanging pictures," which had been given to them at the American Institute's (mechanics') fair, then one of the city's main attractions. Keokuk, "chief of the confederated tribes of Sauks and Foxes" (whom Catlin had painted several years earlier), and "his favorite squaw" were the central figures, sitting on a carpet a bit away from the rest.

More remarkable was the defeated Black Hawk, recently released from a prison in Virginia and being returned to the Plains. He seemed to have "lost caste," sitting with his son at one corner of the square assemblage, wrapped in a bright scarlet blanket, "silent, surly, and picturesque." His son was more impressive, a "perfect Ajax Telemon."[20] Hone greeted these "Herculeses and Apollos of the woods," by whose strong physical appearance he was much impressed, all except for the hands: Keokuk's felt "like the hand of a woman," he wrote, and young Black Hawk's was not as large as his own. Hone explained this by noting that warriors "perform no manual labor," even as their large, well-developed lower bodies indicated that they excelled "in the chase and other field exercises." He saw the large party in their last hours in New York—at four in the afternoon they departed for Boston.[21]

The theatricality of this appearance contrasts to the experience of young George Templeton Strong, not yet the prominent attorney he would become, who a few months earlier, while on a day-long "ramble" to Hoboken, New Jersey, encountered a very different group of Native Americans. "Saw a sort of Indian colony over there," he wrote in his diary, "consisting of a couple of Indians, a squaw and a lot of papooses, horrid little loafers in appearance." The adults "carried on the trade of basket-making," he continued, "and look altogether philosophical and comfortable." "What fools!" he exclaimed, "as if Hoboken could be to a true-blooded and true-hearted Indian any sort of approximative likeness to his woods and rocks and lakes at home."[22] Strong implies that "real "Indians had to conform to the Plains stereotype, not to what Apess represented, which suggests how far the erasure of eastern Indians in the popular mind had come by this point.

Such encounters with bona fide Indians or simulacra such as Catlin's were not the only ways New Yorkers encountered Native people. They were as well a frequent topic of speakers on the fledgling lyceum circuit. Reports of one lecturer in particular appeared frequently in the public prints late in the winter of 1837. "A Rabbi in the Rostrum," read the catchy header in James Gordon Bennett's *New York Herald*, a paper he had started two years earlier and already made successful as the nation's first tabloid. Bennett loved to regale the city's august tastemakers with sensational stories, like that of the murder of the prostitute Helen Jewett. He sent reporters to transcribe court testimony and frequently commissioned woodcuts to illustrate the news.[23] If people wanted to be au courant of events, low and high, they read the *Herald*.[24]

In this case, Bennett was having fun at the expense of Mordecai Manuel Noah, the country's most famous Jewish citizen and, variously, a playwright, diplomat, journalist, and erstwhile utopian.[25] He first became known when, after a brief career as a merchant, President James Madison appointed him consul to Tunis, where he won the release of some Americans whom Moroccans had enslaved. Subsequently, however, he was shocked because Secretary of State James Monroe summarily removed him from the position because he considered Noah's religion a stumbling block to his consular work. Despite a letter-writing campaign of several years' duration, by him and by equally outraged supporters, Noah gave up attempts to get reinstated and moved to New York, where in 1826 he started a pro-Jackson newspaper, the *Inquirer* (later, the *New York Courier and Inquirer*). He also authored plays for the city's growing theater scene. *She Would Be a Soldier; or, The Plains of Chippewa* (1819), probably based on the widely known true story of Deborah Sampson, who had dressed as a woman to fight in the American Revolution, proved to be his most popular and was on and off the stage for thirty years.[26]

Noah became most notorious in 1825 for his plan to start a utopian community for Jews—literally, a Zionist mini-homeland he called "Ararat"—on Grand Island in the middle of the Niagara River near Buffalo. With his own funds, he purchased the island and planned an elaborate ceremony, including the laying of a cornerstone with appropriate Masonic ritual and a parade of militia companies. But after all this hoopla, and without his ever having set foot on the island, he abandoned the plan—he had not been able to draw many fellow Jews to the idea—and returned to New York City.

He never lost interest in the Jewish people's future, however, and in the 1830s he turned his attention to the perennially revisited idea that the American Indians were descendants of the Ten Lost Tribes of Israel, who had to be converted before the Jewish restoration of Jerusalem. Bennett's barb in the *Herald* was aimed directly at Noah's recently published *Discourse on the Evidences of the American Indians Being the Descendants of the Lost Tribes of Israel* (1837), in which he added his own ruminations in regard to ideas that had been bandied about in one form or another since the discovery of the New World.

Bennett announced that "Rabbi Noah of the Evening Star" (a New York newspaper that Noah had published from 1833 to 1835) was to deliver a lecture that evening in Clinton Hall, "shewing that the Indian races of this continent are the legitimate descendants of the ten lost Tribes of Israel," dispersed after the Assyrian conquest. Noah, he hoped, would illustrate his "peculiar theory with several pretty specimens of live Black Hawks," Bennett continued, "a young Oceola [the Seminole leader], a Jumper [another Seminole tribe], and two or three Black Dirts [members of Seminole Chief Black Dirt's tribe]."[27] Noah should produce these specimens, Bennett observed, "for the benefit of science and inductive philosophy."

After sparring a bit with Noah on the matter of the ritual of circumcision—a key matter because some Native American tribes practiced the rite, thus supposedly linking them to Jews—Bennett continued his report, tongue in cheek. Everyone knew Noah's goal was praiseworthy, he deadpanned, for the Jew was endeavoring to link the identity of the Indians with his own people "in order to organize all the Indian Tribes west of the Mississippi, and to become their Messiah or Moses, and to lead them into a new Canaan, under the brow of the Rocky Mountains." Bennett did not object to this, he explained, if Noah could convince people of his theory. "If he can get up a Holy Land beyond the Mississippi, discover a river Jordan, build up a new Jerusalem, and adorn another Temple," Bennett quipped, "he will have some thousand excellent building lots to dispose of in Wall Street," implying that other Jewish businessmen would gather up families and pull up stakes and join Noah. Bennett closed by noting drily that during the ensuing evening, "Professor Stillman [perhaps Benjamin Silliman, of Yale]" intended to "controvert the Rabbi's theory."[28]

HANDSOME LAKE REDIVIVUS

The next notice of such matters is more surprising, for it links Apess to this well-publicized discussion of speakers who took Native Americans as their subject. A week after Bennett's screed, the *New-York Spectator* promised its readers "novelty" in a course of "Indian Lectures," to begin the following evening. "An Indian named Gos-kuk-wa-na-kou-ne-di-yu," the paper noted, "by some purported to be a Mohawk, and by others a Pequot, proposes to give a course of lectures on the subject of Indian history, wars, manners, customs, religion, &c. &c." The first lecture was the next evening, also at Clinton Hall.[29]

A few days later, the *New-York Evangelist*, a weekly newspaper that regularly covered antislavery news as well as missionary work and that was edited by Joshua Leavitt, an associate of the Tappans in their anti-slavery crusade, chimed in. "Indians! Indians! Again!" read the header. "Gos-kuk-wa-na-kon-ne-di-yu, one of the Indian orators, and a descen-dant of one of the most celebrated tribes of Indians, will give four lec-tures, in Clinton Hall, on the origin of the American Indians—manners and customs—wars and treaties—the injuries they have received under proposed measures for their benefit." The newspaper noted that two lec-tures would be given that week and two the following week, all commenc-ing at 7:30 P.M. "The avails of these lectures will go to aid an academy for the education of Indians," and the paper encouraged "those friendly to this depressed people" to attend.[30]

On March 1, Bennett's *Herald* added to the chorus. "Metacomet, a Mo-hawk Indian, and what is more, a very gentlemanly savage, gives a lecture in Clinton Hall, tomorrow evening." Obviously finding this speaker more credible than Noah, he added, "We shall go and hear him."[31] By the next day, the news had reached Pittsfield, Massachusetts. "Mr. Gos-kuk-wa-na-kon-ne-di-yu, an Indian, is delivering lectures in New York on the origins of the wars, treaties, and injuries of the American Indians."[32]

On March 8, Bennett had the last word, writing with his characteristic humor. "Rabbi Noah at a Discount.—Indian Lecture at Clinton Hall." The editor announced that the following evening "the Indian warrior, Mete-comet [Metacomet]," would lecture "upon the most important events and treaties between the Indians and whites—also combating the notions of Major Noah on the ten tribes." It should be a "a highly interesting and novel" presentation, he added, for "the bare fact of an aboriginal address-ing and instructing an audience of whites on a subject so involving the fate of his own unfortunate race, is an epoch in the progress of civilization." "In the course of the evening," Bennett continued, "the lecturer will descant on the character of Oceola, the agitator of the south, and investigate and trace the causes of the war now devastating that portion [Florida] of our country." "Altogether," he concluded, "these lectures form one of the most attractive evening amusements now going." Tickets were 50 cents, at the door. "We hope he won't spoil Major Noah's theories," Bennett quipped.[33]

These announcements present a body of evidence for Apess's activities in New York after he left Mashpee, for it is all but certain that he was the speaker. In fact, Bennett perhaps said more than he knew, for Apess had dealt with the question of the Natives' relation to the Lost Tribes in his earlier sermon, *The Increase of the Kingdom of Christ* (1831). He was well known as a Pequot and recently had given his eulogies on King Philip, otherwise known as Metacomet. Further proof linking these presentations to Apess appears in his obituary in the *Boston Christian Watchman*, a weekly newspaper issued in Boston by the Baptist Missionary Society of Massachusetts. There readers learned that Apess, "the Indian preacher," had "delivered orations in Clinton Hall a year or two since, and solicited funds to build a church and academy for the remnant of an Indian tribe" in Massachusetts.[34] Corroborating this, at the inquest into his death, Apess's wife testified that recently "he [had] lectured on the history of the Indians."[35]

Other evidence similarly points to Apess and what amounted to his considerable reputation. Bennett called the speaker "Metacomet" and a "gentlemanly savage," suggesting that he knew him. Similarly, the reference in the *Spectator* mentions that some thought him a Pequot and others thought him to be a Mohawk, again suggesting personal knowledge of the speaker. It is possible that Apess's New Bedford friend Johnson had mentioned to the Reverend Williams that Apess was coming to New York. Williams (or perhaps Johnson himself) could have then put him in touch with the Tappans or other reformers, who would have appreciated someone who had given considerable thought to matters of Indian history and policy and who was also a powerful speaker.

Apess's venue for this lecture series also is important, for Clinton Hall was the location of New York's Mercantile Library, one of the largest subscription libraries in the nation and the center of cultural life for clerks and other low-level white-collar workers. It also was one of the city's prime venues for lecturers—the Tappans, for example, frequently used it for antislavery meetings and lectures.[36] Given that the Tappans knew Joshua Leavitt of the *Evangelist*—they backed this newspaper when their own effort at such a journal, the *Commercial Advertiser*, failed—they may have expedited Apess's lectures at Clinton Hall, particularly when they realized that what he had to say on matters of race jibed neatly with their own.[37]

In 1833, for example, in a letter to the secretary of the American Colonization Society in which Arthur Tappan explained his opposition to colonization, he asked rhetorically, "Shall eight or nine millions of 'pale-faced' human beings, arrogate to themselves the right to trample under foot of their fellow-men, because the color of their skin is different, when, too, a

Mashpee to Washington Street

vast majority of mankind is on the side of the colored man?" Apess marshaled basically the same argument in his "Looking-Glass" against duplicitous Christians who discriminated against Natives.[38]

But what of the sobriquet "Gos-kuk-wa-na-kon-ne-di-yu"? With the exception of one missing syllable, this is how Samuel Gardner Drake and other writers on Indian history and affairs spelled Handsome Lake's name—"Gos-kuk-*ke*-wa-na-kon-ne-di-yu."[39] Why Apess assumed this name remains a mystery, but by that time Handsome Lake's fame was familiar to New Yorkers because of the Seneca tribe's ongoing difficulties with the state. The Methodist Native activist Apess would have appreciated Handsome Lake's resistance to missionaries' attempts at complete Christianization of the Senecas, even as he had urged them to make some accommodation to white civilization.

Negotiations with this tribe and others in New York that eventuated in the Treaty of Buffalo Creek (1838), which putatively would make more lands near Lake Erie available for white settlement, were already ongoing, again putting the Senecas in the public eye. Steeped in history as he had come to be in the course of preparing his lectures, Apess appreciated the Senecas' parallel to the exploitation of the Mashpees, just as he recognized the relevance of the recent defeat of Osceola.

LOST IN THE PANIC

On the cusp of what promised to be new and greater fame—not merely for having argued a local Indian tribe's rights but as a chief spokesperson for Native people generally in the nation's largest city—Apess simply dropped from sight. Notices of his lectures promised that he would discourse on "Indian history, wars, manners, customs, religion," including the U.S. government's various treaty obligations and its neglect or willful breaking of the same, topics that in Massachusetts he had framed through Mashpee and Pequot experience. In New York, a city literally enflamed by the issue of race, he would add his voice to those in the American Anti-Slavery Society or the New York Anti-Slavery Society who also were committed to the cause of wider, more inclusive liberty for people of color, all the while maintaining his belief in the sovereignty of Native tribes.

There is no hard evidence available, but Apess's disappearance from the scene may well have been related to the widespread social and economic dislocation caused by the Panic of 1837, the nation's worst economic depression up to that time. National in scope, it had been preceded by several years of easy credit, improved transportation, booming land sales, and rising cotton prices. Then, in February, a crisis began when international brokerage houses failed in London and Paris and then in American cities. By May, banks in New York, Philadelphia, New Orleans, and other chief American trading cities suspended specie payments and called in their loans, leaving businessmen with worthless paper and scrambling to pay their own debts to creditors. By the summer, all sorts of companies were failing.[40]

This crisis devastated New York, which after the opening of the Erie Canal in 1827 had emerged as the throbbing heart of the country's burgeoning economy. No class seemed immune from the Panic's disruption, as a look at Arthur Tappan's experience shows. He was high in the pecking order of the city's mercantile barons; his silk jobbing business, quartered at 122 Pearl Street, had recovered after a devastating fire in 1835 that had ruined many of the city's commercial establishments. After that setback, Tappan tried to be prudent and conduct as much of his business in cash as possible; but, generous as he was, as the depression spread he used some reserves to help other business associates.

When money became tighter and the discount rate on commercial paper from Wall Street grew dangerously high, he sent his brother Lewis to Philadelphia to ask Nicholas Biddle, president of the Second Bank of the United States, to guarantee a loan of $150,000 in order that so important a firm would not fail. Biddle granted this personal request but refused a second a few months later. In May, Tappan, like so many other New York businessmen, suspended his payments.

To survive, he proposed to his major creditors that they accept new notes, due in six, twelve, or eighteen months, with an attractive rate of interest, in exchange for their existing ones. Tappan's debts totaled over a million dollars, but, given his reputation for honesty, his creditors accepted the proposal, enabling his firm to emerge from the immediate crisis. But then, in the Panic's aftermath—its ill effects were felt for several years—with his personal funds he made what he later acknowledged to be ill-judged real estate investments, and in 1840 he went bankrupt personally, even as his firm survived with new leadership.[41]

As Tappan's difficulties suggest, the Panic's depth and pervasiveness temporarily derailed reform movements, making attendance at lectures like those of Apess seem frivolous luxuries. Even the well-known Catlin suffered. By December 1837, unable to persuade the U.S. government to purchase his entire Indian Gallery, he shipped it to Europe, where the exhibit, and his career, found new life.

But Apess had neither a safety net of goodwill, as did Tappan, nor the novelty of Catlin's paintings and artifacts. Nor did he have much, if any, liquid capital. The income of his neighbors in the Washington Street boardinghouses consisted of wages. When those were suspended, as many were in the Panic of 1837, workers no longer could pay for rent, food, or fuel.[42] At the end of 1837, Apess very likely shared the fate of these individuals. The next notices of him were the grim, clinical reports of a coroner's inquest.

EIGHT

Living with "Color"

William Apess died a tragically early death. In all likelihood, he was laid to rest in an unmarked grave in New York's Potter's Field, at Forty-ninth Street and Fourth Avenue, then at the far northern edge of the city. His corpse may even have suffered the indignity of being exhumed in the early 1850s when the city decided to extend Forty-ninth Street through the graveyard and moved many of the remains to new Potter's Fields on Randall's and Ward's Islands in the East River. The work at this scene was macabre, and citizens with a concern for common decency began to complain about how long—the work went on for several years—they had to tolerate sights like the one the *New York Times* reported one year as winter turned to spring: "The thin layer of earth which covered some hundred half-decayed coffins has fallen away, and . . . crowds of urchins assemble there daily and play with the bones of the dead; troops of hungry dogs prowl about the grounds and carry off skulls and detached parts of human bodies."[1]

How many Native American lives ended in a similarly melancholy way, given the government's and citizenry's attendant neglect or, worse, overt persecution? But it need not have been that way.

Consider the very different life and resting place of Apess's half brother, Elisha Apes, the child of his father and his third wife, whose history has recently been recovered.[2] Along with his two brothers, Solomon and Leonard, all three born in southeastern Connecticut, Elisha became a whaleman. He and Solomon went to sea in the same year, 1832, when Elisha was seventeen, on different vessels; but after one more voyage, Solomon dropped from the historical record. Leonard, the youngest, shipped six years later and rose rapidly in the trade to the position of first mate. He remained in the industry for several decades and retired well off. Crew lists on their vessels variously described the brothers as "Indian," "Dark," or "Florid," indicating that complexion was as much an identifying marker as race.

Elisha Apes first shipped out of Norwich, Connecticut, and then embarked three more times from Connecticut ports. His last voyage was in 1839, when he signed on to the *Ann Maria* under Captain Nathaniel Middleton Jr. for a two-year whaling voyage to the South Seas. Because of what he regarded as irrational and life-endangering commands from his captain, though, with a friend (the ship's carpenter) he jumped ship at Waikouaiti (now Karitane, about thirty-five kilometers north of Dunedin) on the east coast of New Zealand's South Island.

Both men liked what they saw, settled there, and married Maori women.[3] As ethnohistorian Nancy Shoemaker notes, the most remarkable thing about Elisha Apes's story is that in New Zealand he was not considered "Indian" or "colored," but "a foreigner and a settler, categorically 'European' or 'white'" in local records. She continues: "It was not just that nineteenth-century New England and New Zealand employed different racial categorizing schemes but more importantly that colonialism used indigeneity to construct racial categories." In New Zealand, "the indigenous and the settler became racialized opposites," but not on the grounds of race. There were natives, and there were Europeans.[4]

Although Elisha Apes was darker than other Europeans, the Maori always considered him *pakeha*, a word that is now most commonly translated as "foreigner," but in the nineteenth century connoted "foreigner," "European," or "white," and that had more to do with things that made the newcomers different *culturally* from the natives—their ships, clothing, languages, manners, goods—everything, in short, *but* their skin color.[5] By all accounts, his own life on New Zealand's South Island was happy and full, not vexed by the kinds of troubles, personal and institutional, that his older brother William experienced in the northeastern United States.[6]

What made the difference in the lives of these two siblings? In 1836, in his eulogy on King Philip, William Apess dramatically articulated the answer, one he probably had intuited since he was a child. He discovered what he needed to know in his family history and in the larger lessons of New England's past, for he placed the guilt for what his people had endured squarely on the New England settlers' religion. This is why it was so important for him to proclaim himself a descendant of Pequot warriors and to describe King Philip as a member of that tribe: the American history he learned from Puritan apologists such as Increase Mather, William Hubbard, and Mary Rowlandson provided a passe-partout to understanding contemporary attitudes and events.

Apess also rhetorically linked New England history to both the horror of contemporary southern slavery and to the rampant prejudice against free blacks in the North, where their plight was intertwined with that of Native Americans, both of whom appeared in census records as "colored." "I do not hesitate to say," Apess declared in the *Eulogy*, that "the prayers, preaching, and examples of those pretended pious [the Puritans] has been the foundation of all the slavery and degradation in the American colonies toward colored people" (304).

What did he mean? Apess found the Gospel as the Methodists presented it exhilarating—indeed, liberating—because it described equality in the Spirit that obviated arbitrary divisions among people. These, he learned from critically studying New England history, were based in nothing but raw, arbitrary power of the sort the Puritans displayed when they drew and quartered and then beheaded King Philip.

Apess first experienced such abuse of power—admittedly in a small way—in the service of ideology when the Methodist Church hierarchy refused to grant his license to preach, a temporary obstacle he overcame by joining with the more democratic Protestant Methodists. Then, when he lived in Providence and Boston and traveled among abolitionists and other reformers and read more about President Jackson's destructive Indian policy, he increasingly understood what he, as a Pequot, had in common with *all* Native peoples. News of the federal government's progressive dispossession of the Cherokees, as well as of the Methodist Episcopal Church's progressive retrenchment of its missionary activities among the tribe through the 1830s, opened his view on national problems.

The fact that among many of his own Methodist brethren land was of more interest than the harvest of souls provoked him to speak truth in the face of the power that sought nothing more than to pronounce the New England Natives extirpated. Among the Mashpees, he saw the white peoples' cupidity at the most local level, among the tribe's overseers; and he learned that once he declared solidarity with this tribe, he would be tarred indiscriminately with the same brush that Cape Cod's white population used daily to dispirit the Mashpees.

The immediate precipitating factor for Apess's *Eulogy on King Philip* may well have been the eruption of the Second Seminole War in 1835 as he was wearing out his welcome on Cape Cod.[7] In the First Seminole War (1817–18), then-general Jackson found that in his attempts to take Florida from the Spanish, his progress was slowed by the Seminoles' alliance with the foreign power. In 1818, after Jackson had destroyed their major villages, he declared victory; but he was far from having defeated the Seminole people, who fled into the Florida backcountry. According to the subsequent Treaty of Camp Moultrie (1823), the governor of Florida granted

Living with "Color"

the Seminoles lands further south, in the Everglades, and required them to stop harboring slaves; but in this they were recalcitrant.

Empowered by the Indian Removal Act, in 1835 the U.S. Army, now at President Jackson's command, marched against the tribe to make it accept lands across the Mississippi in exchange for its claims in Florida. The result was bloodshed and treachery—the Seminole leader Osceola, for example, was taken and imprisoned when he came under a flag of truce to negotiate with the army—and news of this conflict filled the newspapers, making it likely that this is what Apess had in mind when in his *Eulogy* he mentioned that "we often hear of the wars breaking out upon the frontiers." For these troubles, too, he blamed the Puritans' legacy: such warfare was inevitable "because the same spirit reigns there [on the "frontiers," that is, in Florida] that reigned in New England" (307).

By "same spirit," Apess had in mind first and foremost the sense of divine mission through which the Puritans had understood and justified their activities in the New World. He criticized his contemporaries for celebrating December 22, Forefathers' Day, for in so doing they implicitly approved "the works of their fathers" against the Natives—their bringing them powder and ball, rum, and diseases, as well as the Gospel—all to the end of extinguishing them, through all the bloodshed proclaiming that they were "executing the judgments of God by so doing" (286). "The seed of iniquity and prejudice" sown in that day continued to bear its poisonous fruit in the American government's ongoing efforts to make the Native people "vanish." Thus, to rationalize their violent actions, whites held "a deep-rooted popular opinion" that Indians were "made for destruction, to be driven out by white Christians, and they to take their places," what John L. O'Sullivan soon would proclaim to be part of the nation's "Manifest Destiny" (287).

Apess could not comprehend how such behavior could be termed "Christian," yet the Puritans' "haughty divines and orators" devoted themselves to perfecting this rhetoric of extinction, particularly by promulgating the belief that the passing of the Native was part of God's larger plan for human redemption. "O Christians," Apess asked, "can you answer for those beings that have been destroyed by your hostilities, and beings too that lie as endeared to God as yourselves, his Son being their Savior as well as yours, and alike to all men," whatever their color (286)? Racial prejudice would end only when white Christians took this to heart and acted on it.

Natives were no more barbarous or "savage" than white men; sinfulness of both lay in their both having lost sight of their common humanity. King Philip was not a "beast." He saw and felt like any Puritan, or like any enslaved African, for that matter (285). Apess admitted puzzlement at "what divinity men were made of in those days," so callous they seemed in the face of the horror their theology enabled. As long as contemporaries refused, as the Puritans had for over a century, to acknowledge their common humanity with people of color, tragedies like that of King Philip's War, then being replicated in Florida, would continue. They would continue to sacrifice Indians and African Americans to what whites—now not Puritans but citizens—irrationally continued to claim was the greater glory of God (288).

As this national sense of divine mission accepted and absorbed a labor system based on slavery, the matter of race was inflected in novel, horrific ways. Yet again, religion was the complicating and enabling factor, for in the British island colonies of Barbados and Jamaica, as well as in the French, Spanish, and Dutch Caribbean and in the Portuguese colony on the South American mainland—as in New Zealand and Australia—there was nothing comparable to the Puritans' self-righteousness about divine mission. Over two centuries, this belief had been transformed into an irrational refusal to alter a way of life that, bombastically defended on the grounds of leading the United States to divine glory, only marked a path to the gates of hell. Apess's prescience lay in his discernment of and unflinching challenge to this fact, another Jeremiah calling America to judgment.

The astute cultural critic Edward Dahlberg warned, "We cannot perceive what we canonize," for "the citizen secures himself against genius by icon worship."[8] William Apess, who lay in obscurity for a century and a half, has enjoyed no such fate, and that is why I do not end his biography with a call for an enshrinement that would only defang him.

Progress toward the achievement of equality in human rights often proceeds dialectically. We need to see our limits transgressed, to be challenged by ideas that, while at first are seemingly so outré that no "sane" man would adopt them, in fact inoculate us against ever-more-virulent forms of prejudice. Apess—dying in a crowded room in a boardinghouse in lower Manhattan at the too-young age of forty-one—is one of the nation's great prophetic voices. He deserves all our attention but none of the mindless adulation that would turn him into a speechless monument rather than a painful reminder of what the United States might have been and still might be.

EPILOGUE

F or a century and a half, William Apess virtually dropped from American history. Unlike, say, in the case of the pioneering feminist Margaret Fuller, whose premature death by drowning similarly robbed the nation of one of its most important voices for democratic inclusiveness, no one stepped forward to continue his work, as Caroline Dall, Elizabeth Cady Stanton, and others did in the case of Fuller. After 1839, Apess's contributions to Native American rights were almost completely unacknowledged. But not wholly.

We know that in the 1850s Iroquois leaders Ely and Nicholson Parker knew Apess's *Eulogy on King Philip* and used it in some of their writings.[1] But an even more striking instance of the reach of Apess's work came in 1845 when Thomas Commuck, a Narragansett convert to Methodism, published *Indian Melodies*, a collection of hymns, most of whose words he composed and which Thomas Hastings (1784–1872), a well-known American composer, then "harmonized," that is, set to music. Commuck had worked on the project, he told the reader, for seven years. He named the hymns after "noted Indian chiefs, Indian females, Indian names of places, &c." and also tribes, as a "tribute of respect to the[ir] memory" because some were "now nearly if not quite extinct," and "as a mark of courtesy" to some groups "with whom the author is acquainted." Thus, the reader finds "Osceola" and "Pocahontas," for example, and "Wampanoag" and "Yamassee," among scores of others. Following "Tuscarorah," there is one called "Apes."

Commuck was a member of the Brothertown Indian Nation, comprised of Mohegan from the Stockbridge, Massachusetts, mission and members of the Pequot and other southeastern New England tribes who, after the Revolutionary War, moved to Oneida County in New York to lands set aside for them. But soon white settlers were clamoring for these lands, too. Thus, in the early 1820s, the U.S. government offered lands in Wisconsin in exchange for those making up the Brothertown reservation. The tribe agreed but shortly after moving west again felt vulnerable. Commuck was one of the tribe's five delegates, and they petitioned the federal government to become American citizens, in exchange for relinquishing group ownership of their land. Their request was successful.[2] The price was their adapting to a new way of relating to the land.

Commuck's tunes' names display a deep familiarity with the history of the nation's Native peoples and a sharp condemnation of their treatment at the hands of whites who tried to "civilize" them.[3] His inclusion of the tune "Apes" speaks to his belief that, six years after William Apess's death, he deserved a place in a compilation that included, among others, Uncas, the great Mohegan leader, and Samson Occom, pioneering Native American clergyman. Commuck may even have met Apess and he certainly knew his *Son of the Forest*, for in his preface Commuck writes that, to his knowledge, "no 'son of the forest'"—the quotation marks are his— had ever undertaken such a musical compilation.

Commuck, too, shared Apess's experience of the prejudice under which a Native author labored. Commuck suffered, he wrote, under "the circumstance of having been born, not only in obscurity," but as a descendant of "that unfortunate and proscribed people, the Indians, with whose name a considerable portion of the enlightened American people are unwilling to associate even the shadow of anything like talent, virtue, or genius." With his *Indian Melodies*, Commuck bravely appeared "at the bar of public opinion, not knowing but Judge Prejudice may preside, and condemn his work to the deep and silent shades of everlasting oblivion, without even a hearing."[4] Apess's song ends thus:

> Are not thy mercies large and free! May not a sinner trust in thee?
> Happy the man that finds the grace, The blessing of God's chosen race;
> The wisdom coming from above, The faith that sweetly works by love.

Apess would have appreciated the sentiment, so accurately reflecting what he had come to believe.

NOTES

PROLOGUE

1. Coroner's Inquest for William Apes, April 10, 1839, New York County Coroner Inquests, roll no. 16, July 1838–August 1840, Department of Records and Information, Municipal Archives of the City of New York, New York.

2. For New York's growth in this period, see Elizabeth Blackmar, *Manhattan for Rent, 1785–1850* (Ithaca, N.Y.: Cornell University Press, 1989). In *The Boardinghouse in Nineteenth-Century America* (Baltimore: Johns Hopkins University Press, 2007), Wendy Gamber provides detailed descriptions of life in city boardinghouses; see especially 20–24, 44–55, and 98–103 for New York City.

3. *Philadelphia North American*, April 12, 1839, p. 2.

4. Theodore Romeyn Beck and John B. Beck, in *Elements of Medical Jurisprudence* (2 vols. [1823; Philadelphia: Thomas, Copperthwait, 1838], 2:530–31), state that they "do not exaggerate" that from 1828 to 1838 "thousands of individuals in the United States have been murdered by the combined use of capsicum [hot pepper] and lobelia, administered by Thompsonian quacks."

5. James. C. Mohr, *Doctors and the Law: Medical Jurisprudence in Nineteenth-Century America* (New York: Oxford University Press, 1993), 89–90.

6. Coroner's Inquest for William Apes. For an example of how the coroner's report was redacted, see "Death of a Pequod Indian," *Albany Evening Journal*, April 14, 1839, p. 2.

7. See, for example, W. Beach, M.D., *The Family Physician; or, The Reformed System of Medicine: On Vegetable or Botanical Principles* (New York, 1845), 661; and S. Remington, M.D., *The Family Doctor . . . to Which Is Added a Dispensatory of American Botanical Medicines* (New York: H. Phelps, 1848), 89. Although whites had practiced "Indian medicine" since the period of settlement, in the early nineteenth century Samuel Thomson popularized such treatment; see his *A New Guide to Health; or, Botanic Family Physician* (Boston: For the author, 1832); and John S. Haller Jr., *The People's Doctors: Samuel Thompson and the American Botanical Movement, 1790–1860* (Carbondale: Southern Illinois University Press, 2000), especially part 2. Thompson himself was brought to trial in 1809 for supposedly murdering a patient with lobelia; see ibid., 127–28.

8. See Remington, *Family Doctor*, 91.

9. See Beck and Beck, *Elements of Medical Jurisprudence*, 2:41–44, 665–66. A

modern diagnosis would suggest a case of acute pancreatitis, often linked to heavy drinking.

10. Barry O'Connell, ed., *On Our Own Ground: The Complete Writings of William Apess, a Pequot* (Amherst: University of Massachusetts Press, 1992).

11. Robert Warrior, *The People and the Word: Reading Native Nonfiction* (Minneapolis: University of Minnesota Press, 2005), 3.

CHAPTER 1

1. William Apess, *A Son of the Forest: The Experience of William Apes, A Native of the Forest, Comprising a Notice of the Pequod Tribe of Indians; Written by Himself* (New York: Published by the author, 1829), 7. Unless noted, quotations in the text are keyed to the first edition of this work, not to the second. The entirety of the second edition is included in *On Our Own Ground: The Complete Writings of William Apess, a Pequot*, ed. Barry O'Connell (Amherst: University of Massachusetts Press, 1992), 1–98; I quote from the second edition only if the quotation is not found in the first edition.

2. Alfred A. Cave, *The Pequot War* (Amherst: University of Massachusetts Press, 1996). In the nineteenth century, "Pequod" and "Pequot" were used interchangeably to refer to the tribe.

3. John W. De Forest, *History of the Indians of Connecticut* (Hartford, Conn.: Hamersley, 1851), 159–60; Treaty of Hartford, March 21, 1638, reprinted in Alden T. Vaughan, *New England Frontier: Puritans and Indians, 1620–1675* (Boston: Little, Brown, 1965), 340–41.

4. Daniel R. Mandell, *Tribe, Race, History: Native Americans in Southern New England, 1780–1880* (Baltimore: Johns Hopkins University Press, 2008), 9.

5. See David J. Silverman, "The Impact of Indentured Servitude on the Society and Culture of Southern New England Indians, 1680–1810," *New England Quarterly* 74, no. 4 (December 2001): 654–55.

6. See Mandell, *Tribe, Race, History*, chap. 1, passim; and Donna Keith Baron, J. Edward Hood, and Holly V. Izard, "They Were Here All Along: The Native American Presence in Lower-Central New England in the Eighteenth and Nineteenth Centuries," *William and Mary Quarterly*, 3rd Series, 53, no. 3 (July 1996): passim.

7. Mandell, *Tribe, Race, History*, 9–16.

8. See John Lauritz Larson, *The Market Revolution in America: Liberty, Ambition, and the Eclipse of the Common Good* (New York: Cambridge University Press, 2012), 12–38.

9. See, for example, Jack Campisi, "The New England Tribes and Their Quest for Justice," in *The Pequots in Southern New England: The Fall and Rise of an American Indian Nation*, ed. Laurence M. Hauptman and James D. Wherry (Norman: University of Oklahoma Press, 1990), 179–93; Jack Campisi, *The*

Mashpee Indians: Tribe on Trial (Syracuse, N.Y.: Syracuse University Press, 1991), 9–67; and Jean M. O'Brien, *Firsting and Lasting: Writing Indians Out of Existence in New England* (Minneapolis: University of Minnesota Press, 2010), 117–20.

10. In his *Landscape and Material Life in Franklin County, Massachusetts, 1770–1860* (Knoxville: University of Tennessee Press, 1991), chap. 1, J. Ritchie Garrison offers a good overview of this region's history and geography.

11. Elmer F. Davenport, *The Puzzle of Catamount Hill* (N.p., 1969); Charles H. McClellan, *The Early Settlers of Colrain, Massachusetts* (Greenfield, Mass.: W. S. Cason, 1885).

12. See Josiah Gilbert Holland, *History of Western Massachusetts*, 2 vols. (Springfield, Mass.: Samuel Bowles, 1855), 2:336–45; John Warner Barber, *Massachusetts Historical Collections* (Worcester, Mass.: Dorr, Howland, 1839), 242–44; Elias Nason, *A Gazetteer of the State of Massachusetts* (Boston: B. B. Russell, 1874), 164–65; David P. Szatmary, *Shays's Rebellion: The Making of an Agrarian Insurrection* (Amherst: University of Massachusetts Press, 1980); and Leonard L. Richards, *Shays's Rebellion: The American Revolution's Final Battle* (Philadelphia: University of Pennsylvania Press, 2002).

13. He repeats this claim in the second edition of his autobiography but obviously conflates the two great seventeenth-century wars between Puritans and Native Americans: the Pequot War and King Philip's War. King Philip (also known as Metacom, Metacomet, and Metamora) was not a Pequot, however, but a leader of the Pokanokets (Narragansetts) of Rhode Island. I spell his grandfather's and father's names "Apes" to distinguish them from William Apess, who added the "s" to his name sometime in the mid-1830s.

14. A "colored" woman by this name admitted to Christ Church in Norwich on May 4, 1834, may be she: "William married to Jerusha Maria Apes from Norwich, Connecticut, possibly an African American." See Robert C. Bates, ed., *Rolls of Connecticut Men in the French and Indian War, in Collections of the Connecticut Historical Society, vols. 9 and 10* (Hartford, Conn., 1903, 1905), 9:191, 10:307.

15. An article in the *Greenfield (Mass.) Gazette* (published nearby) lists among the deceased a "son of William Apes, an Indian." In addition to white people who perished in the same epidemic, the paper also noted two daughters, ages four and two, of Peter Green, "a black man," and a son of Peter James, "a black man," age five, facts that suggest the small hill country community's complex interracial makeup. See *Greenfield Gazette*, September 12, 1803. According to Nancy Shoemaker, in "Race and Indigeneity in the Life of Elisha Apes" (*Ethnohistory* 60, no. 1 [Winter 2013]: 29), William Apes had at least one sibling, Desire Apes (b. ca. 1765). In 1850 she was listed as a widow in Lebanon, Connecticut, and she died at age eighty-five.

16. See Shoemaker, "Race and Indigeneity," 29, citing census records. Incomplete records indicate that Elias married Louisa Worthington, "colored," in Hartford in 1827. By 1850, Gilbert had moved to Brooklyn, New York; Griswold stayed in Colchester.

17. See Mandell, *Tribe, Race, History*, 6, 146; and Daniel R. Mandell, "Shifting Boundaries of Race and Ethnicity: Indian-Black Intermarriage in Southern New England, 1760–1880," *Journal of American History* 85 (1998): 466–501. See John W. Sweet, *Bodies Politic: Negotiating Race in the Antebellum North, 1730–1830* (Baltimore: Johns Hopkins University Press, 2003), passim, for the complex typology of race in New England among its various peoples.

18. Shoemaker, "Race and Indigeneity," 29. Throughout this section I am indebted to Shoemaker's admirable detective work among admittedly fragmentary local and state records. See also Barbara W. Brown and James M. Rose, *Black Roots in Southeastern Connecticut, 1650–1900*, Gale Genealogy and Local History Series vol. 8 (Detroit: Gale, 1980), 9–11.

19. William Apess, *The Experiences of Five Christian Indians of the Pequod Tribe* (1833), in *On Our Own Ground: The Complete Writings of William Apess, a Pequot*, ed. Barry O'Connell (Amherst: University of Massachusetts Press, 1992), 120.

20. Timothy Dwight, *Travels through New England and New York*, 4 vols. (New Haven, Conn.: S. Converse, 1822), 3:14.

21. Kevin A. McBride, "The Historical Archaeology of the Mashnantucket Pequot Tribe, 1637–1975," in *The Pequots in Southern New England: The Fall and Rise of an American Indian Nation*, ed. Laurence M. Hauptman and James D. Wherry (Norman: University of Oklahoma Press, 1990), 111–12.

22. See O'Brien, *Firsting and Lasting*, 105–40.

23. Dwight, *Travels*, 3:14; Mandell, *Tribe, Race, History*, 45.

24. John Warner Barber, *Connecticut Historical Collections* (New Haven, Conn.: Durrie and Peck, 1836), 303–6.

25. [Anonymous], "Bacon Academy," *Connecticut Quarterly* 2, no. 2 (1896): 120–39.

26. See Hilary E. Wyss, *English Letters and Indian Literacies: Reading, Writing, and New England Missionary Schools* (Philadelphia: University of Pennsylvania Press, 2012).

27. Its first instructor had been Prince Hall, founder of the first African American Masonic lodge in the country.

28. Van Wyck Brooks, *The Flowering of New England, 1815–1865* (New York, 1936), 11. In addition to being Saunders's father-in-law, Paul Cuffe was a prominent mixed-blood (Native and African) Connecticut merchant and an early advocate of the repatriation of the country's African Americans to Africa, specifically, Sierra Leone.

29. On the Haitian Revolution, see Laurent Du Bois, *Avengers of the New World:*

The Story of the Haitian Revolution (Cambridge, Mass.: Harvard University Press, 2004).

30. Hubert Cole, *Christophe: King of Haiti* (London: Eyre and Spotswood, 1967), 240–42.

31. Arthur White, "Prince Saunders: An Instance of Social Mobility among Antebellum New England Blacks," *Journal of Negro History* 40, no. 4 (1975): 526–35; Arthur White, "The Black Leadership Class and Education in Antebellum Boston," *Journal of Negro Education* 42, no. 4 (1973): 504–15. In 1820, Saunders returned to Haiti and persuaded Emperor Christophe to send a ship to Philadelphia to transport African American emigrants to the island. But a coup in Haiti halted these plans. Emperor Christophe committed suicide, and the new leader showed little interest in furthering Saunders's educational program for the country. The next year, Saunders returned to Philadelphia, but in 1822, disgusted by the degree of racial discrimination blacks experienced in the United States, he moved back to Haiti. He died in Port-au-Prince in 1839.

32. Shoemaker, "Race and Indigeneity," 45, n. 9.

33. Apess, *Experiences*, in O'Connell, *On Our Own Ground*, 120.

34. See Shoemaker, "Race and Indigeneity," 45, n. 6, for the uncle's name.

35. See Laurel Thatcher Ulrich, "A Woodsplint Basket," in *The Age of Homespun: Objects and Stories in the Creation of an American Myth* (New York: Knopf, 2001), 340–73.

36. John Avery, *History of the Town of Ledyard, 1650–1900* (Norwich, Conn.: Noyes and Davis, 1901), 259–60. A pamphlet called *Poor Sarah; or, The Indian Woman* (New York: American Tract Society, ca. 1820s) told the story of one such impoverished Native who "lived in the eastern part of Connecticut," between Tolland and Ellington (suggesting that she was indeed a Pequot) and who found solace in the message of Christianity. This was a popular tract, reprinted in its entirety in A. Mott, compiler, *Biographical Sketches and Interesting Anecdotes of Persons of Colour* (New York: Mahlon Day, 1826), 12–22, and also contained a poem about her.

37. See Nan Wolverton, "'A Precarious Living': Basket Making and Related Crafts among New England Indians," in *Reinterpreting New England Indians and the Colonial Experience*, ed. Colin G. Calloway and Neal Salisbury (Boston: Colonial Society of Massachusetts, 2003), 341–68; Jean M. O'Brien, "'Divorced' from the Land: Resistance and Survival of Indian Women in Eighteenth-Century New England," in *After King Philip's War: Presence and Persistence in Indian New England*, ed. Colin G. Calloway (Hanover, N.H.: University Press of New England, 1997), 144–61; and Ruth B. Phillips, *Trading Identities: The Souvenir in Native American Art from the Northeast, 1700–1900* (Seattle: University of Washington Press, 1998).

38. Shoemaker, "Race and Indigeneity," 45, n. 6.

39. February 8, 1802, Colchester Treasurer's Records, 1801–2, New London County, Connecticut, Archives, http://files.usgwarchives.org/ct/newlondn/history/other/townpoor224gms.txt, accessed July 11, 2013. Elsewhere in these records, when medical care was reimbursed, the title "Doctor" often was affixed to the individual's name, suggesting that Gates was not a doctor.

40. On November 8, 1802, the town of Colchester reimbursed David "Firmin" for "keeping William Apes. an Indian boy, 18 weeks in 1802," and for providing him with clothing. See ibid.

41. See Ruth Wallis Herndon and John E. Murray, eds., *Children Bound to Labor: The Pauper Apprentice System in Early America* (Ithaca, N.Y.: Cornell University Press, 2009); and David J. Silverman, "The Impact of Indentured Servitude on the Society and Culture of Southern New England Indians, 1680–1810," *New England Quarterly* 74, no. 4 (2001): 622–66.

42. Ruth Wallis Herndon and John Murray, "'A Proper and Instructive Education': Raising Children in Pauper Apprenticeship," in Herndon and Murray, *Children Bound to Labor*, 3–18; and Ruth Wallis Herndon, "'Proper' Magistrates and Masters: Binding Out Poor Children in Southern New England, 1720–1820," in ibid., 39–51.

43. Herndon, "'Proper' Magistrates," 51.

44. The Pequot language persisted into the twentieth century, however; see Frank G. Speck, "Native Tribes and Dialects of Connecticut: A Mohegan-Pequot Diary," *Forty-third Annual Report of the Bureau of Ethnology, 1925–1926* (Washington, D.C.: Government Printing Office, 1928), 199–287.

45. See Silverman, "Impact of Indentured Servitude," 656–63. Apess gave the recitation in 1836 in Boston after his lecture on King Philip (see below); an advertisement for the lecture in the *Boston Daily Evening Transcript*, January 6, 1836, noted that "at the close he will give a specimen of Philip's language."

46. W. J. Rorabaugh, *Alcoholic Republic: An American Tradition* (New York: Oxford University Press, 1979), passim.

47. See David J. Silverman, *Faith and Boundaries: Colonists, Christianity, and Community among the Wampanoag Indians of Martha's Vineyard, 1600–1871* (New York: Cambridge University Press, 2007), 185–222; and Silverman, "Impact of Indentured Servitude," 649–50.

48. [Samuel Elliott], *New England's Chattels: or, Life in the Northern Poor-House* (New York: H. Dayton, 1858), 35–36.

49. Eunice Mahwee, a one-hundred-year-old Pequot woman who was visited by historian Benson J. Lossing in 1859, reported a very similar experience. Born in 1759 in Derby, Connecticut, she remembered that her father always "wore the costume of the white people." When her grandfather and a few of his friends visited the family when she was a small child, they were "dressed in the Indian manner," and "their wild appearance frightened her and she hid in the bushes

for fear of being eaten up by them." She also was surprised that they took dinner "with their fingers out of a huge kettle of meat and vegetables, all sitting around it on the ground." Benson J. Lossing, "The Last of the Pequots," in *The Indian Miscellany*, ed. W. W. Beach (Albany, N.Y.: J. Munsell, 1877), 458.

50. See Nathan O. Hatch, *The Democratization of American Christianity* (New Haven, Conn.: Yale University Press, 68–81); and for Smith's own thoughts, see Elias Smith, *The Clergyman's Looking-Glass: Being a History of the Birth, Life, and Death of Anti-Christ* (Portsmouth, N.H., 1803).

51. *Herald of Gospel Liberty*, October 26, 1810, p. 263.

52. On Hillhouse, see *Historical and Genealogical Collections Relating to the Descendants of Rev. James Hillhouse* (New York: Wright, 1924), 43ff.

53. On Williams, see J. Oliver Williams, *A Genealogy of Williams Families* (Brookline, Mass., 1938).

54. Apess, *Experiences*, in O'Connell, *On Our Own Ground*, 124–25.

55. Dee R. Andrews, *The Methodists and the American Revolution, 1760–1800: The Shaping of an Evangelical Culture* (Princeton: Princeton University Press, 2000), 156–61; Hatch, *Democratization of American Christianity*, 49–56, 81–93, 103–10; Julia Stewart Werner, *The Primitive Methodist Connexion: Its Background and Early History* (Madison: University of Wisconsin Press, 1984), passim.

56. Anna M. Lawrence, *One Family under God: Love, Belonging, and Authority in Early Methodism* (Philadelphia: University of Pennsylvania Press, 2011), 81, 91–92.

57. See David Hempton, *Methodism: Empire of the Spirit* (New Haven, Conn.: Yale University Press, 2005), 131–50.

58. Apess, *Experiences*, in O'Connell, *On Our Own Ground*, 126.

59. The *Connecticut Courant*, on April 21, 1813, noted that "Indian boy William Apes ae. 15, ran away, from William Williams of New London, 1813." See also Brown and Rose, *Black Roots*, 9–11.

CHAPTER 2

1. See *Register of Enlistments in the US Army, 1798–1814*, vols. 1 and 2 (A, B), 1798 on (A, B), p. 203, for Apess's recruitment record. He was first put under the command of Captain J. McKeon in the Artillery Corps.

2. Alan Taylor, *The Civil War of 1812: American Citizens, British Subjects, Irish Rebels, and Indian Allies* (New York: Knopf, 2010), 349.

3. Ibid., 347.

4. See ibid., 3–14; Donald R. Hickey, *The War of 1812: A Short History* (Urbana: University of Illinois Press, 1995); and J. C. A. Stagg, *Mr. Madison's War: Politics, Diplomacy and Warfare in the Early American Republic* (Princeton: Princeton University Press, 1983), and *The War of 1812: Conflict for a Continent* (New York: Cambridge University Press, 2012).

5. For the tribes' conflicted allegiances during the war, see Carl Benn, *The Iroquois in the War of 1812* (Toronto: University of Toronto Press, 1998); and "Iroquois External Affairs, 1807–1815: The Crisis of the New Order," in *The Sixty Years War for the Great Lakes, 1754–1814*, ed. David Curtis Skaggs and Larry L. Nelson (East Lansing: Michigan State University Press, 2001), 291–302.

6. Clay to Thomas Bodley, December 18, 1813, in *The Papers of Henry Clay: The Rising Statesman, 1797–1814*, ed. James Hopkins (Louisville: University of Kentucky Press, 1959), 842.

7. Taylor, *Civil War*, 325; Hickey, *War of 1812*, 21.

8. Hickey, *War of 1812*, 21.

9. Taylor, *Civil War*, 329–30.

10. Ibid., 342–44.

11. See ibid., 203–33, for discussion of scalping and other tortures used during the war by both sides.

12. Hickey, *War of 1812*, 43–44; and see Carl Benn, *Native Memoirs of the War of 1812: Black Hawk and William Apess* (Baltimore: Johns Hopkins University Press, 2014), 79–118, for Apess's participation in the war.

13. Francis H. Beirne, *The War of 1812* (New York: E. P. Dutton, 1949), chap. 23; Hickey, *War of 1812*, 56–59; Taylor, *Civil War*, 402–3.

14. See John R. Elting, *Amateurs to Arms! A Military History of the War of 1812* (Chapel Hill: Workman, 1991); and Charles G. Muller, *The Proudest Day: Macdonough on Lake Champlain* (New York: John Day, 1960).

15. See, for example, Karim M. Tiro, *The People of the Standing Stone: The Oneida Nation from the Revolution through the Era of Removal* (Amherst: University of Massachusetts Press, 2011), chaps. 5 and 6.

16. See Fred L. Engerman, *The Peace of Christmas Eve* (New York: Harcourt, 1960); and Frank A. Updyke, *The Diplomacy of the War of 1812* (Baltimore: Johns Hopkins University Press, 1915).

17. Army records show, however, that he deserted on September 14, 1814 (though he may have left earlier). If he had not obtained a discharge, this would have made him ineligible for the land grant bounty promised soldiers. See Benn, *Native Memoirs*, 163, n. 112; and O'Connell, "Introduction," *On Our Own Ground*, xxxii.

18. See Carl Benn, *The Iroquois in the War of 1812* (Toronto: University of Toronto Press, 1998), chap. 8, for a description of the state of Haudenosaunee in this area after the war; and also Matthew Dennis, *Seneca Possessed: Indians, Witchcraft, and Power in the Early American Republic* (Philadelphia: University of Pennsylvania Press, 2010), 156–57, and chap. 5 passim; and Benn, *Native Memoirs*, 114, n. 117.

19. See Dennis, *Seneca Possessed*, 144–46.

20. See ibid., 195–200, for population of tribes in these parts of Canada.

21. See Anthony F. C. Wallace, *The Death and Rebirth of the Seneca* (New York:

Knopf, 1970), especially chap. 8; and Dennis, *Seneca Possessed*, especially 53–80. On Handsome Lake's doctrine, see Arthur C. Parker, "The Code of Handsome Lake," in *Parker on the Iroquois*, ed. William N. Fenton (Syracuse, N.Y.: Syracuse University Press, 1968), book 2. On Tecumseh, see R. David Edmunds, *Tecumseh and the Quest for Indian Leadership* (New York: Pearson Longman, 2007). On the Shawnee, see Colin G. Calloway, *The Shawnees and the War for America* (New York: Viking, 2007); and Stephen Warren, *The Worlds the Shawnee Made: Migration and Violence in Early America* (Chapel Hill: University of North Carolina Press, 2014).

22. Wallace, *Death and Rebirth of the Seneca*, chap. 9.

23. Audra Simpson has addressed such issues for the Mohawk. See, for example, "Paths towards a Mohawk Nation: Narratives of Citizenship and Nationhood in Kahnawake," in *Political Theory and the Rights of Indigenous Peoples*, ed. Duncan Ivison, Paul Patton, and Will Sanders (London: Cambridge University Press, 2000), chap. 6.

24. See Konkle, *Writing Indian Nations*, chap. 4 passim; and Laurence M. Hauptman, *The Tonawanda Senecas: Conservative Indian Activists* (Albany: State University of New York Press, 2011).

25. See Whitney Cross, *The Burned-Over District: The Social and Intellectual History of Enthusiastic Religion in Western New York, 1800–1850* (Ithaca, N.Y.: Cornell University Press, 1950); and Michel Barkun, *Crucible of the Millennium: The Burned-Over District of New York in the 1840s* (Syracuse, N.Y.: Syracuse University Press, 1986).

26. Konkle, *Writing Indian Nations*, 263–64, 257.

27. See, for example, "Mission to the Senecas," *Christian Monitor* 2, no. 13 (1817): 198, where, in extracts from an account of a missionary tour among the Seneca made by the Reverend Timothy Alden, the name is spelled "Gos-kuk-ke-wa-na Kon-ne-di-yo" and translated as "Large Beautiful Lake." On Apess's use of the cognomen, see chap. 7.

28. See Dennis, *Seneca Possessed*; and Laurence M. Hauptman, *Conspiracy of Interests: Iroquois Dispossession and the Rise of New York State* (Syracuse, N.Y.: Syracuse University Press, 1999), especially part 2.

29. See B. W. Gorham, *Camp Meeting Manual* (Boston: H. V. Degen, 1854).

30. Catherine Williams, *Fall River: An Authentic Narrative* (1833; New York: Oxford University Press, 1993), 143–67. See also David Richard Kasserman, *Fall River Outrage: Life, Murder, and Justice in Early Industrial New England* (Philadelphia: University of Pennsylvania Press, 1986).

31. William Apess, *Experiences of Five Christian Indians* (1833), in *On Our Own Ground: The Complete Writings of William Apess, a Pequot*, ed. Barry O'Connell (Amherst: University of Massachusetts Press, 1992), 148.

32. Ibid., 149.

33. Ibid., 150.

34. [George A. Spywood], *The Experience of George A. Spywood* (Middletown, Conn.: Charles H. Pelton, 1843).

35. Ibid., 26–27. Spywood "got up" his book because he needed money, "having m[e]t with several los[s]es by bad notes" since he entered the ministry. The sum was "small," he told his readers, only $80, but if not "immediately met," he would lose his "house and lot" (title page). In this, too, Spywood's experience closely parallels that of Apess.

36. See Thomas Robbins, *A View of All Religions, and the Religious Ceremonies of All Nations at the Present Day* (Hartford, Conn.: Oliver Cooke, 1824), 167.

37. Drawn from her autobiography, in Apess, *Experiences*, in O'Connell, *On Our Own Ground*, 133–44.

38. See Chauncy Edwin Peck, *History of Wilbraham, Massachusetts* (Wilbraham: The Town, 1913), passim, for discussions of its Methodist history.

39. William J. Brown, *Life of William J. Brown* (1883); reprinted with an introduction by Joan Pope Melish (Hanover, N.H.: University Press of New England, 2006), 50.

40. See John Wood Sweet, *Bodies Politic: Negotiating Race in the American North, 1730–1830* (Baltimore: Johns Hopkins University Press, 2003), 371–74.

41. In 1827, for example, the Narragansett Joseph Nocake was "warned out" as a person of "bad fame and reputation" but ran off before the municipal constable could apprehend him. Ibid., 372.

42. Ibid., chap. 9 passim, and 373–74, 403, 461–62, n. 37.

43. Brown, *Life*, 50–51.

44. Cited in Sweet, *Bodies Politic*, 376.

45. See Robert J, Cottrol, *The Afro-Yankees: Providence's Black Community in the Antebellum Era* (Westport, Conn.: Greenwood Press, 1982), 58. In turn, one of Thomas Paul's parishioners was black abolitionist David Walker, whose incendiary 1828 pamphlet, *An Appeal to the Coloured People of the World*, may well have contributed to Apess's own radicalization.

46. See George R. Price and James Brewer Stewart, eds., *To Heal the Scourge of Prejudice: The Life and Writings of Hosea Easton* (Amherst: University of Massachusetts Press, 1999), for biographical information. The editors reprint this "Thanksgiving Sermon."

47. See Maureen Konkle, *Writing Indian Nations: Native Intellectuals and the Politics of Historiography, 1827–1863* (Chapel Hill: University of North Carolina Press, 2004), 104.

48. Hosea Easton, in Price and Stewart, *To Heal the Scourge of Prejudice*, 54–56, 60.

49. On Methodism in the city at this time, see William McDonald, *History of Methodism in Providence, Rhode Island, from Its Introduction in 1787 to 1867* (Boston, 1868), especially 60–64.

50. See Mark J. Miller, "'Mouth for God': Temperate Labor, Race, and Methodist Reform in William Apess's *A Son of the Forest*," *Journal of the Early Republic* 30 (Summer 2010): 225–51, which offers an important summary of what the reformist Methodists meant to Apess.

51. Nathan O. Hatch, *The Democratization of American Christianity* (New Haven, Conn.: Yale University Press, 1989), 85.

52. See, for example, Leigh Eric Schmidt, *Hearing Things: Religion, Illusion, and the American Enlightenment* (Cambridge, Mass.: Harvard University Press, 2000).

53. Russell Richey, *Early American Methodism* (Bloomington: Indiana University Press, 1991), 82–83.

54. David Hempton, *Methodism: Empire of the Spirit* (New Haven, Conn.: Yale University Press, 2005), 22.

55. See John Lauritz Larson, *The Market Revolution in America: Liberty, Ambition, and the Eclipse of the Common Good* (New York: Cambridge University Press, 2012), 42–45.

56. See ibid., chaps. 1 and 4, especially 30–31.

57. See Hatch, *Democratization of American Christianity*, 201–3.

58. Eventually, dissident groups organized as Associated Reformers and then, in the 1830s, as Methodist Protestants. See ibid., 102–4; and William R. Sutton, *Journeyman for Jesus: Evangelical Artisans Confront Capitalism in Jacksonian Baltimore* (University Park: Pennsylvania State University Press, 1998), 76–77.

59. At this point, Apess's spiritual autobiography, published in 1829 as *A Son of the Forest*, ends; a lengthy appendix completes the book. In this appendix, borrowing liberally from Elias Boudinot's *A Star in the West* (Trenton, N.J.: Fenton, Hutchinson, and Dunham, 1816), he offered "general observations" on his Native brethren's recent experiences.

60. Indeed, he may even have recorded it for them in "The Indian's Prayer," a hymn which was first published in 1829 in Methodist Reuben Peaslee's *Choice Selection of Hymns and Spiritual Songs, Designed to Aid in the Devotions of Prayer, Conference, and Camp Meeting* and which Apess put at the end of the Appendix to the 1831 edition of *A Son of the Forest*. It was much reprinted, both in subsequent hymnals and (in the 1830s) as a broadsheet. Hezekiah Butterworth, in *The Story of the Hymns; or, Hymns That Have a History* (New York: American Tract Society, 1875), 181–82, attributes it to Apess. In the late nineteenth century, in the *Congregationalist*, there were mentions of the hymn by the editor and readership, some people again attributing it to Apess, although the editor thought "some white friend of the Indians" more likely wrote it. See *Congregationalist* 78, no. 25 (June 22, 1893): 984; and 85, no. 28 (July 12, 1900): 51. It also appeared in the *Red Man* (June 1889), a newspaper published at the Carlisle Indian School in Pennsylvania. Barry O'Connell, in *On Our Own Ground*,

p. 97, says that the hymn is "from Boudinot." If so, it is not in *A Star in the West*. And if it were in some work of Boudinot's, why would Apess have not included it in the first edition of his autobiography? He may have written it in that same year, 1829, after the publication of his book but in time for it to appear in the Methodist hymnal. In 1845, in his pioneering collection of Native American hymns, *Indian Melodies* (New York: Thomas Hastings, 1845), Brotherton Indian Thomas Cummock included another, different selection, which he named "Apes" (p. 28). See Epilogue.

61. 1830 U.S. Manuscript Census. I thank Professor Nancy Shoemaker for this reference.

62. In the 1830 census all in the Apess family were denominated "white."

CHAPTER 3

1. See Barry O'Connell, "Introduction," *On Our Own Ground: The Complete Writings of William Apess, a Pequot*, ed. Barry O'Connell (Amherst: University of Massachusetts Press, 1992), 3, for the preface to the second edition, in which Apess apologizes for how hastily the book was produced and offers thanks to those who helped him publish it.

2. On religious publishing in this period, see Candy Gunther Brown, *The Word in the World: Evangelical Writing, Publishing, and Reading in America, 1789–1880* (Chapel Hill: University of North Carolina Press, 2004), 46–78; David Paul Nord, "Benevolent Capital: Financing Evangelical Book Publishing in Early Nineteenth-Century America," in *God and Mammon*, ed. Mark A. Noll (New York: Oxford University Press, 2001), 147–70; and David Paul Nord, *Faith in Reading: Religious Publishing and the Birth of Mass Media in America* (New York: Oxford University Press, 2004).

3. After a lecture in Hartford, for example, in the early autumn of 1830, he sold copies for fifty cents and for the same price a year later in Salem, Massachusetts. "Notice," *Christian Secretary* (Hartford), September 25, 1830, p. 143; "A Son of the Forest," *Salem Gazette*, October 11, 1831, p. 3.

4. On Paradise, see Dee Andrews, *The Methodists and Revolutionary America, 1760–1800: The Shaping of an Evangelical Culture* (Princeton: Princeton University Press, 2000), 336, n. 48. Among his paintings is one of the great Methodist leader Francis Asbury, in the Methodist Collection at Drew University. *Methodist Magazine* 2 (1819) carried an engraving of William McKendree, a bishop of the Methodist Episcopal Church, from Paradise's painting of him.

5. [Samuel Gardner Drake], "A Son of the Forest," *American Monthly Review* 2 (August 1832): 149–50.

6. Frank Lambert, *Inventing the "Great Awakening"* (Princeton: Princeton University Press, 1999), offers the best discussion of the Great Awakening's textuality.

7. See below.

8. See Daniel Williams, *Pillars of Salt, Monuments of Grace: New England Crime Literature and the Origins of American Popular Culture, 1674–1860* (New York: Oxford University Press, 1993).

9. David Hempton, *Methodism: Empire of the Spirit* (New Haven, Conn.: Yale University Press, 2005), 60, 61–68 passim.

10. These omissions are described in O'Connell, *On Our Own Ground*, 314–24.

11. Peter Jones (Kahkewaquonaby), *Life and Journals of Kah-ke-wa-quo-na-by (Rev. Peter Jones), Wesleyan Missionary* (Toronto: Anson Green, 1860); and Donald B. Smith, *Sacred Feathers: The Reverend Peter Jones (Kahkewaquonaby) and the Mississauga Indians* (Lincoln: University of Nebraska Press, 1987).

12. On this topic, see the essays in *Native Americans, Christianity, and the Reshaping of the American Religious Landscape*, ed. Joel Martin and Mark A. Nicholas (Chapel Hill: University of North Carolina Press, 2010); and Michael D. McNally, *Ojibwe Singers: Hymns, Grief, and Native Culture in Motion* (New York: Oxford University Press, 2000).

13. This view had currency from the seventeenth century onward, in the works of Roger Williams, John Eliot, and Samuel Sewall and then in the eighteenth century in the works of James Adair and Jonathan Edwards Jr., on the Mohegan language. See Richard Lyman Bushman, *Joseph Smith: Rough Stone Rolling* (New York: Knopf, 2005), 96.

14. See George Boyd, *Elias Boudinot: Patriot and Statesman, 1740–1821* (Westport, Conn.: Greenwood Press, 1969). On the mission school, see John Demos, *The Heathen School: A Story of Hope and Betrayal in the Age of the Early Republic* (New York: Knopf, 2014).

15. Elias Boudinot, *A Star in the West* (Trenton, N.J.: Fenton, Hutchinson, and Dunham, 1816), i–ii, xxi.

CHAPTER 4

1. *New York Evangelist*, June 26, 1830, p. 51; John Petty, *The History of the Primitive Methodist Connexion* (London: Richard Davies, 1860), 249–52. See also Julia Stewart Werner, *The Primitive Methodist Connexion: Its Background and Early History* (Madison: University of Wisconsin Press, 1984), passim.

2. On Lorenzo Dow, see Nathan O. Hatch, *The Democratization of American Christianity* (New Haven, Conn.: Yale University Press, 1989), 130–33.

3. *Connecticut Gazette*, October 12, 1831, p. 3; *Portland (Maine) Eastern Argus*, July 16, 1834, p. 3.

4. *Mutual Rights and Methodist Protestant*, October 14, 1831, p. 45.

5. *Baltimore Gazette and Daily Advertiser*, March 9, 1831, p. 3; *Baltimore Patriot*, March 23, 1831, p. 4.

6. See Jean M. O'Brien, *Firsting and Lasting: Writing Indians Out of Existence in New England* (Minneapolis: University of Minnesota Press, 2010), 178–80, for a discussion of who Apess may have been influenced by in Boston.

7. James Oliver Horton and Lois E. Horton, *Black Bostonians: Family Life and Community Struggle in the Antebellum North* (1979; New York: Holmes and Meier, 1999), chap. 3.

8. See William S. Parson and Margaret A. Drew, *The African Meeting House in Boston: A Sourcebook* (Boston: Museum of Afro American History, 1990).

9. Roy E. Finkenbine, "Boston's Black Churches: Institutional Centers of the Anti-slavery Movement," in *Courage and Conscience: Black and White Abolitionists in Boston*, ed. Donald M. Jacobs (Bloomington: Indiana University Press, 1993), 169–90.

10. The best biography and assessment of Walker's importance is Peter P. Hinks, *To Awaken My Afflicted Brethren: David Walker and the Problem of Antebellum Slave Resistance* (University Park: Pennsylvania State University Press, 1997).

11. Henry Highland Garnet, *Walker's Appeal, with a Brief Sketch of His Life* (New York, J. H. Tobitt, 1848), v.

12. On Nat Turner, see James Thomas Baker, *Nat Turner: Cry Freedom in America* (New York: Harcourt, Brace, 1998); and Kenneth S. Greenberg, ed., *Nat Turner: A Slave Rebellion in History and Memory* (New York: Oxford University Press, 2003).

13. David Walker, *David Walker's Appeal to the Coloured Citizens of the World*, ed. Peter P. Hinks (University Park: Pennsylvania State University Press, 2000), 30.

14. Ibid., 44–45.

15. Marilyn Richardson, ed., *Maria W. Stewart, America's First Black Political Writer—Essays and Speeches* (Bloomington: Indiana University Press, 1987), 60. Richardson's introduction provides biographical information.

16. Maria Stewart, "Lecture Delivered at Franklin Hall," in ibid., 46.

17. Maria Stewart, *Productions of Mrs. Maria W. Stewart* (New York, 1835), 61, in *Spiritual Narratives*, ed. Susan Hutchins (New York: Oxford University Press, 1988).

18. Hosea Easton, *A Treatise on the Intellectual Character, and Civil and Political Condition of the Colored People of the U. States; And the Prejudice Exercised Towards Them* (1837), 40, in *Negro Protest Pamphlets: A Compendium*, ed. Dorothy Porter (New York: Arno Press, 1969). See also George R. Price and James Brewer Stewart, eds., *To Heal the Scourge of Prejudice: The Life and Writings of Hosea Easton* (Amherst: University of Massachusetts Press, 1999).

19. Easton, *Treatise on the Intellectual Character*, 5. See also John Ernest, *Liberation Historiography: African American Writers and the Challenge of History, 1794–1861* (Chapel Hill: University of North Carolina Press, 2004), passim.

20. Donald M. Jacobs, "David Walker and William Lloyd Garrison: Racial Coopera-

tion and the Shaping of Boston Abolitionism," in Jacobs, *Courage and Conscience*, 1–21.

21. See *Liberator*, January 1, 8, 22, 29, February 5, 19, April 30, and May 14, 28, 1831. Stewart's first publication was *Religion and the Pure Principles of Morality: The Sure Foundation in Which We Must Build* (Boston, 1831).

22. Horton and Horton, *Black Bostonians*, 88–96.

23. On these controversies, see Francis Paul Prucha, *American Indian Treaties: The History of a Political Anomaly* (Berkeley: University of California Press, 1994), 165–68 and 156–82 passim.

24. *Boston Advertiser*, April 24, 25, 1832.

25. Samuel Gardner Drake, *Indian Biography, Containing the Lives of More Than Two Hundred Chiefs* (Boston: Josiah Drake, 1832), 268.

26. *Liberator*, May 19, 1832, p. 3; May 26, 1832, p. 3.

27. See Dorothy Porter Wesley and Constance Porter Uzelac, eds., *William Cooper Nell: Selected Writings* (Boston: Black Classics Press, 2002), 444.

28. *Liberator*, June 9, 1832, p. 3; July 17, 1832, p. 3; July 14, 1832, p. 3.

29. *Boston Evening Transcript*, April 15, 1832.

30. Louisa Jane Park to Agnes Major Park, April 29, 1832, Park Family Papers (1800–1890), American Antiquarian Society, Worcester, Mass.

31. *Newburyport Herald*, October 9, 1832.

32. *Norwich (Conn.) Courier*, January 9, 1833.

33. He dropped the "Looking-Glass" from the second edition he issued in 1837, substituting a briefer "Indian's Thought."

34. This suggests that he may have composed the "Looking-Glass" before 1831.

35. Daniel R. Mandell, *Tribe, Race, History: Native Americans in Southern New England, 1780–1880* (Baltimore: Johns Hopkins University Press, 2008), 42–69.

36. "Savage," *Boston Investigator*, April 27, 1832.

37. Jack Campisi, *The Mashpee Indians: Tribe on Trial* (Syracuse, N.Y.: Syracuse University Press, 1991), 73. See also Donald M. Nielsen, "The Mashpee Indian Revolt of 1833," *New England Quarterly* 58, no. 3 (September 1985): 400–420.

38. See Jean M. O'Brien, *Dispossession by Degrees: Indian Land and Identity in Natick, Massachusetts, 1650–1790* (New York: Cambridge University Press, 1997), in which the author offers another example of how such coherence was maintained, in this case, in another "praying town," that is, a community of Native Americans who had been converted to Christianity.

39. The estimate of worth comes from Benjamin F. Hallett, *Rights of the Marshpee Indians* (Boston: Jonathan Howe, 1834), 25.

40. *Records of the Colony of New Plymouth in New England*, 6 vols. (Boston: William White, 1855–61), 6:159–60.

41. Massachusetts Historical Society, *Collections*, 1 ser., 10 (1809): 133.

42. See O'Brien, *Dispossession by Degrees*, passim.

43. *Acts and Resolves of the Massachusetts Bay Company* (Boston, 1746–47), chap. 12, pp. 306–7.

44. Ibid. (Boston, 1763), chap. 3, p. 640.

45. See Mark A. Nicholas, "Mashpee Wampanoags of Cape Cod, the Whalefishery, and Seafaring's Impact on Community Development," *American Indian Quarterly* 26 (2002); and Nancy Shoemaker, ed., *Living with Whales: Documents and Oral Histories of Native New England Whaling History* (Amherst: University of Massachusetts Press, 2014).

46. Jedediah Morse, *A Report to the Secretary of War of the United States . . . for the Purpose of Ascertaining for the Use of the Government, the Actual State of the Indian Tribes of Our Country* (New Haven, Conn.: S. Converse, 1822), 69.

47. See Conrad Wright, *Beginnings of Unitarianism in America* (Boston: Starr King Press, 1955). Fish's overall career was undistinguished; his only publications were three sermons, two for ordinations and one for a funeral, all local to Cape Cod.

48. Morse, *Report to the Secretary of War*, 70.

49. Massachusetts Senate, 1834, Document no. 14, p. 5.

CHAPTER 5

1. Francis G. Hutchins, *Mashpee: The Story of Cape Cod's Indian Town* (West Franklin, N.H.: Amarta Press, 1979), 115–16. One of the best readings of this episode is Lisa Brooks, *The Common Pot: The Recovery of Native Space in the Northeast* (Minneapolis: University of Minnesota Press, 2008), 163–97.

2. See William Apess, *Indian Nullification of the Unconstitutional Laws of Massachusetts Relative to the Mashpee Tribe* (Boston: Jonathan Howe, 1835), in *On Our Own Ground: The Complete Writings of William Apess, a Pequot*, ed. Barry O'Connell (Amherst: University of Massachusetts Press, 1992), 233, for this description of Amos, provided by Hallett. Further page references to this text in this chapter are keyed to O'Connell's edition and are in parentheses.

3. On Enoch Pratt, see his *Comprehensive History, Ecclesiastical and Civil, of Eastham, Wellfleet, and Orleans, County of Barnstable, Massachusetts* (Yarmouth: W. S. Fisher, 1844).

4. See *Biographical Sketch, Personal and Descriptive, of Sylvanus B. Phinney* (Boston: Rand Avery, 1888).

5. Patrick Jung, *The Black Hawk War of 1832* (Norman: University of Oklahoma Press, 2007); Kerry A. Trask, *Black Hawk: The Battle for the Heart of America* (New York: Henry Holt, 2006).

6. "Black Hawk," *Barnstable Patriot*, June 26, 1833.

7. "Documents Relative to the Marshpee Indians," Senate Document, no. 14, p. 5, in *Documents Printed by Order of the Senate of the Commonwealth of Massachusetts* (Boston: Dutton and Wentworth, 1834).

8. Information about Apess's children is scanty and inconclusive, but in the early twentieth century Mrs. Rhoda Attaquin Sturgis of Mashpee recalled that "two daughters of William Apes, the well-known Indian minister," had married into the Chummuck family of Herring Pond Indians, who lived on a reservation twelve miles from Plymouth, Massachusetts. See Frank G. Speck, "Territorial Subdivisions and Boundaries of the Wampanoag, Massachusetts, and Nauset Indians," *Indian Notes and Monographs* no. 44 (New York: Museum of the American Indian, 1928), 90. Also, Providence town records indicate that when Apess lived there in 1825 he had "a wife and two children and is to follow trucking for a living." See Providence Town Papers, Rhode Island Historical Society, vol. 127, p. 26, item 004197, March 25, 1825. Reference courtesy of John Wood Sweet.

9. The Mashpees to Fish, June 26, 1833, Massachusetts Indian Guardian Accounts and Correspondence, Massachusetts Archives, box 1, file 1, cited in Daniel R. Mandell, *Tribe, Race, History: Native Americans in Southern New England, 1780–1880* (Baltimore: Johns Hopkins University Press, 2008), 100.

10. See, for example, Robert M. Owens, *Mr. Jefferson's Hammer: William Henry Harrison and the Origins of American Indian Policy* (Norman: University of Oklahoma Press, 2007).

11. *Washington Globe*, July 19, 1833, from the *New York Evening Post*.

12. *Documents Printed by Order of the Senate of the Commonwealth of Massachusetts*, 11–12; Levi Lincoln to Josiah Fiske, June 20, 1833, Folder 1–1, Marshpee Disturbance, 1833–34, Guardians of Indian Plantations, Massachusetts Archives, Boston; cited in Maureen Konkle, *Writing Indian Nations: Native Intellectuals and the Politics of Historiography, 1827–1863* (Chapel Hill: University of North Carolina Press, 2004), 121.

13. Josiah Fiske to Levi Lincoln, July 3–4, 1833, Folder 1–2, Marshpee Disturbance, 1833–34, Massachusetts Indian Guardian Accounts and Correspondence Indian Plantations, Massachusetts Archives, Boston; cited in Konkle, *Writing Indian Nations*, 121.

14. The accused were Apess; Joseph, Jacob, and Nicholas Pocknett; Aaron Keater; Charles De Grasse; and Abraham Jackson. The last six were all described as "Labourers." Barnstable Court of Common Pleas, September Term, 1833, p. 489.

15. See Richard E. Ellis, *The Union at Risk: Jacksonian Democracy, States Rights, and the Nullification Crisis* (New York: Oxford University Press, 1987), passim.

16. *Liberator*, July 20, 1833.

17. Donald B. Trayser, *Barnstable: Three Centuries of a Cape Cod Town* (Hyannis, Mass., 1939), 69–70.

18. Ronald P. Formisano, *The Transformation of Political Culture: Massachusetts Politics, 1790–1840* (New York: Oxford University Press, 1983), 436, n. 48.

19. *Barnstable Patriot*, July 10, 1833.

20. *Washington Globe*, July 18, 1833.

21. See *United States Telegraph*, August 19, 1833.

22. Phineas Fish to Josiah Quincy, December 6, 1833, Marshpee Indians, 1811–41, UAI.20.811, Harvard University Archives; cited in Konkle, *Writing Indian Nations*, 127.

23. Benjamin F. Hallett, *Rights of the Marshpee Indians* (Boston: Jonathan Howe, 1834), 16; see also Konkle, *Writing Indian Nations*, 126.

24. Hallett, *Rights of the Marshpee Indians*, 35.

25. In the beginning of his presentation to the legislature, Hallett used the same word, "vassalage," to describe the relation of the Mashpees to the overseers; see ibid., 3; and Jeremiah Evarts, *Cherokee Removal: The "William Penn" Essays and Other Writings*, ed. Francis Paul Prucha (Knoxville: University of Tennessee Press, 1981).

26. *Boston Advocate*, December 27, 1833.

27. *Liberator*, January 25, 1834.

28. Ibid.

29. Ibid.

30. Ibid.

31. *Boston Courier*, January 28, 1834.

32. Benjamin Hallett, in *Boston Advocate*, in O'Connell, *On Our Own Ground*, 225.

33. *Barnstable Patriot*, February 5, 1834.

34. Hallett, *Rights of the Marshpee Indians*, 32.

35. On Shays' Rebellion, see David P. Szatmary, *Shays's Rebellion: The Making of an Agrarian Insurrection* (Amherst: University of Massachusetts Press, 1980).

36. See Mandell, *Tribe, Race, History*, 262, nn. 89, 90.

37. "Trouble in the Wigwarm [*sic*]," *Barnstable Patriot*, July 10, 1833.

38. Konkle, *Writing Indian Nations*, 126.

39. *Liberator*, January 25, 1834.

40. *Lowell Evangelist and Journal of Religion and Literature* 4, no. 3 (1834): 24.

CHAPTER 6

1. *The Family Magazine; or, Monthly Abstract of General Knowledge*, April 1835, p. 2.

2. *New-York Weekly Mirror: A Weekly Gazette of Literature and the Fine Arts* 15, no. 18 (1837): 143.

3. Fish to Quincy, December 7, 1833, Marshpee Indians 1811 to 1841, Harvard University Archives; cited in Donald M. Nielsen, "The Mashpee Indian Revolt of 1833," *New England Quarterly* 58, no. 3 (September 1985): 418.

4. *Boston Daily Advocate*, December 27, 1833.

5. James Walker, "Facts in Regard to the Difficulties in Mashpee," October 17, 1835, Marshpee Indians 1811 to 1841, Harvard University Archives; cited in Nielsen,

"Mashpee Indian Revolt," 418. Jean M. O'Brien has much to say about this kind of rhetoric as emblematic of the erasure of Native American authority and sovereignty—indeed, even of presence—in New England; see *Firsting and Lasting: Writing Indians Out of Existence in New England* (Minneapolis: University of Minnesota Press, 2010), passim.

6. Benjamin Hallett to James Walker, September 11, 1835, Marshpee Indians 1811 to 1841, Harvard University Archives; cited in Nielsen, "Mashpee Indian Revolt," 418.

7. *Boston Recorder*, February 16, 1838, p. 26.

8. *Family Magazine*, April 1835, p. 2.

9. Phineas Fish to James Walker, October 3, 1835, UAI 20.811, Marshpee Indians, 1811–41, Harvard University Archives; cited in Maureen Konkle, *Writing Indian Nations: Native Intellectuals and the Politics of Historiography, 1827–1863* (Chapel Hill: University of North Carolina Press, 2004), 131.

10. *Boston Morning Post*, June 19, 1835.

11. *New England Magazine* 9, no. 1 (July 1835): 79.

12. *Boston Pearl and Literary Gazette* 4, no. 40 (June 1835).

13. John H. Sheppard, *A Memoir of Samuel G. Drake, A.M.* (Albany: Munsell, 1863), 33–34.

14. Samuel Gardner Drake, *Indian Biography, Containing the Lives of More Than Two Hundred Chiefs* (Boston: Josiah Drake, 1832), 268.

15. *American Monthly Review* 2 (August 1832): 149–50.

16. See Konkle, *Writing Indian Nations*, 232–33.

17. William J. Snelling, "Life of Black Hawk," *North American Review* 40, no. 86 (1835): 70. The book was *Life of Ma-ka-tai-me-she-kia-kiak, or Black Hawk* (1833), as told through an interpreter, Antoine LeClaire.

18. This misattribution of *Indian Nullification* to Snelling took on extended life after the sale of Drake's considerable library in 1846. The auction catalog noted that in his own copy of Apess's book Drake had observed, "This work was written by William J. Snelling, who often consulted me during the progress of it. It was done at the request of Wm. Apes, whose name appears in the Title." See Barry O'Connell, "Introduction," in *On Our Own Ground: The Complete Writings of William Apess, a Pequot*, ed. Barry O'Connell (Amherst: University of Massachusetts Press, 1992), xliii, n. 38. See *Catalogue of the Private Library of Samuel G. Drake* (Boston, 1845), 33 (no. 544).

19. The attribution is repeated in "Snelling," entry no. 18425, *Bibliography of American Literature*, comp. Jacob Blanck, vol. 7, edited and completed by Virginia L. Smyers and Michael Winship (New Haven, Conn.: Yale University Press, 1983). The editors also note, however, that the copyright is in Apess's name.

20. Cited in Konkle, *Writing Indian Nations*, 149.

21. Ibid., 135–38.

22. See Jill Lepore, *The Name of War: King Philip's War and the Origins of American Identity* (New York: Knopf, 1998).

23. See John Augustus Stone, *Metamora and Other Plays*, ed. Eugene R. Page (Princeton: Princeton University Press, 1941).

24. Gabriel Harrison, *Edwin Forrest: The Actor and the Man* (Brooklyn, N.Y., 1889), 39.

25. William Alger, *Life of Edwin Forrest, the American Tragedian* (Philadelphia: Lippincott, 1877), 240.

26. See advertisement in the *Critic*, November 28, 1828, cited in Lepore, *Name of War*, 194.

27. James Wallis Eastburn and Robert Charles Sands, *Yamoyden, a Tale of the Wars of King Philip: In Six Cantos* (New York: Eastburn, 1820).

28. George Bancroft, *History of the United States, from the Discovery of the American Continent*, vol. 2 (1837; Boston: Little, Brown, 1841), 101.

29. Benjamin Church, *Entertaining History of King Philip's War* (1716), in *The History of Philip's War, Commonly Called the Great Indian War of 1675 and 1676* (Exeter, N.H.: J. and B. Williams, 1829), 125–26.

30. "Indian Biography," *North American Review* 33 (October 1831): 407–49.

31. Later in the nineteenth century, another Native, Zerviah Gould Mitchell, stepped forward and claimed to be a direct descendant of Philip. In 1878, Ebenezer Weaver Pierce, with her assistance, published *Indian History, Biography, and Genealogy Pertaining to the Good Sachem Massasoit* (North Abington, Mass.: Zerviah Gould Mitchell, 1878), a detailed examination of Native history from European settlement of New England through King Philip's War. In the preface, Mitchell explained that she was a "literal descendant, in the seventh generation," from the great and good Massasoit, Philip's father. In addition to spelling out that connection, though, she wished "to make record of the wrongs which during all the generations have been endured by [her] race." Further, her personal complaint was eerily similar to that of the Mashpees. For the past twenty-five years, she explained, she had been "seeking redress for the wrongs done to [her] and [hers], by petitioning the Massachusetts Legislature to remove the State's guardians from [her] lands; and to pay [her] for wood cut therefrom by their agent." The excuse of the man who cut the wood was that he did not think any heirs to the land were still alive, but "it seemed as though, when it was thought by him that all the Indians were dead, one was dug right up out of the grave," in her person. "There seems," she concluded, "to be no law for the Indian" (iii–v).

32. *Christian Register and Boston Observer*, January 2, 1836.

33. Notices appeared in the January 2 issue of the *Liberator* and in the *Daily Advocate*, *Morning Post*, and *Evening Transcript* on January 6 and 7. The other two stores were those of Benjamin Mussey and Charles Stimpson.

34. "The Boston Academy of Music," *Family Minstrel* 1, no. 15 (September 1, 1835). "Moreen" is a sturdy, ribbed fabric, often embossed, suitable for upholstery. Abel Bowen, *Bowen's Picture of Boston*, 3rd ed. (1837; Boston: Otis, Broaders, 1838), 71–73.

35. Bowen, *Bowen's Picture of Boston*, 71.

36. *Boston Morning Post*, January 25, 1836; *Daily Advocate*, January 25, 1836.

37. *Hartford (Conn.) Courant*, March 7, 1836.

38. On the whole matter of the Indians' disappearance or nondisappearance, see O'Brien, *Firsting and Lasting*, especially chap. 2.

39. Edward Everett, "The Battle of Bloody Brook," *Orations and Speeches on Various Occasions*, 2 vols. (Boston: Little, Brown, 1850), 1:634–69. "The "Flower of Essex" refers to the young men from Essex County, Massachusetts, who had been sent to the Connecticut River Valley to defend the frontier settlements from King Philip's incursions.

40. Ibid., 1:637.

41. *Liberator*, June 6, 1837, p. 108.

42. William Apess, *A Eulogy on King Philip* (1836), in O'Connell, *On Our Own Ground*, 277; further page references in this chapter are to this edition.

43. *Ezra Toby v. Wm Apess*, Barnstable Court of Common Pleas, April 1837 Term, case no. 1069. I am indebted to Maureen Konkle for sharing copies of this and the following four documents.

44. *Phebe Ann Weden (by Pro Ami) v. William Apes*, Barnstable Court of Common Pleas, September 1836 Term, case no. 1168.

45. *William Pope v. Williams Apess*, Barnstable Court of Common Pleas, April 1836 Term, case no. 1035.

46. *Enos Ames v. William Apess and Trustee*, Barnstable Court of Common Pleas, September 1837 Term, case no. 1199.

47. Mortgage, William Apess to Richard Johnson, September 11, 1836, First Book of Personal Property Mortgaged, Marshpee Indian District, Mashpee Historical Commission, Mashpee, Mass.

48. Apess's library included a six-volume set of English Methodist Adam Clarke's *Commentary on the Bible*, valued at $24; Joseph Benson's five-volume *Holy Bible, Containing the Old and New Testaments . . . with Notes, Critical, Explanatory, and Practical* (1811–18), valued at $20; a concordance to scripture; William Whiston's two-volume *Works of Flavius Josephus* (1829); a three-volume set of Josephus's *History of the Jews*; George Horne's *Commentary on the Book of Psalms* (1825); and P. P. Sanford's *Help to Faith; or, A Summary of the Evidence of the Genuineness, Authenticity, Credibility, and Divine Authority of the Holy Scriptures* (1828). He also had acquired Richard Watson's *Life of the Rev. John Wesley* (1831) and an edition of Wesley's sermons; Congregationalist Nehemiah Adams's *Remarks on the Unitarian Belief* (1832); English

Nonconformist clergyman Simeon Ashe's *Primitive Divinity: A Treatise on Divine Contentment* (1670; probably in the 1823 edition); Jonathan Crowder's *A True and Complete Portraiture of Methodism* (1813); *A Treatise of the Faith of the Freewill Baptists*, issued by prominent Free Will Baptist John Colby (1834); English Baptist J. G. Pike's *Persuasives to Early Piety, Interspersed with Suitable Prayers* (1830s); English religious writer Hannah More's *Practical Piety; Constitution and Discipline of the Methodist Protestant Church* (1830); Congregationalist Orin Fowler's *Lectures on the Mode and Subjects of Baptism* (1835); Nonconformist Philip Doddridge's *Rise and Progress of Religion in the Soul* (1830s); Universalist Elhanan Winchester's *Universal Restoration* (1804); Spanish poet and Unitarian Joseph Blanco White's *Letter to Charles Butler: On His Notice of the Practical and Internal Evidences against Catholicism* (1826); a volume of "Episcopal sermons"; two volumes of Methodist hymns; Providence, Rhode Island, Congregationalist James Wilson's *Apostolic Government Displayed; and the Government and System of the Methodist Episcopal Church Investigated* (1798); *Confession of Faith by a Calvinist* (perhaps *The History, Constitution and Confession of Faith of the Calvinistic Methodists* [1823]); the Book of Common Prayer; and a volume on the "foundation of the church." Finally, the library also included an edition of Noah Webster's unabridged dictionary; a Latin grammar; a "map of the United States" and "Maps of the World" in an atlas; and "the book of monsters with pictures" (perhaps John Boynton's *The Great Sea-Serpent, Upon the Coast of New-England, in 1817* [1818]).

49. On Richard Johnson, see Kathryn Grover, *The Fugitive's Gibraltar: Escaping Slaves and Abolitionists in New Bedford, Massachusetts* (Amherst: University of Massachusetts Press, 2001), 88, 121; and William C. Nell, *Colored Patriots of the American Revolution, with Sketches of Distinguished Colored Persons* (Boston: Robert E. Walcutt, 1855), 90–91.

50. On Paul Cuffe, see Sheldon H. Harris, *Paul Cuffe: Black America and the African Return* (New York: Simon and Schuster, 1972); Lamont D. Thomas, *Paul Cuffe: Black Entrepreneur and Pan-Africanist* (Urbana: University of Illinois Press, 1986); Jace Weaver, "The Red Atlantic: Transoceanic Cultural Exchanges," *American Indian Quarterly* 35, no. 3 (Summer 2011): 437–39; and Nell, *Colored Patriots*, 73–89. In *Red Atlantic: American Indigenes and the Making of the Modern World, 1000–1927* (Chapel Hill: University of North Carolina Press, 2014), Jace Weaver extends his analysis of Cuffe's importance. He positions Cuffe as an indigenous figure first, rather than as an African American, and argues that the latter category was of less significance to Cuffe's identity. Thus, while some scholars may think half-blooded Indians are less Indian, Weaver argues powerfully that there was no diminishment of Cuffe's Wampanoag identity as he journeyed around the world. In this reading, as happens for

Apess, Cuffe becomes an example of an indigenous person connecting to the wellspring of abolitionism for political and other purposes.

51. On one occasion, for example, he provided his sister Ruth with British abolitionist Thomas Clarkson's *History of the Rise, Progress, and Accomplishment of the Abolition of the Slave-Trade by the British Parliament* (1808). See Grover, *Fugitive's Gibraltar*, 74.

52. Nell, *Colored Patriots*, 91.

53. *Liberator*, May 14, 1836.

54. See Grover, *Fugitive's Gibraltar*, especially pp. 106–13.

55. Record of Names and Ages of the People Who Are Not Proprietors in Mashpee District for the Year 1834, Mashpee Town Records.

CHAPTER 7

1. Gerda Lerner, *The Grimké Sisters from South Carolina: Pioneers for Women's Rights and Abolition* (1967; Chapel Hill: University of North Carolina Press, 2004); Robert H. Abzug, *Passionate Liberator: Theodore Dwight Weld and the Dilemma of Reform* (New York: Oxford University Press, 1980). On public lectures, see Carl Bode, *The American Lyceum: Town Meeting of the Mind* (Carbondale: Southern Illinois University Press, 1956); and Angela G. Ray, *The Lyceum and Public Culture in the Nineteenth-Century United States* (East Lansing: Michigan State University Press, 2005).

2. See *Liberator*, March 18, May 5, 16, 23, June 30, July 28, 1837, and March 16, May 18, June 22, October 12, 19, 1838, for news of or items about Native Americans.

3. *Liberator*, June 6, 1837, p. 108.

4. On Paul Cuffe, see Lamont D. Thomas, *Rise to Be a People: A Biography of Paul Cuffe* (Urbana: University of Illinois Press, 1986), and chap. 6, n. 50.

5. On Peter Williams Sr., see J. B. Wakeley, *Lost Chapters Recovered from the Early History of American Methodism* (New York: For the author, 1858), 438–73; and Craig D. Townsend, *Faith in Their Own Color: Black Episcopalians in Antebellum New York* (New York: Columbia University Press, 2005), 10–17.

6. On St. Philip's Church, the second black Episcopal Church in the United States (after one in Philadelphia overseen by Absalom Jones), and on Williams's career there, see Townsend, *Faith in Their Own Color*, 18–52.

7. Bertram Wyatt Brown, *Lewis Tappan and the Evangelical War against Slavery* (Cleveland: Case Western Reserve University, 1969), 115–21.

8. Townsend, *Faith in Their Own Color*, 44–45.

9. See Christopher Rush and George Collins, *A Short Account of the Rise and Progress of the African Methodist Episcopal Church in America* (New York: W. Marks, 1843), passim, for both Williamses' importance. On Williams's resignation, see Townsend, *Faith in Their Own Color*, 53–58; and, for an example, see *New York Journal of Commerce*, July 15, 1834, p. 1.

10. The varieties of positions within the black antislavery movement are nicely distinguished in Leslie M. Alexander, *African or American? Black Identity and Political Activism in New York City, 1784–1861* (Urbana: University of Illinois Press, 2008). In this period, some blacks began to prefer the term "colored" rather than "African." The nineteenth-century African American intellectual, James McCune Smith, for example, recalled that as more black Americans protested against the Colonization Society, "the term 'African' fell into disuse and finally discredit." See James McCune Smith, "Introduction," in Henry Highland Garnet, *A Memorial Discourse Delivered in the Hall of the House of Representatives, Washington City, D.C. . . . February 12, 1865* (Philadelphia: J. M. Wilson, 1865), 24; and Alexander, *African or American*, 76–96.

11. Peter S. Williams Jr., "Discourse Delivered in St. Philip's Church," cited in Alexander, *African or American*, 79. Toward this end, Williams catechized church youth before services and encouraged them to attend the city's African Free School. Among those he tutored were two future African American intellectuals. One was the Episcopal theologian and abolitionist Alexander Crummell, who, after being denied admission to the General Theological Seminary and the Andover Theological Seminary because of his race, attended the Oneida Institute in upstate New York, founded by Presbyterians in 1827 as a manual labor college that accepted blacks. See Wilson Jeremiah Moses, *Alexander Crummell: A Study of Civilization and Discontent* (New York: Oxford University Press, 1989). The other was the illustrious abolitionist and medical doctor Dr. James McCune Smith. He, too, had experienced educational discrimination firsthand. Rejected for admission at Columbia College, at Williams's encouragement he applied to and was admitted to the University of Glasgow, where he received a medical degree, the first African American to hold one. See Townsend, *Faith in Their Own Color*, chap. 8; and John Stauffer, *The Black Hearts of Men: Radical Abolitionists and the Transformation of Race* (Cambridge, Mass.: Harvard University Press, 2002).

12. The letter is docketed "Richard M. Johnson New Bedford / to / Rev. Peter Williams / Nov 18/37 / asking him to call on me / respecting a colored boy / who left him. / [I had a current acco / unt with Johnson and / [?]."

13. William H. Truettner, *The Natural Man Observed: A Study of Catlin's Indian Gallery* (Washington, D.C.: Smithsonian Institution Press, 1979), 36. Also see Benita Eisler, *The Red Man's Bones: George Catlin, Artist and Showman* (New York: W. W. Norton and Company, 2013), 214–59.

14. See Paul Reddin, *Wild West Shows* (Urbana: University of Illinois Press, 1999).

15. *New York Morning Herald*, November 28, 1837, pp. 1–2. See George Gurney and Therese Thau Heyman, eds., *George Catlin and His Indian Gallery* (Washington, D.C.: Smithsonian American Art Museum, 2002), which includes several interpretive essays on the exhibit.

16. *Diary of Philip Hone, 1828–1851*, December 6, 1837, 2 vols. (New York: Dodd, Mead, 1927), 1:290–91.

17. Patrick J. Jung, *The Black Hawk War of 1832* (Norman: University of Oklahoma Press, 2007), 192–97.

18. *Diary of Philip Hone*, 1:97–98.

19. *Baltimore Sun*, December 4, 1837.

20. Ajax, son of Telemon and cousin of Achilles, plays a role in the *Iliad*. He was of great stature and strongest of all the Achaeans.

21. *Diary of Philip Hone*, October 27, 1837, 1:280–81.

22. George Templeton Strong, *The Diary of George Templeton Strong*, July 26, 1837, ed. Alan Nevins and Milton Halsey Thomas, 4 vols. (New York: Macmillan, 1952), 1:72.

23. Patricia Cline Cohen, *The Murder of Helen Jewett: The Life and Death of a Prostitute in Nineteenth-Century America* (New York: Knopf, 1998).

24. James L. Crouthamel, *Bennett's New York Herald and the Rise of the Popular Press* (Syracuse, N.Y.: Syracuse University Press, 1989).

25. On Noah, see Jonathan D. Sama, *Jacksonian Jew: The Two Worlds of Mordecai Noah* (New York: Holmes and Meier, 1981).

26. See Michael Schuldiner and Daniel J. Kleinfeld, eds., *The Selected Writings of Mordecai Noah* (Westport, Conn.: Greenwood Press, 1999), 11–25.

27. "A Rabbi in the Rostrum," *New York Herald*, February 14, 1837.

28. Ibid.

29. *New-York Spectator*, February 21, 1837.

30. *New-York Evangelist*, February 25, 1837.

31. *New York Herald*, March 1, 1837.

32. *Pittsfield Sun*, March 2, 1837.

33. *New York Herald*, March 8, 1837.

34. *Boston Christian Watchman*, April 19, 1839.

35. Coroner's Inquest for William Apes, April 10, 1839, New York County Coroner Inquests, roll no. 16, July 1838–August 1840, Department of Records and Information, Municipal Archives of the City of New York, New York.

36. Indeed, in October 1833 they had scheduled a meeting of the friends of emancipation there but had to move it to the Chatham Street Chapel when antiabolitionists threatened violence and the proprietors of Clinton Hall canceled the lease. When the Tappans' detractors discovered where they had moved, they marched on the Chatham Street Chapel and incited the violence that led to the first of the "Tappan Riots." See [Lewis Tappan], *The Life of Arthur Tappan* (New York: Hurd and Houghton, 1870), 169–70.

37. See Brown, *Lewis Tappan*, passim.

38. Ibid., 131.

39. See Samuel Gardner Drake, *Book of the Indians of North America* (Boston: Josiah Drake, 1833), 98.

40. On the Panic of 1837 and its effects, see Alasdair Roberts, *America's First Great Depression: Economic Crisis and Political Disorder after the Panic of 1837* (Ithaca, N.Y.: Cornell University Press, 2012), 13–48; and John Lauritz Larson, *The Market Revolution in America: Liberty, Ambition, and the Eclipse of the Common Good* (New York: Cambridge University Press, 2012), 92–97.

41. [Lewis Tappan], *Arthur Tappan*, 279–82, 296–98.

42. See Larson, *Market Revolution*, 92–93, 98–140, passim.

CHAPTER 8

1. Cited from *New York Times*, 1858, in Thomas Bahde, "The Common Dust of Potter's Field: New York City and Its Bodies Politic, 1800–1860," *Common-Place* 6, no. 4 (July 2006), www.common-place.org, accessed July 8, 2013.

2. Here I am much indebted to Nancy Shoemaker's important article, "Race and Indigeneity in the Life of Elisha Apes," *Ethnohistory* 60, no. 1 (Winter 2013): 27–50.

3. Elisha's spouse was Mata Punahere, an Ngai Tahu woman from Arowhenua to the north, likely a refugee driven down the island because of the raids of Te Rauparaha, a belligerent tribal leader on the North Island. Beginning with a girl, Mary, born in 1842, the couple eventually had six children who survived to adulthood; the others were William, George, James, Thomas, and Kitty. Elisha lived in Waikouaiti for the next fifty years, continuing to engage in offshore whaling and in farming a small plot of land. His children remained nearby or, at the farthest, on the North Island; the men worked as sheep shearers on the increasingly large ranches; the women married and raised families.

4. Shoemaker, "Race and Indigeneity," 27–28.

5. Ibid., 34–35. His children and other descendants, however, were designated in a new category: "half-caste." Later, when indigenous people petitioned the government for lands supposedly due them, such offspring were eligible for the benefit; *pakeha*, no matter what their race, never were. They remained foreigners.

6. See T. B. Kennard, *The First White Boy Born in Otago: The Story of T. B. Kennard*, ed. J. Herries Beattie (1939; Christchurch, New Zealand, 1998), 24–25, 47–48, for reminiscences about the Apes family. From the 1790s through the 1830s, the Maori faced similar kinds of challenges to their culture—brought on by foreign "discovery"—as had the Pequots and other tribes in New England in the 1630s. First came seemingly unthreatening outsiders, whalers in this case— in New England, they had been adventurous fishermen—from Great Britain, France, Germany, Portugal, and the United States, who put into locations in Waikouaiti Bay for supplies. There and elsewhere in villages along the coasts

of both the North and the South Islands, the Maori had long practiced shore whaling, hunting from large dugout canoes the right whales, which cruised by on their migrations. The early visitors brought the Maori all sorts of novel and welcome skills, such as boat-building—the Maori used large dugout canoes—and goods—tobacco, different kinds of cloth, metal knives and axes, and, most insidiously, guns. In turn, the natives supplied the whalemen with bales of flax for the European market and, later, foodstuffs, primarily potatoes and pork. Before long, there also appeared new specimens of produce from the commerce: the offspring of whalemen and Maori women.

Next came a second wave of Europeans, seeking land. By 1830, Australian and British entrepreneurs began purchasing large tracts from the different Maori tribes and transporting workers to farm these new investments. Missionaries accompanied this wage of immigration. The first clergyman in Apes's region, a Wesleyan Methodist, came in 1840; and soon Church of England priests arrived. Thereafter, these two denominations divided God's work between them, ministering in the villages to the European settlers and to Maori who converted to Christianity. In 1848, for example, Apes's wife, Mata Punahere, taking the name Caroline, was baptized in the local Methodist Church.

The greatest threat to Maori culture came that same year when, with the consent of various Maori chiefs in the Treaty of Waitangi, Britain assumed sovereignty over all New Zealand. The Maori freely entered into this agreement, in which they promised to halt intertribal conflict and become subject to British law. In turn, Britain gained control of the distribution of the islands' rich lands to stop what threatened to become an indiscriminate stampede for them. What rights the Maori retained as a result of this negotiation were (and still are) vexed. While the British assumed primary legal authority, indigenous people expected to exercise certain of their traditional rights as well as assume those that came with citizenship in and the protection of the British Empire. This would be fought out by future generations.

After his wife's death in 1874, Elisha remarried, perhaps twice. He rests in a graveyard near where the old Methodist mission church stood in what is now Karitane. Mata Punahere/Caroline Apes (both names are on her stone), however, is buried in a cemetery at Puketeraki, near the site of a Maori *pa* (fortified building), high above the sea, with the remains of her children and grandchildren. The reason for this separation from her husband is unclear. It may have been because Elisha remarried or, more likely, because even in death he remained a *pakeha*. See the notes to Shoemaker's "Race and Indigeneity" for bibliographical guidance, especially Harry C. Evison, *Te Wai Pounamu, The Greenstone Island: A History of the Southern Maori during the European Colonization of New Zealand* (Christchurch: Aoraki Press, 1993); Peter Entwisle, *Behold the Moon: The European Occupation of the Dunedin District, 1770–1848*

(Dunedin: Fort Daniel Press, 1998); and Angela Wanhalla, *In/visible Sight: The Mixed-Descent Families of Southern New Zealand* (2009; Seattle: University of Washington Press, 2010).

7. John Missall and Mary Lou Missall, *The Seminole Wars: America's Longest Indian Conflict* (Gainesville: University Press of Florida, 2004); William S. Belko, ed., *America's Hundred Years' War: U.S. Expansion to the Gulf Coast and the Fate of the Seminole* (Gainesville: University Press of Florida, 2011).

8. Edward Dahlberg, *Can These Bones Live* (1941; Ann Arbor: University of Michigan Press, 1967), 13.

EPILOGUE

1. Maureen Konkle, *Writing Indian Nations: Native Intellectuals and the Politics of Historiography, 1827–1863* (Chapel Hill: University of North Carolina Press, 2004), 257, 263–64. There is one other odd survival. In the October 8, 1911, issue of the newspaper the *Oregonian*, Mary Marshall published a brief story about "William Apes" called "A Little Indian Outcast," copyrighted to the Associated Literary Press. Based on firsthand knowledge of Apess's *Son of the Forest*, the column relates the story of how Apes had been a happy child, helping his mother in her basket work, until she began selling her craft for whiskey. She and Apes's father then began to neglect their son and soon left him with his grandmother. Marshall then relates how this woman abused the boy, virtually starving and freezing him, and then one day asked him if he "hated" her. As Marshall interprets the moment, Apes, "never imagining that he was to speak anything but the truth," kept answering, "yes," because he *did* hate her. Marshall's version proceeds through his rescue by his uncle, and his discovery and eventual adoption by Mr. Furman, who took him into his family "and made him the happiest little Indian boy in the country." The effect is that of a children's morality tale, but Marshall does not appear to have continued the story in later issues.

2. David J. Silverman, *Red Brethren: The Brothertown and Stockbridge Indians and the Problem of Race in Early America* (Ithaca, N.Y.: Cornell University Press, 2010); Brad D. E. Jarvis, *The Brothertown Nation of Indians: Land Ownership and Nationalism in Early America, 1740–1840* (Lincoln: University of Nebraska Press, 2010).

3. Later, Commuck penned a brief history of the Brothertown band in which he expressed the same outrage at the whites' treatment of Natives that Apes had. See Thomas Commuck, "Sketch of the Brothertown Indians," *Wisconsin Historical Collections* 4 (1859): 291–98.

4. Thomas Commuck, *Indian Melodies by Thomas Commuck, a Narragansett Indian, Harmonized by Thomas Hastings, Esq.* (New York: G. Lane and C. B. Tippett, 1845), iii–iv.

SELECT BIBLIOGRAPHY

Apess, William. *Eulogy on King Philip, as Pronounced at the Odeon, in Federal Street, Boston*. Boston: Published by the author, 1836.

———. *Eulogy on King Philip, as Pronounced at the Odeon, in Federal Street, Boston*. 2nd ed. Boston: Published by the author, 1837.

———. *The Experiences of Five Christian Indians of the Pequod Tribe*. Boston: James B. Dow, 1833.

———. *The Experience of Five Christian Indians of the Pequod Tribe*. 2nd ed. Boston: Printed for the author, 1837.

———. *The Increase of the Kingdom of Christ*. New York: G. F. Bunce, 1831.

———. *Indian Nullification of the Unconstitutional Laws of Massachusetts Relative to the Mashpee Tribe; or, The Pretended Riot Explained*. Boston: Jonathan Howe, 1835.

———. *On Our Own Ground: The Complete Writings of William Apess, a Pequot*. Edited by Barry O'Connell. Amherst: University of Massachusetts Press, 1992.

———. *A Son of the Forest: The Experience of William Apes, A Native of the Forest, Comprising a Notice of the Pequod Tribe of Indians. Written by Himself*. New York: Published by the author, 1829.

———. *A Son of the Forest*. 2nd ed. New York: G. F. Bunce, 1831.

Bayers, Peter L. "William Apess' Manhood and Native Resistance in Jacksonian America," *MELUS* 31, no. 1 (2006): 123–46.

Benn, Carl. *Native Memoirs from the War of 1812: Black Hawk and William Apess*. Baltimore: John Hopkins University Press, 2014.

Bizzell, Patricia. "(Native) American Jeremiad: The 'Mixedblood' Rhetoric of William Apess." In *American Indian Rhetorics of Survivance*, edited by Ernest Stromberg, 34–49. Pittsburgh: University of Pittsburgh Press, 2006.

Black Hawk. *Black Hawk: An Autobiography*. Edited by Donald Jackson. 1955; reprint, Urbana: University of Illinois Press, 1990.

Boudinot, Elias. *A Star in the West; or, A Humble Attempt to Discover the Long Lost Ten Tribes of Israel*. Trenton, N.J.: Fenton, Hutchinson, and Dunham, 1816.

Brodeur, Paul. *Restitution: The Land Claims of Mashpee, Passamaquoddy, and Penobscot Indians of New England*. Boston: Northeastern University Press, 1985.

Brooks, Lisa. *The Common Pot: The Recovery of Native Space in the Northeast*. Minneapolis: University of Minnesota Press, 2008.

Brown, Barbara W., and James M. Rose. *Black Roots in Southeastern Connecticut, 1650–1900.* Gale Genealogy and Local History Series vol. 8. Detroit: Gale, 1980.

Brumble, H. David, III. *American Indian Autobiography.* Berkeley: University of California Press, 1988.

Campisi, Jack. *The Mashpee Indians: Tribe on Trial.* Syracuse, N.Y.: Syracuse University Press, 1991.

Calloway, Colin G., ed. *After King Philip's War: Presence and Persistence in Indian New England.* Hanover, N.H.: University Press of New England, 1997.

Calloway, Colin G., and Neal Salisbury, eds. *Reinterpreting New England Indians and the Colonial Experience.* Boston: Colonial Society of Massachusetts, 2003.

Commuck, Thomas. *Indian Melodies by Thomas Commuck, a Narragansett Indian, Harmonized by Thomas Hastings, Esq.* New York: G. Lane and C. B. Tippett, 1845.

Copway, George (Kahgegagahbowh). *Life, Letters, and Speeches.* Edited by A. LaVonne Brown Ruoff and Donald B. Smith. Lincoln: University of Nebraska Press, 1977.

Cuffe, Paul, Jr. *Narrative of the Life and Adventures of Paul Cuffe, a Pequot Indian.* Vernon, N.Y.: Horace N. Bill, 1839.

Dannenberg, Anne Marie. "'Where, Then, Shall We Place the Hero of the Wilderness': William Apess' Eulogy on King Philip and Doctrines of Racial Destiny." In *Early Native American Writing: New Critical Essays,* edited by Helen Jaskoski, 66–82. New York: Cambridge University Press, 1996.

Donaldson, Laura. "Making a Joyful Noise: William Apess and the Search for Postcolonial Method(ism)." In *Messy Beginnings: Postcoloniality and Early America Studies.* edited by Malini Johar Schueller and Edward Watts, 29–44. New Brunswick: Rutgers University Press, 2003.

Drake, Samuel Gardner. *Indian Biography, Containing the Lives of More Than Two Hundred Chiefs.* Boston: Josiah Drake, 1832.

Earle, John Milton. *Report to the Governor and Council Concerning the Indians of the Commonwealth.* Boston: William White, 1861.

Forbes, Jack D. *Africans and Native Americans: The Language of Race and the Evolution of Red-Black Peoples.* Urbana: University of Illinois Press, 1993.

Freeman, Frederick. *The History of Cape Cod: The Annals of Barnstable County; Including the District of Mashpee.* 2 vols. Boston: Printed for the author, 1860.

Gaul, Theresa Strouth. "Dialogue and Public Discourse in William Apess' *Indian Nullification.*" *American Transcendental Quarterly* 15 (2001): 275–92.

Grover, Kathryn. *The Fugitive's Gibraltar: Escaping Slaves and Abolitionism in New Bedford, Massachusetts.* Amherst: University of Massachusetts Press, 2001.

Gussman, Deborah. "'O Savage, Where art Thou?': Rhetorics of Reform in

William Apess's *Eulogy on King Philip.*" *New England Quarterly* 77, no. 3 (2004): 451–77.

Gustafson, Sandra. "Nations of Israelites: Prophecy and Cultural Autonomy in the Writings of William Apess." *Religion and Literature* 26 (1994): 31–53.

Hallett, Benjamin F. *Rights of the Marshpee Indians.* Boston: Jonathan Howe, 1834.

Hauptman, Laurence M., and James D. Wherry, eds. *The Pequots in Southern New England: The Fall and Rise of an American Indian Nation.* Norman: University of Oklahoma Press, 1990.

Hayes, Carolyn. "'A Mark for Them All to . . . Hiss At': The Formation of Methodist and Pequot Identity in the Conversion of William Apess." *Early American Literature* 31, no. 1 (1996): 25–44.

Hutchins, Francis G. *Mashpee: The Story of Cape Cod's Indian Town.* West Franklin, N.H.: Amarta Press, 1979.

Jones, Peter. *Life and Journals of Kah-ke-way-quo-na-by (Rev. Peter Jones), Wesleyan Missionary.* Toronto: Anson Green, 1860.

Konkle, Maureen. "Indian Literacy, U.S. Colonialism, and Literary Criticism." *American Literature* 69, no. 3 (1997): 457–86.

———. *Writing Indian Nations: Native Intellectuals and the Politics of Historiography, 1827–1863.* Chapel Hill: University of North Carolina Press, 2004.

Lepore, Jill. *The Name of War: King Philip's War and the Origins of American Identity.* New York: Knopf, 1998.

Lopenzina, Drew. "What to the American Indian Is the Fourth of July?: Moving beyond Abolitionist Rhetoric in William Apess's *Eulogy on King Philip.*" *American Literature* 82, no. 4 (2010): 674–99.

Mandell, Daniel R. *Behind the Frontier: Indians in Eighteenth-Century Eastern Massachusetts.* Lincoln: University of Nebraska Press, 1996.

———. "Shifting Boundaries of Race and Ethnicity: Indian-Black Intermarriage in Southern New England, 1760–1880." *Journal of American History* 85 (1998): 466–501.

———. *Tribe, Race, History: Native Americans in Southern New England, 1780–1880.* Baltimore: Johns Hopkins University Press, 2008.

———. "'We as a Tribe, Will Rule Ourselves': Mashpee's Struggle for Autonomy, 1745–1840." In *Reinterpreting New England Indians and the Colonial Experience,* edited by Colin Calloway and Neal Salisbury, 299–340. Boston: Colonial Society of Massachusetts, 2003.

McQuaid, Kim. "William Apes, Pequot: An Indian Reformer in the Jackson Era." *New England Quarterly* 50 (1977): 605–25.

Mielke, Laura L. "'Native to the Question': William Apess, Black Hawk, and the Sentimental Context of Early Native American Autobiography." *American Indian Quarterly* 26, no. 2 (2002): 246–70.

Miller, Mark J. "'Mouth for God': Temperate Labor, Race, and Methodist Reform in William Apess's *A Son of the Forest.*" *Journal of the Early Republic* 30 (Summer 2010): 225–51.

Moon, Randall. "William Apess and Writing White." *Studies in American Indian Literature* 5, no. 4 (Winter 1993): 45–54.

Murray, David. *Forked Tongues: Speech, Writing, and Representation in North American Indian Texts.* Bloomington: Indiana University Press, 1991.

Nicholas, Mark A. "Mashpee Wampanoags of Cape Cod, the Whalefishery, and Seafaring's Impact on Community Development." *American Indian Quarterly* 26 (2002): 165–97.

Nielsen, Donald M. "The Mashpee Indian Revolt of 1833." *New England Quarterly* 58, no. 3 (September 1985): 400–20.

O'Brien, Jean M. "'Divorced' from the Land: Resistance and Survival of Indian Women in Eighteenth-Century New England." In *After King Philip's War: Presence and Persistence in Indian New England,* edited by Colin G. Calloway, 144–61. Hanover, N.H.: University Press of New England, 1997.

———. *Firsting and Lasting: Writing Indians Out of Existence in New England.* Minneapolis: University of Minnesota Press, 2010.

O'Connell, Barry. "Introduction." In *On Our Own Ground: The Complete Writings of William Apess, a Pequot,* edited by Barry O'Connell, xiii–lxxviii. Amherst: University of Massachusetts Press, 1992.

———. "'Once More Let Us Consider': William Apess in the Writing of New England Native American History." In *After King Philip's War: Presence and Persistence in Indian New England,* edited by Colin G. Calloway, 162–77. Hanover, N.H.: University Press of New England, 1997.

———. "William Apess and the Survival of the Pequot People." In *Algonkians of New England: Past and Present; The Dublin Seminar for New England Folklife Proceedings,* edited by Peter Benes and Jane Montague Benes, 57–64. Boston: Boston University Press. 1993.

Peyer, Bernd. *The Tutor'd Mind: Indian Missionary Writers in Antebellum America.* Amherst: University of Massachusetts Press, 1997.

Prucha, Francis Paul. *American Indian Treaties: The History of a Political Anomaly.* Berkeley: University of California Press, 1994.

———. *The Great Father: The United States Government and the American Indians,* vol. 1. Lincoln: University of Nebraska Press, 1984.

Rosen, Deborah A. *American Indians and State Law.* Lincoln: University of Nebraska Press, 2007.

Round, Phillip H. *Removable Type: Histories of the Book in Indian Country, 1663–1880.* Chapel Hill: University of North Carolina Press, 2010.

Sayre, Gordon. "Defying Assimilation, Confounding Authenticity: The Case of William Apess." *a/b: Auto/Biography Studies* 11 (Spring 1996): 1–18.

Select Bibliography

Shoemaker, Nancy. "Race and Indigeneity in the Life of Elisha Apes." *Ethnohistory* 60, no. 1 (Winter 2013): 27–50.

———, ed. *Living with Whales: Documents and Oral Histories of Native New England Whaling History*. Amherst: University of Massachusetts Press, 2014.

Silverman, David J. *Faith and Boundaries: Colonists, Christianity, and Community among the Wampanoag Indians of Martha's Vineyard, 1600–1871*. New York: Cambridge University Press, 2007.

———. "The Impact of Indentured Servitude on the Society and Culture of Southern New England Indians, 1680–1810." *New England Quarterly* 74, no. 4 (2001): 622–66.

Smith, Donald B. *Sacred Feathers: The Reverend Peter Jones (Kahkewaquonaby) and the Mississauga Indians*. Lincoln: University of Nebraska Press, 1987.

"A Son of the Forest." *American Monthly Review* 2 (August 1832): 149–50.

Speck, Frank G. "Native Tribes and Dialects of Connecticut: A Mohegan-Pequot Diary." In *Forty-third Annual Report of the Bureau of American Ethnology, 1925–1926*, 199–287. Washington, D.C.: Government Printing Office, 1928.

———. "Territorial Subdivisions and Boundaries of the Wampanoag, Massachusetts, and Nauset Indians." *Indian Notes and Monographs* no. 44. New York: Museum of the American Indian, 1928.

[Spywood, George A.] *The Experience of George A. Spywood*. Middletown, Conn.: Charles H. Pelton, 1843.

Stevens, Scott Manning. "William Apess's Historical Self." *Northwest Review* 35, no. 3 (1997): 67–84.

Sweet, John Wood. *Bodies Politic: Negotiating Race in the American North, 1730–1830*. Baltimore: Johns Hopkins University Press, 2003.

Thomas, Lamont D. *Rise to Be a People: A Biography of Paul Cuffe*. Urbana: University of Illinois Press, 1986.

Tiro, Karim M. "Denominated 'Savage': Methodism, Writing, and Identity in the Works of William Apess, a Pequot." *American Quarterly* 48, no. 4 (1996): 653–79.

Warrior, Robert. *The People and the Word: Reading Native Nonfiction*. Minneapolis: University of Minnesota Press, 2005.

Weaver, Jace. *The Red Atlantic: American Indigenes and the Making of the Modern World, 1000–1927*. Chapel Hill: University of North Carolina Press, 2014.

———. "The Red Atlantic: Transoceanic Cultural Exchanges." *American Indian Quarterly* 35, no. 3 (Summer 2011): 418–63.

———. *That the People Might Live: Native American Literatures and the Native American Community*. New York: Oxford University Press, 1997.

Wyss, Hilary E. *Writing Indians: Literacy, Christianity, and Native Community in Early America*. Amherst: University of Massachusetts Press, 2000.

ACKNOWLEDGMENTS

Memory is a crafty grand master, often not revealing the logic of its moves until near the endgame. So it was in the case of this book, for it was not until I had almost completed it that I realized fully why I came to write it and understood more what it means to me. In 1977, as a young professor at the University of Colorado at Boulder, I published an essay in *American Literature* called "Thoreau's Maine Woods Indians: More Representative Men," which I had written in graduate school. I was thrilled when it won the Norman Foerster Prize of the Modern Language Association that year.

How did I come to write it? As a teenager, I had been fascinated by the fact that Thoreau spent so much time talking about his Penobscot guides in the essays that subsequently were published as *The Maine Woods* (1864). I played off the title of Ralph Waldo Emerson's book of essays, *Representative Men* (1850), and argued that Thoreau found his friend's pantheon insufficient for his needs, just as Emerson had published his book as an answer to Thomas Carlyle's *On Heroes, Hero Worship, and the Heroic in History* (1841). In Thoreau's accounts of his travels in the Allagash wilderness, he offered his own candidates for representativeness, the Maine Natives, as men whose closeness to the natural world had won his admiration.

As I recently reviewed this piece, I was embarrassed to see how little I knew at the time about New England Native Americans, indeed, how little *any* of us who taught American literature and history then knew about the subject. The pioneering work of James Axtell, Francis Jennings, and Robert Berkhoffer was just appearing—that of James Merrell, Daniel Richter, Neal Salisbury, and others was just being formulated. I was truly a babe in the woods. But I had a hunch that Thoreau's interest was significant.

There also was the coincidence that my sophomore-year tutor in my major, American History and Literature, was none other than Barry O'Connell, whose edition of all of Apess's works (1992) later pushed this figure onto the main stage of nineteenth-century Native American history. But when O'Connell taught me, he was working on a dissertation on nineteenth-century politics, and Apess was not yet on his radar. So, ironically, O'Connell's personal guidance, which meant so much to me in other ways, had little to do with my interest in Apess.

This project began in earnest when two of my dissertation students got interested in topics in which Native Americans played large parts. The first was Hilary Wyss, at Auburn, who wrote about the conversion narratives of the so-called Praying Indians of early New England; she has since become a leader in the study of seventeenth- and eighteenth-century Native American literature and culture. Laura Mielke, now at the University of Kansas, wrote a dissertation on literary domesticity, published as *Moving Encounters: Sympathy and the Indian Question*, in which Apess figured directly. To guide such work, I had to educate myself in what for me was a new field of inquiry.

Things accelerated. Aware that North Carolina has the largest Native American population of any state east of the Mississippi, the University of North Carolina at Chapel Hill began a major initiative in Native American Studies and subsequently based many of the faculty in one of my home departments, American Studies. The university's biggest coup was to hire the team of Michael Green and Theda Perdue, senior scholars and remarkable teachers in the field. I had prided myself in knowing a lot about nineteenth-century New England history, but Mike in particular made me aware of my utter ignorance of the region's Native American history. Remembering how excited Laura Mielke had been about Apess and now having O'Connell's edition and lengthy introduction before me, I eventually decided to take on this most important nineteenth-century Native American intellectual. I had written on other New Englanders who had contributed to the deep texture of U.S. history, so why not Apess, still so little known, yet so absolutely central to an understanding of nineteenth-century American history?

As has become habitual, I thank the unmatched staff of the American Antiquarian Society, who for three decades have expedited my work. On this go-round, Jacki Penny has been particularly helpful. Thanks, too, to the University of North Carolina at Chapel Hill for providing research grants and released time, and particularly to the Department of English and Comparative Literature, which has always allowed me free rein to pursue my varied interests. Colleagues in Native American Studies, particularly Dan Cobb and Chris Teuton, have been very supportive and founts of knowledge. Old friend Bob Cantwell has kept me on an even keel all these years. I also heartily thank Maureen Konkle, whose contributions on Apess are so important and who generously shared research notes and ideas with me.

In 1977, that same year in which I published my essay on Thoreau's Maine Woods Indians, the literary scholar Robert Sayre published *Thoreau and the American Indians*, a much more detailed and powerful work. Because the subject was on my mind, I gave his book as a gift to the person to whom this book is dedicated. By what can only be understood as evidence of God's free grace, almost four decades later this individual returned unannounced to my life.

INDEX

The abbreviation WA refers to William Apess.

Index

Irving, Washington, 106, 111
Izard, George, 25

Jackson, Abraham, 157 (n. 14)
Jackson, Andrew: Indian policy of, 61, 62, 88, 108, 136, 137; and Cherokees, 64; WA on, 66, 94, 113; and Black Hawk, 124–25; and Noah, 127; and First Seminole War, 136
Jackson, Daniel, 126
James, Peter, 143 (n. 15)
Jefferson, Thomas, 58, 60
Jewett, Helen, 127
Jews and Judaism, 127–28
Johnson, Elizabeth, 29
Johnson, Jimmy, 29
Johnson, Richard, 81, 115–16, 118–19, 121, 123, 130
John Street Methodist Church (New York City), 42
Jones, Peter (Kahkewaquonaby), 48
Josephus, 161 (n. 48)

Keater, Aaron, 157 (n. 14)
Kecter, Hetty, 115
Kendall, James, 77
Keokuk (chief of Sauks and Foxes), 126
King Philip's War (1675–76), xvi, 73, 106, 108, 109, 112–13, 138, 143 (n. 13), 160 (n. 31), 161 (n. 39). *See also* Metacom
Knowles, Caroline, 66
Konkle, Maureen, 161 (n. 43)

Leavitt, Joshua, 129, 130
LeClaire, Antoine, 159 (n. 17)
Liberator, xv, 60–61, 63–64, 92, 98, 107, 110, 118, 119
Lincoln, Abraham, 65
Lincoln, H., 91
Lincoln, Levi, 76, 81, 83, 91, 93, 96

Lobelia, xii, 141 (nn. 4, 7)
Lord's Prayer, WA's recitation in Massachusetts language, 12, 114, 146 (n. 45)
Loring, James, 107
Lossing, Benson J., 146–47 (n. 49)
Lumpkin, Wilson, 62

Macdonough, Thomas, 25
Madison, James, 127
Mahwee, Eunice, 146–47 (n. 49)
Manifest Destiny, 108, 137
Maori, 135, 166–67 (n. 6)
Market economy, 2, 42, 43. *See also* Panic of 1837
Marshall, John, 61, 62
Marshall, Mary, 168 (n. 1)
Marston, Charles, 95
Martineau, Harriet, 110
Mashnatuck Pequots, 1
Mashpee Indians: self-governance of, xiii, xv, xvi, 72, 74, 75–76, 81, 82, 90, 96; WA's contact with, 54, 77; WA as spokesperson for, 68, 87, 89, 131, 136; WA's assistance of, 71–72, 76, 79, 81, 82; history of, 71–76, 155 (n. 38); control of tribal lands, 72–73, 74, 75, 79, 81, 83–84, 90–91; Massachusetts government's relationship with, 72–73, 74, 75–76, 77, 78–79, 80, 81, 82, 83, 90–93, 97, 98, 158 (n. 25); population of, 73, 74–75, 100; intermarriage with African Americans, 74–75; occupations of, 74–75, 100; WA preaching to, 77–79, 80, 81, 87, 96; WA adopted into tribe, 80–81, 100; incorporation as district, 96, 100; trade vessel of, 100; WA's popularity diminished among, 101
Mashpee Revolt (1833–34): WA's leadership of, xiii, xv, 83–85, 87,

88–89, 91, 92, 93–98, 101, 105, 107;
petition to Massachusetts governor,
81–82, 84, 90–91, 94, 95, 102; Fish's
warning of, 83; newspaper coverage of, 83, 86–87, 88, 91–95, 97–98,
101, 102; and Sampson brothers,
83–84; and WA's arrest, 85–86, 89,
157 (n. 14); and redress of grievances,
86–95; Mashpee Indians' triumph in,
95–97, 120; WA's analysis of, 97, 102;
as pyrrhic victory, 97–99; Mitchell's
story similar to, 160 (n. 31)
Massachusetts: abolition in, 4; Mashpee Indians' relationship with, 72–
73, 74, 75–76, 77, 78–79, 80, 81, 82,
83, 90–93, 97, 98, 158 (n. 25); WA
preaching in, 77–80, 81, 98, 102. *See
also specific cities and towns*
Mather, Increase, 111, 135
McKendree, William, 152 (n. 4)
Medical practice, regulation of, xii, xiii
Mercantile Library (New York City),
130
Metacom (King Philip): family of, 4,
143 (n. 13); Drake on, 45, 63, 103,
105; WA's lecture on, 105, 106–8, 110–
14, 117, 118, 119, 120, 135, 146 (n. 45);
John Stone's drama on, 105–6, 108,
111; memorialization of, 105–8; Everett on, 109–10; Puritans' treatment
of, 136, 137–38; descendants of, 160
(n. 31)
Methodism: WA's conversion, xiv, 20,
32–33, 43, 47; WA's circuit as exhorter, xv, 34, 39–40, 44; WA's
leaving ministry, xvi; in Colrain, 4;
revival meetings of, 17, 34; growth in,
17, 41, 42; WA's discovery of, 17–18,
31–33; circuits of, 18, 34, 44; egalitarian message of, 29, 41, 42, 46, 69;
and camp meetings, 31, 32–33, 34,

35, 41, 42, 69; and African Americans, 31, 33, 41, 42, 56, 57, 60, 121;
WA's six month "trial," 31–32; stigma
of, 32, 35, 42; WA as exhorter, 33,
38, 40, 43, 150 (n. 35); and class
issues, 33, 41, 42–43, 46; and licenses for exhorters, 33–34, 38, 39,
40, 43, 68, 136; and racial issues,
34, 35, 41; conferences of, 34, 40,
43, 52, 54; theology of, 39, 40; WA
as ordained minister, 39–43, 46–47,
48, 52, 53–54, 101, 116; discipline
of, 40–41, 42, 43; and cottage meetings, 41; factions of, 41, 42–43, 46,
48, 52; and republican ideology, 41,
69; and emotionalism, 42, 43, 46, 52;
and respectability, 42, 46; and Great
Awakening, 46; and WA's library, 116,
117; in New Zealand, 167 (n. 6). *See
also* Methodist Episcopal Church;
Methodist Society; Protestant Methodist Church
Methodist Book Concern, 44, 46
Methodist churches in Boston: May
Street, 56; Center Street, 56, 60
Methodist Episcopal Church: and
opposition to WA's licensing, 40–41,
68; WA on, 41, 43, 45, 46, 47–48, 69;
and slavery, 42, 46; book publica-
tion program of, 44; conservatism of,
52; and missionary activities among
Native Americans, 136
Methodist Magazine, 45, 152 (n. 4)
Methodist Society, 41, 42, 43, 44, 46,
48. *See also* Protestant Methodist
Church
Mexico, 109
Middleton, Nathaniel, Jr., 135
Miner, John, 18–19
Missassauga Ojibwes, 27
Missionaries: and Native Americans, 4,

28, 136; and Native American land division, 27, 62; WA's as missionary for Pequots, 53–54, 67–68; and Mashpee Indians, 73; and Senecas, 104, 131; WA's criticism of, 107, 108, 111–12; and New Zealand, 167 (n. 6)

Mitchell, Zerviah Gould, 160 (n. 31)

Mohawks, 27

Mohegans, 1, 11, 105, 139, 153 (n. 13)

Monroe, James, 75, 127

Monthly Repository and Library of Entertaining Knowledge, 52–53

Moore, Martin, 117

Moor's Charity School (Hanover, N.H.), 7, 11

Morality: and WA's early life, 11; colonial laws on, 36; and racial issues, 36–37, 71; and African Society, 55; Stewart on, 59; and Garrison's abolitionism, 61, 71; WA on, 70, 71, 98; and slavery, 122

More, Hannah, 162 (n. 48)

Morgan, Lewis Henry, 29

Morris, Thomas, 52

Morse, Jedediah, 75

Mutual Rights and Methodist Protestant, 54

Narragansetts, xiii, 1, 34, 105, 109, 143 (n. 13)

National Republican Party, 88

Native American rights: WA as spokesperson for, xiii, xiv, xv, xvi, 54, 66–67, 85–86, 97, 99, 102, 120, 125, 131; and Boudinot, 50; WA's role in securing, 54, 80–81, 139; Supreme Court cases on, 61–62, 64, 72; WA preaching on, 79, 81; erasure of authority and sovereignty, 159 (n. 5)

Native Americans: traditional medicine of, xii, 141 (n. 7); housing of, 2, 6; whites' attitudes toward, 2, 6–7, 13, 23, 50, 78, 85, 87, 88, 105–6, 108–9, 110, 112–14, 123–28, 137, 138, 140, 168 (n. 3); diet of, 2, 12; clothing of, 2, 12, 66, 146–47 (n. 49); education for, 7, 69, 75, 78, 85–86, 96, 100, 102; and basket making, 9, 27, 75, 85, 126; corporal punishment frowned upon by, 12; WA's childhood fears of, 13–14; and racial categories, 16, 36–37, 136; and War of 1812, 21, 26; Canadian encampments, 27; and identity, 28; WA's lectures on Native history and culture, 29, 129–31; and Methodism, 33, 41, 46–47; WA on whites' treatment of, 45, 48, 49, 51, 53, 70, 71, 102, 125, 136; WA on Christianity providing arguments against American society, 47, 48–49; Boudinot on, 49, 50; as descendants of Ten Lost Tribes of Israel, 49, 50, 52, 53, 127–28, 153 (n. 13); and Christianity, 50, 53, 73, 75, 110–11, 113, 131, 137, 155 (n. 38); removal policies, 61, 62, 109, 111–12, 120, 136, 137; and European diseases, 72; conversion of, 73, 75, 112; paternalism toward, 77, 83, 113; William Joseph Snelling on, 104; vanishing Indian myth, 105, 106, 108, 109, 123, 137; histories of, 108–14, 117, 160 (n. 31); captives of, 112–13; Catlin on, 123–24; and New York City Indian appearances, 123–28; treaties with U.S. government, 124–25, 131; erasure of eastern Indians and, 126

Nat Turner's Rebellion, 58

Negro Masons of America, 8

Nell, William C., 118

New Bedford, Mass., 118–19

Newburyport Herald, 67

Index

Praying towns, 73, 155 (n. 38)
Presbyterian Church, 4, 16–17, 34, 35, 41, 46, 49
Prévost, George, 25
Primitive Methodist Connexion, 52
Prince Hall Lodge, 55–56
Print culture, proliferation of, 44, 46
Protestant Methodist Church, 48, 52, 54, 68, 69, 136. *See also* Methodist Society
Providence, R.I.: WA living in, 36, 136, 157 (n. 8); racial issues in, 36–37, 38, 119; and class segregation, 37
Puritans: and Pequot War, 1, 11, 143 (n. 13); and spiritual autobiography, 45, 70; and Mashpee Indians, 73; portrayals of, 106, 108, 109, 111; on American history, 135; WA on, 136, 137; and Metacom, 136, 137–38; divine mission of, 137, 138. *See also* King Philip's War

Quakers, 28, 81
Quincy, Josiah, 89, 101

Racial categories: and mixed ancestry, xiv, xv, 5, 6, 7, 35, 37, 59, 60, 144 (n. 28); fluidity of, 5, 16, 143 (n. 15); and Native Americans, 16, 36–37, 136; in New Zealand, 135
Racial issues: and interracial communities, xiii, 4, 143 (n. 15); WA on, xvi, 54, 70–71, 95–96, 114, 120, 130, 131, 135–36, 137, 138; and pauper apprentice system, 11; and Methodism, 34, 35, 41; in Providence, 36–37, 38, 119; and intermarriage, 37, 71, 74–75, 95–96, 122; and voting rights, 38; discrimination in white churches, 56; David Walker on, 57–59; Hosea Easton on, 60; and racial violence,

119; and delegations of Indians, 125
Red Jacket (Seneca leader), 28
Red Man, 152 (n. 60)
Reed, John, 84, 85
Republican Party, 64
Reynolds, John, 67, 68, 98, 104
Richey, Russell, 41
Ridge, John, 64, 65, 66
Roger's Rangers, 4
Rogue narratives, 47
Rowlandson, Mary, 112–13, 135

St. Philip's Church (New York City), 121, 122
Salaberry, Charles de, 24
Sampson, Deborah, 127
Sampson brothers, 83–84, 85
Sands, Robert Charles, 106
Sanford, P. P., 161–62 (n. 48)
Sauk Indians, 125, 126
Saunders, Prince, 7–8, 10, 37, 56, 145 (n. 31)
Scudder, Levi, 115
Second Great Awakening, 28
Second Seminole War (1835), 120, 136–37
Sedgwick, Catharine Maria, 111
Seminoles, 3, 76, 120, 124, 136–37
Senecas, 27–28, 29, 104, 131
Seven Years' War (1754–63), 4
Sewall, Samuel, 153 (n. 13)
Shays' Rebellion (1786–87), 4, 55, 96
Shoemaker, Nancy, 135, 143 (n. 15), 144 (n. 18)
Sigourney, Lydia, 120
Silliman, Benjamin, 128
Simpson, Alvis, 115
Sioux, 125
Slavery: and Methodist Episcopal Church, 42, 46; David Walker on,

Index

attempts at buying, 28, 50, 136, 139; whites' interest in, 61–62, 73, 113; and treaties, 124–25, 131; and Brothertown Indian Nation, 139–40

Turner, Nat, 58

Tyendinaga Mohawks, 27

Uncas (Mohegan leader), 140

Unitarian Church, 67, 75, 86, 117

United States: Cherokees' relationship with, 3, 61–62, 136; and War of 1812, 20–26; boundary with Canada, 21, 26

U.S. Army, 137

U.S. Supreme Court, 61–62, 64, 72, 80, 90

Utopianism, 127

Van Buren, Martin, 120

Veer, James, xii

Vesey, Denmark, 57

Voting rights, 38

Walker, David, xiv, 56–59, 60, 61, 150 (n. 45)

Walker, James, 60, 71, 101

Wampanoag Indians, 37, 72, 109

Wampy, Anne, 9, 68, 70

War of 1812: WA's enlistment in New York troops, xiv–xv, 20, 21, 22; WA's assignment to drum corps, 20, 22; execution of troops for desertion, 20–21; lack of support for, 21, 22; and Canada, 21–22, 24–25, 26; and battles on Great Lakes, 22, 24, 25; conditions of, 22–23; WA's assignment to infantry, 23; WA's assignment to artillery, 23, 24, 25; and WA's desertion, 23, 26, 148 (n. 17)

Warrior, Robert, xvii

Washington, D.C., 125

Washington, George, xvi, 49, 110, 112

Washington Sun, 125

Watie, Gallegina, 50

Watson, Richard, 162 (n. 48)

Weaver, Jace, 162–63 (n. 50)

Webster, Daniel, 124

Webster, Noah, 162 (n. 48)

Weden, Pebe Ann, 115

Weden, Richard, 115

Weld, Theodore Dwight, 120

Wesley, Charles, 41, 46

Wesley, John, 41, 46, 162 (n. 48)

Wheelock, John, 7

Whig Party, 64, 65

Whiston, William, 161 (n. 48)

White, Joseph Blanco, 162 (n. 48)

Whites: attitudes toward Native Americans, 2, 6–7, 13, 23, 50, 78, 85, 87, 88, 105–6, 108–9, 110, 112–14, 123–28, 137, 138, 140, 168 (n. 3); attempts to buy tribal land, 28, 50, 136, 139; Pequots renting tribal land to, 32; and colonization movement, 38; WA's indictment of whites' prejudice against Native Americans, 45, 48, 49, 51, 53, 70, 71, 102, 125, 136; Boudinot on whites' treatment of Native Americans, 50–51; fear of slave rebellions, 58; Hosea Easton on prejudice toward African Americans, 60; tribal lands sought by, 61–62, 73, 113; and Mashpee tribal land, 74, 76, 78, 81, 82; and Mashpee trading vessel, 100; WA's family listed in census as, 152 (n. 62)

White supremacy, 48

Whitman, Kilburn, 95

Wiggins, Francis B., 53

Wight, John, xii

Wilberforce, William, 8

Wilkinson, James, 24, 25

Williams, Catherine, 31

Williams, Daniel, 75, 81, 82, 86, 96, 101

Williams, Peter, 121

Williams, Peter, Jr., 121–23, 130, 164 (n. 11)

Williams, Roger, 153 (n. 13)

Williams, William, 16, 18, 19

Wilson, James, 162 (n. 48)

Winch, Joel, 35

Winchester, Elhanan, 162 (n. 48)

Wirt, William, 88

Women: and pauper apprentice system, 11; and Methodism, 32, 33; education for, 64; in American Revolution, 127

Women's rights, xiv, 59

Woodbury, Benjamin, 79

Worcester, Samuel, 62, 64, 80

Worcester v. Georgia (1832), 61, 62

Wright, Frances, xiv